# Introducing Social Theory
## Second Edition

For Ellen, my wife and true companion
Pip Jones
and
for Jamie Rufus Le Boutillier, with love from Mummy and Daddy
Liz Bradbury and Shaun Le Boutillier

# INTRODUCING SOCIAL THEORY

Second Edition

## PIP JONES,
## LIZ BRADBURY AND
## SHAUN LE BOUTILLIER

polity

First edition first published in 2003 by Polity Press
This edition first published in 2011 by Polity Press

Polity Press
65 Bridge Street
Cambridge CB2 1UR, UK

Polity Press
350 Main Street
Malden, MA 02148, USA

ISBN-13: 978-0-7456-3522-4
ISBN-13: 978-0-7456-3523-1(pb)

A catalogue record for this book is available from the British Library.

Typeset in 10.5 on 12 pt Times New Roman MT Pro
by Servis Filmsetting Ltd, Stockport, Cheshire
Printed and bound in Great Britain by MPG Books Group Limited, Bodmin, Cornwall

For further information on Polity, visit our website: www.politybooks.com

# CONTENTS

# DETAILED TABLE OF CONTENTS

# 1 AN INTRODUCTION TO SOCIOLOGICAL THEORIES

## Introduction

Humans are social beings. Whether we like it or not, nearly everything we do in our lives takes place in the company of others. Few of our activities are truly solitary and scarce are the times when we are really alone. Thus the study of how we are able to interact with one another, and what happens when we do, would seem to be one of the most fundamental concerns of anyone interested in human life. Yet strangely enough, it was not until relatively recently – from about the beginning of the nineteenth century onwards – that a specialist interest in this intrinsically social aspect of human existence was treated with any seriousness. Before that time, and even since, other kinds of interests have dominated the analysis of human life. Two of the most resilient, non-social approaches to human behaviour have been **'naturalistic'**\* and **'individualistic'** explanations.

Rather than seeing social behaviour as the product of interaction, these theories have concentrated on the presumed qualities inherent in individuals. On the one hand, naturalistic explanations suppose that all human behaviour – social interaction included – is a product of the inherited dispositions we possess as animals. We are, like animals, biologically programmed by nature. On the other hand, individualistic explanations baulk at such grand generalizations about the inevitability of behaviour. From this point of view we are all 'individual' and

\* Where a term or concept is highlighted in the text, you will find it defined in the Glossary at the end of the book.

'different'. Explanations of human behaviour must therefore always rest ultimately on the particular and unique psychological qualities of individuals. Sociological theories are in direct contrast to these 'non-social' approaches. Looking a little closer at them, and discovering what is wrong or incomplete about them, makes it easier to understand why sociological theories exist.

## Naturalistic theories

Naturalistic explanations of human activity are common enough. For example, in our society it is often argued that it is only natural for a man and a woman to fall in love, get married and have children. It is equally natural for this nuclear family to live as a unit on their own, with the husband going out to work to earn resources for his dependants, while his wife, at least for the early years of her children's lives, devotes herself to looking after them – to being a mother. As they grow up and acquire more independence, it is still only 'natural' for the children to live at home with their parents, who are responsible for them, at least until their late teens. By then it is only natural for them to want to 'leave the nest', to start to 'make their own way in the world' and, in particular, to look for marriage partners. Thus they, too, can start families of their own.

The corollary of these 'natural' practices is that it is somehow *un*natural not to want to get married, or to marry for reasons other than love. It is equally unnatural for a couple not to comprise a man and a woman, or not to want to have children, or for wives not to want to be mothers, or for mothers not to want to devote the whole of their lives to child-rearing. Though it is not right or natural for children to leave home much younger than eighteen, it is certainly not natural for them not to want to leave home at all in order to start a family of their own. However, these 'unnatural' desires and practices are common enough in our society. There are plenty of homosexual couples and people who prefer to stay single, or 'marry with an eye on the main chance'. There are plenty of women who do not like the idea of motherhood, and there is certainly any number of women who do not want to spend their lives solely as wives and mothers. Likewise, there are plenty of children who want to leave home long before they are eighteen, while there are also many who are quite happy to stay as members of their parents' households until long after that age.

Why is this? If human behaviour is, in fact, the product of a disposition inherent in the nature of the human being then why are such deviations from what is 'natural' so common? We can hardly put the widespread existence of such 'unnatural' patterns of behaviour down to some kind of large-scale, faulty genetic programming. In any case, why are there so many variations from these notions of 'normal' family practices in other kinds of human societies? Both history and anthropology provide us with stark contrasts in family life. In his book on family life in medieval Europe, *Centuries of Childhood* (1973), Philippe Ariès paints a picture of marriage, the family and child-rearing which sharply contradicts our notions of normality. Families were not then, as they are for us today, private and isolated units, cut off socially, and physically separated from the world at large. Families were deeply embedded in the community, with people living essentially public, rather than private, lives. They lived in households whose composition was constantly shifting: relatives, friends, children, visitors, passers-by and animals all slept under the same roof. Marriage was primarily a means of forging alliances rather than simply the outcome of 'love', while women certainly did not look upon mothering as their sole destiny. Indeed, child-rearing was a far less demanding and onerous task than it is in our world. Children were not cosseted and coddled to anywhere near the extent we now consider 'right'. Many more people – both other relatives and the community at large – were involved in child-rearing, and childhood lasted a far shorter time than it does today. As Ariès puts it, 'as soon as he had been weaned, or soon after, the child became the natural companion of the adult' (Ariès 1973).

In contemporary non-industrial societies, too, there is a wide range of variations in family practices. Here again, marriage is essentially a means of establishing alliances between groups, rather than simply a relationship between individuals. Monogamy – one husband and one wife – is only one form of marriage. Polygyny, marriage between a husband and more than one wife, and polyandry, between a wife and more than one husband, are found in many societies. In such societies, domestic life is also far more public and communal than it is in industrial societies. Each family unit is just a part of a much wider, cooperating group of mainly blood relatives associated with a local territory, usually a village. As in medieval Europe, therefore, child-rearing is not considered the principal responsibility of parents alone, but involves a far greater number of people, relatives and non-relatives.

Clearly, then, to hope to explain human life simply by reference to natural impulses common to all is to ignore the one crucial fact that sociology directs our attention to: human behaviour varies according to the social settings in which people find themselves.

## Individualistic theories

What of individualistic explanations? How useful is the argument that behaviour is the product of the psychological make-up of individuals? The employment of this kind of theory is extremely common. For example, success or failure in education is often assumed to be merely a reflection of intelligence: bright children succeed and dim children fail. Criminals are often taken to be people with certain kinds of personality: they are usually seen as morally deficient individuals, lacking any real sense of right or wrong. Unemployed people are equally often condemned as 'work-shy', 'lazy' or 'scroungers' – inadequates who would rather 'get something for nothing' than work for it. Suicide is seen as the act of an unstable person – an act undertaken when, as coroners put it, 'the balance of the mind was disturbed'. This kind of explanation is attractive for many people and has proved particularly resilient in the face of sociological critique. But a closer look shows it to be seriously flawed.

If educational achievement is simply a reflection of intelligence then why do children from manual workers' homes do so badly compared with children from middle-class homes? It is clearly nonsensical to suggest that your doing one kind of job rather than another is likely to determine the intelligence of your child. Achievement in education must in some way be influenced by the characteristics of a child's background.

Equally, the fact that the majority of people convicted of a crime come from certain social categories must cast serious doubt on the 'deficient personality' theory. The conviction rate is highest for young males, especially blacks, who come from manual, working-class or unemployed backgrounds. Can we seriously believe that criminal personalities are likely to be concentrated in such *social* categories? As in the case of educational achievement, it is clear that the conviction of criminals must somehow be influenced by social factors.

Again, is it likely that millions of unemployed people are typically uninterested in working when the vast majority of them have been forced out of their jobs, either by 'downsizing' or by the failure of the companies they worked for – as a result of social forces quite outside their control?

Suicide would seem to have the strongest case for being explained as a purely psychological act. But if it is simply a question of 'an unsound mind', then why does the rate of suicide vary between societies? Why does it vary between different groups within the same society? Also, why do the rates within groups and societies remain remarkably constant over time? As in other examples, social factors must be exerting some kind of influence; explanations at the level of the personality are clearly not enough.

Variations such as these demonstrate the inadequacy of theories of human behaviour which exclusively emphasize innate natural drives, or the unique psychological make-up of individuals. If nature is at the root of behaviour, why does it vary according to social settings? If we are all different individuals acting according to the dictates of unique psychological influences, why do different people in the same social circumstances behave similarly and in ways others can understand? Clearly there is a social dimension to human existence, which requires sociological theorizing to explain it.

All sociological theories thus have in common an emphasis on the way human belief and **action** is the product of social influences. They differ as to what these influences are, and how they should be investigated and explained. This book is about these differences.

We shall now examine three distinct kinds of theory — *consensus*, *conflict* and *action* theories — each of which highlights specific social sources of human behaviour. Though none of the sociologists whose work we will spend the rest of the book examining falls neatly into any one of these three categories, discussing them now will produce two benefits:

- it will serve as an accessible introduction to theoretical debates in sociology; and
- it will act as a useful reference point against which to judge and compare the work of the subject's major theorists.

## Society as a structure of rules

### The influence of culture on behaviour

Imagine you live in a big city. How many people do you know well? Twenty? Fifty? A hundred? Now consider how many other people you encounter each day, about whom you know nothing. For example, how many complete strangers do people living in London or Manchester or Birmingham come into contact with each day? On the street, in shops, on buses and trains, in cinemas or night clubs — everyday life in a big city is a constant encounter with complete strangers. Yet even if city dwellers bothered to reflect on this fact, they would not normally leave their homes quaking with dread about how all these hundreds of strangers might behave towards them. Indeed, they hardly, if ever, think about it. Why? Why do we take our ability to cope with strangers so much for granted? It is because nearly all the people we encounter in our everyday lives do behave in ways we expect. We expect bus passengers, shoppers, taxi-drivers, passers-by, and so on, to behave in quite definite ways even though we know nothing about them personally. City dwellers in particular – though it is true of all of us to some extent – routinely enter settings where others are going about their business both expecting not to know them, and yet also expecting to know how they will behave. And, more than this, we are nearly always absolutely right in both respects. We are only surprised if we encounter someone who is *not* a stranger – 'Fancy meeting you here! Isn't it a small world!' – or if one of these strangers actually does behave strangely – 'Mummy, why is that man shouting and waving his arms about?' Why is this? Why do others do what we expect of them? Why is *dis*order or the *un*expected among strangers so rare?

## Structural-consensus theory

One of the traditional ways in which sociologists explain the order and predictability of social life is by regarding human behaviour as *learned* behaviour. This approach is known – for reasons that will become apparent – as *structural-consensus* theory. The key process this theory emphasizes is called *socialization.* This term refers to the way in which human beings learn the kinds of behaviour expected of them in the social settings in which they find themselves. From this point of view, societies differ because the kinds of behaviour considered appropriate in them differ. People in other societies think and behave differently because they have learned different rules about how to behave and think. The same goes for different groups within the same society. The actions and ideas of one group differ from those of another because its members have been socialized into different rules.

Consensus sociologists use the term *culture* to describe the rules that govern thought and behaviour in a society. Culture exists prior to the people who learn it. At birth, humans are confronted by a social world already in existence. Joining this world involves learning 'how things are done' in it. Only by learning the cultural rules of a society can a human interact with other humans. Because they have been similarly socialized, different individuals will behave similarly.

Consensus theory thus argues that a society's cultural rules determine, or *structure*, the behaviour of its members, channelling their actions in certain ways rather than others. They do so in much the same way that the physical construction of a building structures the actions of the people inside it. Take the behaviour of students in a school. Once inside the school they will display quite regular patterns of behaviour. They will all walk along corridors, up and down stairs, in and out of classrooms, through doors, and so on. They will, by and large, not attempt to dig through floors, smash through walls, or climb out of windows. Their physical movements are constrained by the school building. Since this affects all the students similarly, their behaviour inside the school will be similar – and will exhibit quite definite patterns. In consensus theory, the same is true of social life. Individuals will behave similarly in the same social settings because they are equally constrained by cultural rules. Though these **social structures** are not visible in the way physical structures are, those who are socialized into their rules find them comparably determining.

The levels at which these cultural rules operate can vary. Some rules, like laws for instance, operate at the level of the whole society and structure the behaviour of everyone who lives in it. Others are much less general, structuring the behaviour of people in quite specific social settings. For example, children in a classroom are expected to behave in an orderly and attentive fashion. In the playground much more licence is given them, while away from school their behaviour often bears little resemblance to that expected of them during school hours. Similarly, when police officers or nurses or members of the armed forces are 'on duty', certain cultural rules structure their behaviour very rigidly. Out of uniform and off duty these constraints do not apply, though other ones do instead – those governing their behaviour as fathers and mothers, or husbands and wives, for instance.

This shows how the theory of a social structure of cultural rules operates. The rules apply not to the individuals themselves, but to the positions in the social structure they occupy. Shoppers, police officers, traffic wardens, schoolteachers or pupils are constrained by the cultural expectations attached to these positions, but only when they occupy them. In other circumstances, in other locations in the social structure – as fathers or mothers, squash players, football supporters, church members, and so on – other rules come into play.

Sociologists call positions in a social structure *roles*. The rules that structure the behaviour of their occupants are called *norms*. There are some cultural rules that are not attached to any particular role or set of roles. Called *values*, these are in a sense summaries of approved ways of living, and act as a base from which particular norms spring. So, for example: 'education should be the key to success'; 'family relationships should be the most important thing to protect'; 'self-help should be the means to individual fulfilment'. All these are values, and they provide general principles from which norms directing behaviour in schools and colleges, in the home and at work, are derived.

According to this sociological theory, socialization into norms and values produces agreement, or *consensus*, between people about appropriate behaviour and beliefs without which no human society can survive. This is why it is called structural-consensus theory. Through socialization, cultural rules structure behaviour, guarantee a consensus about expected behaviour, and thereby ensure social order.

Clearly, in a complex society there are sometimes going to be competing norms and values. For example, while some people think it is wrong for mothers to go out to work, many women see motherhood at best as a real imposition and at worst as an infringement of their liberty. Children often encourage each other to misbehave at school and disapprove of their peers who refuse to do so. Teachers usually see this very much the other way round! The Tory Party Conference will invariably be strident in its condemnation of any speaker who criticizes the police. Some young blacks will be equally furious with any of their number displaying anything other than a strongly belligerent attitude towards the police.

Consensus theorists explain such differences in behaviour and attitude in terms of the existence of alternative cultural influences, characteristic of different social settings. A good example of this emphasis is their approach to educational inequality.

## Educational inequality: a consensus theory analysis

Educational research demonstrates, in the most conclusive fashion, that achievement in education is strongly linked to class membership, gender and ethnic origin. There is overwhelming evidence, for example, that working-class children of similar intelligence to children from middle-class backgrounds achieve far less academically than their middle-class counterparts.

To explain this, consensus theorists turn to stock concepts in their approach to social life – norms, values, socialization and culture. Starting from the basic assumption that behaviour and belief are caused by socialization into particular rules, their explanation of working-class underachievement in education seeks to identify:

• the cultural influences which propel middle-class children to academic success

- the cultural influences which drag working-class children down to mediocrity.

The argument usually goes something like this. The upbringing of middle-class children involves socialization into norms and values that are ideal for educational achievement. Because of their own educational experiences, middle-class parents are likely to be very knowledgeable about how education works and how to make the most of it. Further, they are likely to be very keen for their children to make a success of their own education. These children will thus grow up in a social setting where educational achievement is valued and where they will be constantly encouraged and assisted to fulfil their academic potential.

In contrast, the home background of working-class children often lacks such advantageous socialization. Working-class parents are likely to have had only limited, and possibly unhappy, experiences of education. Even if they are keen for their children to achieve educational success, they will almost certainly lack the know-how of the middle-class parent to make this happen. Indeed, sometimes they may actively disapprove of academic attainment; for instance, they may simply distrust what they do not know. As a result, their children may well be taught instead to value the more immediate and practical advantages of leaving school as soon as possible and finding a 'proper' job.

## Consensus theory: conclusion

Here is a clear example of the application of consensus theory to the facts of social life. From this theoretical point of view, different patterns of behaviour are the product of different patterns of socialization. It might seem that this contradicts the commitment of these theorists to the idea that social order in a society is the outcome of an agreement or a consensus among its members about how to behave and what to think. But consensus theorists say that despite differences of culture between different groups, even despite opposing sub-cultures within the overall culture, in all societies an overall consensus prevails. This is because all societies have certain values about the importance of which there is no dispute. They are called either *central values* or *core values*, and socialization ensures everyone conforms to them.

In Victorian Britain two central values were a commitment to Christian morality and loyalty to the Queen and the British Empire. Today, examples of central values in a Western capitalist society might be the importance of economic growth, the importance of democratic institutions, the importance of the rule of law, and the importance of the freedom of the individual within the law. (Indeed, anything trotted out as 'basic to our country's way of life' at any particular time is usually a central value in a society.)

For consensus theory then, central values are the backbone of social structures, built and sustained by the process of socialization. Social behaviour and social order are determined by external cultural forces. Social life is possible because of the existence of social structures of cultural rules.

# Society as a structure of inequality

## The influence of advantages and disadvantages on behaviour

Other sociologists argue a rather different theoretical case. They agree that society determines our behaviour by structuring or constraining it. But they emphasize different structural constraints. For them, the most important influence on social life is the distribution of advantage and its impact on behaviour. Where advantages are unequally distributed, the opportunities of the advantaged to choose how to behave are much greater than those of the disadvantaged.

## Educational inequality: an alternative analysis

For example, while it is perfectly feasible for two boys of the same intelligence to be equally keen to fulfil their potential in education and to be equally encouraged by their parents, their culturally instilled enthusiasm cannot, by itself, tell us everything about their potential educational successes or failures. If one boy comes from a wealthy home, while the other is from a much poorer one, this will be far more significant for their education than their similar (learned) desire. Clearly, the unequal distribution of advantage – in this case material resources – will assist the privileged boy and hamper the disadvantaged one.

The advantaged boy's parents can buy a private education, while those of the poorer boy cannot. The advantaged boy can be assured of living in a substantial enough house, with sufficient space to study, whereas the disadvantaged boy may have to make do with a room with the television in it, or a bedroom shared with his brothers and sisters. The advantaged boy can rely on a proper diet and resulting good health, whereas the disadvantaged boy cannot. The advantaged boy can be guaranteed access to all the books and equipment he needs to study, whereas the disadvantaged boy cannot. Probably most importantly, the advantaged boy will be able to continue his education up to the limit of his potential unhindered. For those who are less advantaged it is often necessary to leave school and go out to work to add to the family income. This stronger impulse usually brings education to a premature end.

## Structural-conflict theory

So, one primary objection some sociologists have to structural-consensus theory is that where societies are unequal, people are not only constrained by the norms and values they have learned via socialization. Such theorists argue that it has to be recognized that people are also constrained by the advantages they possess – by their position in the structures of inequality within their society. This emphasis on the effects on behaviour of an unequal distribution of advantage in a society is usually associated with *structural-conflict* theory. Why are such theories called conflict theories?

The kinds of inequality structures in a society vary. Ethnic groups can be unequal, young and old can be unequal, men and women can be unequal, people doing different jobs can be unequal, people of different religious beliefs can be unequal, and so on. The kinds of advantages unequally possessed by such groups can vary, too. Different groups can possess unequal amounts of power, authority, prestige, or wealth, or a combination of these and other advantages.

Notwithstanding the different kinds of inequality conflict theories focus on, and the different kinds of advantages they see as unequally distributed, such theories nonetheless have in common the axiom that the origin and persistence of a structure of inequality lies in the domination of its disadvantaged groups by its advantaged ones. Conflict theories are so-called because for them, inherent in an unequal society is an inevitable *conflict of interests* between its 'haves' and its 'have-nots'. As Wes Sharrock puts it:

> The conflict view is . . . founded upon the assumption that . . . any society . . . may provide extraordinarily good lives for some but this is usually only possible because the great majority are oppressed and degraded . . . Differences of interest are therefore as important to society as agreements upon rules and values, and most societies are so organised that they not

only provide greater benefits for some than for others but in such a way
that the accrual of benefits to a few causes positive discomfort to others.
(Sharrock 1977: 515–16)

So conflict theory differs from consensus theory not only because it is
interested in the way an unequal distribution of advantage in a society
structures behaviour, but also because it is interested in the conflict,
not the consensus, inherent in such a society. According to conflict
theory, there is a conflict of interest between a society's advantaged
and disadvantaged, which is inherent in their relationship.

However, there is another objection to consensus theory too.
Conflict theorists not only accuse consensus theorists of putting too
much emphasis on norms and values as determinants of behaviour at
the expense of other influences; they also argue that in any case, consensus theory misunderstands and therefore misinterprets the role of
its key concern – socialization into culture.

## Ideas as instruments of power

Consensus theory argues that people behave as they do because they
have been socialized into cultural rules. The outcome is a consensus
about how to think and behave, which manifests itself in patterns and
regularities of behaviour. In contrast, conflict theorists argue that we
should see the role of cultural rules and the process of socialization
in a very different light. For them, the real structural determinants
of behaviour are the rewards and advantages possessed unequally
by different groups in a society. Other things being equal, those most
disadvantaged would not put up with such a state of affairs. Normally, however, other things are *not* equal. Where a society is unequal,
the only way it can survive is if those who are disadvantaged in it
come to accept their deprivation. Sometimes this involves naked
coercion. Plenty of unequal societies survive because their rulers maintain repressive regimes based on terror. However, the exercise of the
force necessary to maintain unequal advantage need not take such
an obvious or naked form. There are two other related ways in which
structures of inequality can survive – and with a surer future than by
the naked use of force. First, they can do so if those most disadvantaged by them can somehow be prevented from seeing themselves as
underprivileged, or second, even if this is recognized, the disadvantaged can do so if they can be persuaded that this is fair enough – that
the inequality is legitimate. According to the conflict view, the way this
happens is through the control and manipulation of the norms and

values – the cultural rules – into which people are socialized. In effect then, for conflict theorists, far from being the means to social order via consensus, socialization is much more likely to be an instrument of power – producing social order by means of force and domination.

Imagine the following scenario. It is early morning in a Latin American country. A group of agricultural labourers, both men and women, are waiting by a roadside for a bus to arrive to drive them to work. Suddenly two vans draw up and four hooded men jump out. At gunpoint they order the labourers into the backs of the vans, which then race away deep into the surrounding countryside. At nightfall they are abandoned and the labourers transferred into a large covered lorry. This is driven through the night, deep into the mountains. Before daybreak it reaches its destination – a huge underground mine, built deep into the heart of a mountain. Here the labourers are horrified to find a vast army of slaves toiling away, under constant surveillance by brutal guards. After being given a meagre meal, the labourers are forced to join this workforce.

As they live out their desperate lives within this mountain world, some of the slaves try to escape. When caught they are publicly punished as a deterrent to others. Two attempts to escape result in public execution. As the labourers get older, they rely on each other for companionship, and on their memories for comfort. They keep sane by recounting stories of their former lives. In the fullness of time, children are born to them. The parents are careful to tell these children all about their past. As the children grow up and have children of their own, they, too, are told tales of their grandparents' land of lost content. But for them these are handed-down, historical stories, not tales based on experience. As the years go by, though the facts of life within the mountain remain the same, the perception of life in it by the participants alters. By the time five or six generations of slaves have been born, their knowledge of the world of their ancestors' past lives has become considerably diminished. It is still talked about, sometimes. But by now it is a misted world of folklore and myth. All they know from experience is slavery. So far as any of them can remember, they have always been slaves. In their world, slavery is 'normal'. In effect, to be a slave means something very different to them from what it meant to their ancestors.

A similar process occurs with the oppressors. As the slaves' view of themselves has altered over time, so the necessity for naked force has become less and less. As, through socialization, their subordinates have begun to acquiesce in their own subordination, the guards no longer brandish guns and clubs. Because of this, they no longer see themselves as the original guards did. Both the dominant and the subordinate, knowing nothing else, have, through socialization, come to see the inequality in their world in a very different light from the original inhabitants.

Though this story is rather larger-than-life, it does allow us to see the role of socialization into cultural rules as conflict theorists see it. Their argument is that we must be careful not to dismiss the presence of conflict in societies just because a consensus seems to prevail. Naked force is only necessary so long as people see themselves as oppressed. If they can be persuaded that they are not oppressed, or if they fail to see that they are, then they can be willing architects in the design of their own subordination. The easiest way for the dominant to exercise power, and maintain their advantage as a result, is if the dominated are complicit in their own subordination.

Conflict theorists tell us, therefore, that rather than simply describe cultural rules in a society, we must carefully examine their content. We must ask: 'Who *benefits* from the *particular* set of rules prevailing in this society, rather than some other set?' Cultural rules cannot be neutral or all-benevolent. Of course, consensus theorists are right to say that people are socialized into pre-existing norms and values. But for conflict theorists this tells us only half the story. We must also find out whether some groups benefit more than others from the existence of a particular set of rules and have a greater say in their construction and interpretation. If they do, then the process of socialization into these is an instrument of their advantage – it is an instrument of their power.

## Ideas exercising power: the example of gender inequality legitimation

For example, even a cursory glance at the kinds of occupations held by women and the kinds of rewards they receive for doing them clearly indicates the advantages men have over women in our society. Of course, Britain once had a female prime minister, and today has some female civil servants, MPs, judges, and university vice-chancellors as well as an increasing number of women in leading positions in business. But this cannot hide the fact that there is still markedly unequal occupational opportunity, and unequal economic reward, based on gender. The facts are that males dominate the best-rewarded and most prestigious occupations and (despite the Equality and Human Rights Commission) usually receive greater rewards when they perform the same jobs as women.

Clearly, there is a considerable potential conflict of interests between men and women here. It is in men's interests for women not to compete in large numbers for the limited number of highly rewarded jobs. It is in men's interests for women to stay at home and provide domestic services for them. If women were to want something different, this would conflict with the desires, interests and ambitions of men.

So why is it that more women do *not* object to this state of affairs? If women are as systematically deprived of occupational opportunities and rewards by men as this, why do so many of them acquiesce in their deprivation? For example, why are some of the fiercest critics of the feminist movement women? Why do so many women *choose* to be (unpaid) houseworkers for the benefit of their husbands and children? Why is 'starting a family' the main ambition of so many girls? Why do they not wish to explore their potential in other activities more thoroughly?

Clearly, a substantial part of the answers to these questions is that women have been socialized into accepting this definition of themselves. For conflict theorists, this is a clear example of particular norms and values working in the interests of one section of society and against another. Through the ideas they have learned, women have been forced to accept a role that is subordinate to men.

There is one final question to be asked about this theoretical approach. How does the exercise of force by means of socialization into particular ideas happen? Conflict theorists say it can be intentional or unintentional. The rulers of many societies in the world today deliberately employ propaganda to persuade the ruled of the legitimacy of this arrangement. They also often control and censor mass media in their countries, to ensure lack of opposition to this controlled socialization.

The exercise of this kind of force can be less deliberate too. Take our example of the inequality between men and women in our society. To what extent does the image of women presented in advertising promote an acceptance of this inequality? Though the intention is to sell various products – from lingerie and perfume to household goods, alcohol, cars and office equipment – the images of women used in advertising are so specific that there are other, less intentional effects, too. Two images dominate. One is of the woman as the domestic at home, using the 'best' products to clean, polish, launder and cook. The other is of the woman as a sexually desirable object, guaranteed to magically adorn the life of any male who is sensible enough to drink a certain sort of beer, for example.

Such advertising socializes both men *and* women, of course. The outcome is a **stereotypical** view of womanhood and of the place of women in society, a view Raewyn Connell summarizes as that of 'emphasised femininity' (Connell 1987), which is embraced not only by those whom it disadvantages, but also by those who benefit from it. There *is* a consensus about such things. However, it is not the kind of consensus portrayed by the consensus theorist. It is an imposed consensus, preventing the conflict that would break out if people were allowed to see the world as it really is.

## Conflict theory: conclusion

There are a number of sociological theories that can be called structural-conflict theories, in that they are based on two main premises:

* social structures consist of unequally advantaged groups; the interests of these groups are in conflict, since inequality results from the domination and exploitation of the disadvantaged groups by the advantaged ones
* social order in such societies is maintained by force – either by actual force, or by force exercised through socialization.

## Consensus theory versus conflict theory

Structural-consensus theory and structural-conflict theory emphasize different kinds of influences on thought and behaviour. Though both theories see the origin of human social life in structural influences or determinants of society external to the individual, they disagree about what this outside society consists of. Consensus theory emphasizes the primacy of the influence of culture – what we learn to want as a result of socialization. Conflict theory, in contrast, pays most attention to the conflict inherent in the relationship between unequally advantaged groups in society and argues that the content of culture should be seen as a means of perpetuating relationships of inequality.

# Society as the creation of its members

## The influence of interpretation on behaviour

A third kind of sociological theory leads in a rather different direction. It still attempts to explain why human beings in society behave in the orderly ways they do, but instead of looking for the answer in the influence of a social structure which people confront and are constrained by, this theory argues something else. From this point of view, the most important influence on an individual's behaviour is the behaviour of other individuals towards him or her. The focus is not on general cultural rules, or on the unequal distribution of advantage in whole societies. It is on the way individual social encounters work – on how the parties to them are able to understand and thereby interact with one another. This is not to say that structural theories do not try to explain this, too. In consensus theory, for example, people are role players, and act out parts learned through socialization. But how do they decide which roles to play, in which social setting? Consensus theory does not try to explain why people choose one role rather than another. It is assumed that we somehow learn to make the right choices. This third theory, however, argues that the choice of role playing is much more complex than in this rather robotized view. It argues that the essence of social life lies in the quite extraordinary ability of humans to work out what is going on around them – their ability to attach meaning to reality – and then to choose to act in a particular way in the light of this interpretation. This is called **interpretive**, or **action theory**.

## Action theory

Action theorists stress the need to concentrate on the *micro*-level of social life, the way particular individuals are able to interact with one another in individual social encounters, rather than on the *macro*-level, the way the whole structure of society influences the behaviour of individuals. They argue that we must not think of societies as structures existing independently of, and prior to, the interaction of individuals. For action theorists, societies are the end result of human interaction, not its cause. Only by looking at how individual humans are able to interact can we come to understand how social order is created. To see how this happens, let us reflect on the kinds of action of which humans are capable.

Some human action is like the action of phenomena in the inanimate world – purpose*less*, or lacking intention. We all do things involuntarily – like sneezing, blinking or yawning. We do not *choose* to feel fear, excitement, or pain, or choose to react in certain ways to those feelings. So far as we know, the actions of non-human animate phenomena are purely instinctive (automatic or reflex responses to external stimuli). It is true that animals, for example, often appear to act in a purposive way by using their brains. They seem to choose to eat or sleep or be friendly or aggressive, or to choose to evacuate their bladders over the new living-room carpet. Nevertheless, the usual zoo-logical explanation is that even these often quite sophisticated patterns of animal action are involuntary. They are reactive and conditioned, rather than the product of voluntary creative decision-making.

In contrast, a significant amount of human action *is* voluntary. It is the product of a conscious decision to act, a result of thought. Very often, what we do is the result of choosing to act in one way rather than another. Furthermore, this is purposive, or goal-oriented choice. We choose between courses of action because, as humans, we are able to aim at an end or a goal and take action to achieve this. Such human action, therefore, is *intentional* action: we *mean* to do what we do in order to achieve our chosen purposes.

Where do these chosen purposes, or goals, come from? What action theory emphasizes is that we decide what to do in the light of our *interpretation* of the world around us. Being human means making sense of the settings or situations in which we find ourselves and choosing to act accordingly. To use the usual action theory phrase for this, we choose what to do in the light of our 'definition of the situation'. For example, suppose you wake up one summer morning to find the sun shining in a cloudless sky. You decide to sunbathe all day and to mow your lawn in the evening, when it will be cooler. At lunchtime, you see large clouds beginning to form in the distance. Because you decide there is a chance of a thunderstorm, you cut the grass immediately. You get very hot. It does not rain. In the evening, you go for a walk in the country. You come to a country pub and stop for a drink. As you sit outside you notice smoke rising on a hillside some distance away. As you watch the smoke gets thicker and darker. You decide the fire is unattended and out of control. You hurriedly find your mobile phone and ring the fire brigade. Shortly afterwards you hear a fire engine racing to the fire. You climb a nearby hill to have a better look. When you get there you see that the fire is, in fact, deliberate: it is a bonfire in the garden of a house on the hillside which you had been unable to see from the pub. Shortly afterwards you hear the fire engine returning to its base. You go back to the pub to finish your drink. It has been cleared away in your absence. You have no more money. You decide it is not your day. You decide to go home.

Of course, nearly all of the settings we have to make sense of involve more than this because nearly everything we do in our lives takes place in the company of others. Most of the situations we have to define in order to choose how to act are *social*; they involve other humans doing things. You see a very large man shaking his fist and shouting at you, and conclude that he is not overjoyed that you have driven into the back of his car. As a result you decide not to suggest that he was responsible for the accident because of the way he parked. You see a traffic warden slipping a parking ticket under your windscreen-wiper, and decide not to contribute to the Police Benevolent Fund after all. This is *social* action. It is action we choose to take in the light of what we interpret the behaviour of others to mean.

## Meaningful social interaction

There is more to social action than interpretation leading to action, however. Most of the time when we interact with other humans, they *want* us to arrive at certain interpretations of their actions – they *want* us to think one thing of them rather than another. The man whose car has just been damaged is not behaving in the rather distinctive manner described above because he wishes the culprit to come round to his house for tea. The woman scratching her nose in the auction room is not (usually) alleviating an itch. She is communicating her bid to the auctioneer, and she expects that the latter will interpret her actions as she wishes. Pedestrians in London streets do not wave to taxi-drivers because they are, or want to become, their friends. They do so because they want a lift.

Dress can often organize interpretation just as effectively as gestures, of course. Though the goth, the skinhead, the police officer and the traffic warden whom we encounter in the street make no *apparent* attempt to communicate with us, they are certainly doing so, nevertheless. They want us to think certain things about them when we see them, so they choose to communicate by the use of uniforms. They are making a symbolic use of dress, if you like; after all, like gestures, garments symbolize what their users want us to interpret about them.

The most effective symbols humans have at their disposal are words – linguistic symbols. Though dress, gesture, touch and even smell can often communicate our meanings and organize the interpretations of others adequately enough, clearly the most efficient – and most remarkable – way in which we can get others to understand us is through language. This is why action theorists are often interested in the way we use language to exchange meanings with each other. Language, verbal or written, is the uniquely human device which we are able to use to interact meaningfully with one another, and thereby to create society.

From this point of view, societies are made up of individuals engaging in a countless number of meaningful encounters. The result is social order. But this is no *determined* order. It is not the result of the imposition of cultural rules, as the consensus theorist sees it. Nor is it the result of the constraints of a world where advantages are unequally distributed, and where cultural rules legitimate these constraints, as the conflict theorist sees it. Instead, society is an order created, or accomplished, by the capacities of the members themselves. It is the outcome of innumerable occasions of interaction, each one accomplished by interpreting, meaning-attributing actors who can make sense of the social settings in which they find themselves and who choose courses of action accordingly.

## The social construction of reality

There is another important difference between structural and interpretive conceptions of society. For structural theorists, the character of a society – its social structure – is not in doubt. It is a 'real' thing that exists outside of its members. For the interpretivist, however, it is much more difficult to describe a society that is the outcome of interpretation as somehow 'true' or 'real' in this structural sense.

For the interpretivist, being human involves interpreting what is going on around one – saying 'this is what is happening here', and choosing an appropriate course of action in the light of this interpretation. However, such interpretations of 'what is going on here' can only ever be considered 'correct' or 'true' for the particular person doing the interpreting. What is 'really' going on depends on how the individual sees it. Reality is in the eye of the beholder. We act in ways we consider appropriate. What we consider appropriate depends upon what we think the behaviour of others means. It is therefore by no means inconceivable that other people, in exactly the same social situations as ourselves, would have taken the behaviour around them to mean something very different, and would therefore have taken very different courses of action from us.

For example, a car crashes into a wall on a wet winter's evening. The police officer called to the scene discovers a dead driver and a strong smell of alcohol in the car. A search reveals an empty whisky bottle underneath a seat. Like all humans encountering a social situation, the officer engages in a process of interpretation, defining the situation. Weighing up the evidence, he or she decides that the crash was an accident caused by the driver being drunk and losing control of the vehicle in difficult driving conditions. Another officer called to the scene might use this evidence to interpret things rather differently, however. He or she might consider the possibility that the driver deliberately drove the car into the wall as an act of suicide, having first given himself courage to do so by drinking the whisky. The second officer would then make inquiries that the first would not. The dead man's domestic and work affairs would be looked into and it might be discovered that he had become severely depressed about his future. The officer would decide that his suspicions of suicide had been sufficiently confirmed by this additional evidence, and that it should be given at the Coroner's court when the inquest was held.

How the death is finally interpreted depends, of course, upon the decision of the court, when the evidence is reassessed by a new set of interpreters   particularly the Coroner. The Coroner's decision will define the death as either accidental or a suicide. But is this judgment the 'truth'? Who is to say what the 'reality' of the situation was? What 'really' happened here? In the case of this kind of example, of course, no one will ever know for certain.

Even in less dramatic circumstances, actions still always depend upon the interpretation of the beholder. Suppose you come across a group of adults sitting together in a children's playground. Should this situation worry you? If the group is made up of women you are perhaps going to assume they are parents watching their children play; if the group consists of younger men you may be less likely to assume they are related to the playing children and perhaps you look for evidence of alcohol being consumed, or, in some inner-city parks, of drug deals being made. What matters is not so much that you are right, that you see what is *really* happening, but that:

- you cannot help but come to some sort of interpretation or other (even if it is that you do *not* know what is happening); and
- what you decide to do will be the result of this interpretation.

Though subsequent events may 'prove' things one way or another, initial action undertaken by human beings in such social circumstances, though always involving a process of interpretation, can never be assumed to be definitely 'true' or 'real'. It can only ever be how we choose to see things, often on the basis of fairly limited information and assumptions. The world 'is' what we think it is. As W. I. Thomas puts it: if a human 'defines situations as real, they are real in their consequences' (Thomas 1966).

## Action theory: conclusion

In contrast to the structuralist view then, for action theory social 'reality' is not a factual, objective, unambiguous state of affairs. Reality can only ever be what the actors involved in interaction *think* is real, and what they *think* is real determines what they decide to do. Reality is therefore quite definitely the negotiated creation of individuals in interaction with one another. Furthermore, because the social worlds so created are dependent on the interpretations of particular individuals in particular social settings, they are much more precarious constructions than is suggested by the notion of social structures determining behaviour.

Consensus, conflict and action theories thus identify different factors as significant in explaining the nature of social life, and of the relationship between the individual and society. As we shall see, for most of the time sociology has been in existence as a distinct discipline, the kinds of issues highlighted by consensus, conflict and action approaches have been central to sociological theorizing. Although only some of this theorizing falls neatly or exclusively within one of these traditions alone, they are nonetheless useful as reference points from which to understand differences and debates in sociological thought. We need to go back to the nineteenth-century social theorists' attempts to understand the specific features of modern society to see where these differences and debates within social theory begin.

# Classical sociological theorizing: analysing modernity

The work of three nineteenth-century sociologists in particular has reverberated through the twentieth and twenty-first centuries, and it is for this reason that they are regarded as the classic figures in the discipline. They are a Frenchman, Emile Durkheim (1858–1917), and two Germans, Karl Marx (1818–83) and Max Weber (1864–1920). Despite the great differences in the content and direction of their sociological theories, the work of Durkheim, Marx and Weber each represents an intellectual and political response to the same historical circumstances. The most powerful set of forces at work in nineteenth-century Europe was unleashed in the eighteenth century during the period historians call the **Enlightenment**; today these forces are summarized in sociology as **modernity**. Sociology came into being because of modernity, and the theories of many of its major figures in both the nineteenth and twentieth centuries can be seen as different kinds of responses to the birth of the modern world. This is particularly true of the classic writings of Durkheim, Marx and Weber.

As we shall see later (Chapter 9), there are those today who believe that over the last few decades a new set of social changes has once again transformed the world. According to *postmodernists*, the circumstances in which we live now and the ways in which we think – particularly the ways in which we think about ourselves – are so completely different from those described by the theorists of modernity such as Durkheim, Marx and Weber that we should realize that the world of modernity has been superseded by a new world, that of *postmodernity*. However, as Chapter 9 will show, the many critics of **postmodernism** hotly dispute this depiction of contemporary life. Indeed, the debate between modernist theorists and postmodernists has been one of the principal features of recent social theorizing. But we must leave an examination of the ideas of postmodernism and the competing ones of its critics until the end of this book. At this early stage in our journey we need to examine the profound changes to human existence ushered in by the emergence of modern life that gave birth to the discipline of sociology.

## Modernity

The idea of the 'modern' originated as an account of the kinds of institutions, ideas and behaviours that grew out of the decline of medieval society in Europe. Although the seeds of modernity had been sown hundreds of years before, it was not until the nineteenth century that modern life became securely established. The changes involved were so momentous that Karl Polanyi (1973) does not overstate the case when he uses the phrase *The Great Transformation* to describe them. Marx and Engels are even more graphic in their famous depiction of modernity:

> All fixed, fast-frozen relations, with their train of ancient and venerable prejudices and opinions, are swept away, all new-formed ones become antiquated before they can ossify. All that is solid melts into air, all that is holy is profaned, and men at last are forced to face . . . the real conditions of their lives and their relations with their fellow men. (Marx and Engels 2008 [1848])

In very summary form, the changes wrought by modernity involved the emergence and establishment of:

- **capitalism**
- mass production based on the factory
- a hugely increased, and largely urbanized, population
- the nation-state as the modern form of government
- Western domination of the globe
- secular forms of knowledge, particularly science.

## Capitalism

In pre-capitalist economies, though there is some manufacturing and some trade, people more usually produce goods for their own consumption. This is particularly true of pre-capitalist agriculture. Capitalism means something very different. Capitalists employ workers to produce their goods for them, in return for a wage. The point of producing these goods is to sell them in the marketplace for more than the costs involved in their production. That is, capitalist production is about the pursuit of profit. The more efficient the production, the more profitable it can be. In the systematic pursuit of profit, what matters most is the market value of a good, the availability of markets, and the efficiency with which an enterprise is organized. In particular, this involves the rational management of the labour force so that costs are kept down.

Capitalism thus involves the establishment of new ways of thinking and acting, largely absent in the pre-modern world. Workers have to sell their labour to employers as a commodity in a labour market. Their survival depends not on what they produce for themselves but on the wages they receive, with which they have to purchase the goods and services they need. As a result, their life-chances are crucially determined by the rewards they receive for the work they do. That is, a system of class inequality emerges, largely based on occupational rewards. In addition, identity becomes intimately linked to work and class membership; how you see yourself and how you are seen by others becomes defined by the work you do and the rewards this work brings. One of the social expressions of this aspect of modernity is the emergence of a labour movement: organizations, such as trade unions, become established to represent the collectively held interests of workers in similar occupational groupings. Gender inequality develops too. Not only do male workers tend to receive greater rewards than working women but, over time, and as the mechanization of production increases, women become progressively excluded from the workplace. This produces a separation of life and life-chances into, on the one hand, a male-dominated public sphere, of the world of work and wages, and on the other, a female-dominated private sphere, of the world of unwaged domestic labour. Women thus become economically dependent on their husbands and defined principally in terms of their role in managing the domestic world.

Agricultural production and trade became capitalized first and then, in the nineteenth century, capitalism became the dynamic behind the huge and rapid growth in industrial production.

## Techniques of production

Alongside the emergence of capitalism, the so-called Industrial Revolution allowed new ways of working and producing goods to be instituted. Rapid technological advances led to large-scale manufacturing being located in a designated workplace – the factory – and the organization of production became the object of rational calculation. The factory system involved the workers being systematically organized and controlled, with the separation of the process of production into specialized tasks a distinctive feature of this regulation. Later on, and with further technological advances, modern mass production techniques became ever more sophisticated, culminating in what is known as Fordism – the rational and efficient organization of manufacturing. (The name is derived from the founder of the assembly line in motor manufacturing, Henry Ford.) Fordism involves not only the mass production of a standardized product (Ford is famously remembered for saying that his customers could have any colour Model T Ford that they liked so long as it was black), but rigidly bureaucratic organizational structures, the pursuit of high productivity and collective wage bargaining.

## Population change

The Great Transformation included an unprecedented growth in population and its concentration in urban settings. Birth rates rose and death rates fell; according to Kumar (1978), the population of Europe grew from around 120 million in 1750 to around 468 million in 1913. The urbanization of the population was another major feature of modernity; there was mass migration from the countryside to the towns and cities that were springing up around the centres of industrial production. This provided the template for a typical feature of modern twentieth-century life – the urban conurbation.

## The nation-state

Modernity saw a new form of polity – the nation-state – come into being. States have a centralized form of government whose absolute power extends over a national territory. Governmental decrees – laws – are passed which apply to all those living on this territory and the state's ultimate power resides in its monopoly over the use of force, for example, by means of its control of the armed forces. The emergence of state government spawns a civil authority too – a system of political administrators and officials whose task it is to enforce state-sponsored decisions across the national territory. By the twentieth century, global political power resided in the nation-states of the West and ideas of citizenship, nationalism, democracy, socialism, conservatism and liberalism dominated political thinking and discourse.

## Global domination by the West

The establishment of the power of the nation-state triggered the political, economic and cultural domination of the globe by European states. The rapid economic development of the West in the nineteenth century depended crucially on easy access to raw materials from around the globe. The political and military power of these states enabled them to plunder the material and human resources of weaker global areas and began the process of the unequal development of the First and Third Worlds with which we live today. Later on, this Western domination was cemented politically and culturally by colonialism and economically by the control of global markets.

## Cultural change: the rise of rationality and the secularization of knowledge

The Enlightenment provided the cultural shift necessary for the final triumph of modernity. An historical moment of the eighteenth century, the Enlightenment refers to the emergence of a new confidence in the power of human reason. Knowledge production before the Enlightenment typically involved experts translating religious texts or signs. In this way it became possible for people to know what their God or gods had in mind for them. In complete contrast, the Enlightenment promoted the essentially secular view that by using reason, by thinking rationally, humans could, for the first time in human history, produce certain knowledge and could therefore harness this knowledge in the pursuit of progress. The exemplar of rationality was scientific thinking and scientific activity. The intellectual engine of modernity was thus the belief that nothing could remain a mystery, nothing would remain undiscovered, if reason were made the guide. Moreover, this would allow humankind not only to know things for certain but to know how to make things better – to achieve progress. The pre-modern dependence on the virtues of tradition and continuity gave way to a commitment to the benefits of reason-inspired change, innovation and progress. This way of thinking is called **modernism**. It is the rise of modernism, a cultural change in belief about what constitutes knowledge and what knowledge is for, that directly promoted the rise of sociology and sociological theorizing.

## Modernism and sociology

Modernist thinking involves the idea that the purpose of acquiring knowledge is, as Giddens puts it: 'To influence for the better the human condition' (Giddens 1987). Modernity implies the constant pursuit of improvement in human lives and the pursuit of progress. Unlike traditional settings, where virtue lies in things remaining the same, in modern worlds change, development and improvement are the goals. As Cheal has pointed out, believing in the ideal and possibility of progress means 'believing that things tomorrow can always be better than they are today, which in turn means being prepared to overturn the existing order of things in order to make way for progress. It means, in other words, being prepared to break with tradition' (Cheal 1991: 27).

How should this progress be achieved? Underpinning the belief in the possibility of progress is a belief in the power of reason – in the ability of humans to think about themselves, their condition and their society reflexively and rationally, and to improve it in the light of such rational thought. The idea that humans can not only think about, and explain, their lives – produce *social theories* in fact – but can employ reason to change society for the better, is a specifically modern notion. The idea that reason can provide an agenda and a set of prescriptions for living, rather than relying on divine intervention and instruction, only began to prevail after the Enlightenment. Summarizing the effects of the Enlightenment, Badham says:

> It was during this period that faith in divine revelation, and the authority of the Church as interpreter of God's will, were increasingly undermined by this new confidence in the ability of human reason to provide an understanding of the world and a guide for human conduct. Similarly, the

understanding of history as the chronicle of the fall of man from God's
grace, with spiritual salvation only attainable in the next world, was
largely replaced by a belief in human perfectibility and the increasing faith
in man's power and ability to use his new-found knowledge to improve
mankind's state. The importance of these two assumptions should not
be underestimated. Without the faith in reason, social theory could not
be regarded as playing any important role in society. Without the belief
in the possibility of progress, whatever reason's ability to understand the
nature of society, social theory would not be able to fulfil any positive role
in improving upon man's fate. (Badham 1986: 11)

So sociology is not only a product of modernity – of a belief in the
power of human reason to create knowledge which can be used to
achieve progress. In addition, the world created by modernity is its
principal subject matter: Giddens has said that, in sociology, the
'prime field of study is the social world brought about by the advent
of modernity' (Giddens 1987: vii–viii). As he also puts it, the very
existence of sociology is 'bound up with the "project of modernity"'
(Giddens 1987: 26). The construction of social theories thus reflects
a concern not only with *how* we live, but with how we *should* live;
social theories of modern society try not only to describe and explain
our social world, but to diagnose its problems and propose solutions.
According to Giddens, this places sociology in the 'tensed zone of transition between diagnosis and prognosis' (Giddens 1987: 17).

The obvious problem, of course, concerns the goal and direction of
desirable change. The following chapters attempt to summarize the
contributions of some influential nineteenth-, twentieth- and twenty-
first-century sociological figures to this enterprise – the contribution of
sociology to the '**project of modernity**'.

## Further reading

What you use as further reading and how you use the books suggested
at the end of each chapter depends on the stage you have reached in
your studies. A-level students will get most benefit from the theory
textbooks as will undergraduates in other subjects taking sociology
modules. First-year undergraduates reading sociology should try and
go beyond a reliance on such texts and also use at least the famous
extracts contained in the readers. Second- and third-year undergraduates should consult the original texts and major works themselves
discussed in the chapters, as well as the books dedicated to particular
theorists.

## Textbooks

Some of these are more difficult than others. Decide for yourself which ones you find most accessible and helpful.

Baert, Patrick and Carreira da Silva, Filipe (2009): *Social Theory in the Twentieth Century and Beyond*, Polity.

Bauman, Zygmunt and May, Tim (2001): *Thinking Sociologically*, 2nd edn, Blackwell.

Cuff, E. C., Francis, D. W. and Sharrock, W. W. (2006): *Perspectives in Sociology*, 5th edn, Routledge.

May, Tim and Powell, Jason (2008): *Situating Social Theory*, 2nd edn, Open University Press.

Ritzer, George (2007): *Sociological Theory*, 7th edn, McGraw-Hill.

Seidman, Steven (2008): *Contested Knowledge*: *social theory today*, 4th edn, Blackwell.

### Readers including extracts from the classic works

Calhoun, Craig et al. (2007a): *Classical Sociological Theory*, 2nd edn, Blackwell's Readers in Sociology, Blackwell.

Calhoun, Craig et al. (2007b): *Contemporary Sociological Theory*, 2nd edn, Blackwell's Readers in Sociology, Blackwell.

Farganis, James (ed.) (2007): *Readings in Social Theory: the classic tradition to postmodernism*, 5th edn, McGraw-Hill.

Lemert, Charles (ed.) (2004): *Social Theory: the multicultural and classic readings*, 3rd edn, Westview.

### Readers on theories and theorists

Ritzer, George (ed.) (2002): *The Blackwell Companion to Major Social Theorists*, Blackwell.

Turner, Bryan (ed.) (2000): *The Blackwell Companion to Social Theory*, 2nd edn, Blackwell.

# 2 MARX AND MARXISM

**Karl Marx:** born Trier, Rhineland, 1818, died London, 1883

## Major works

*The Poverty of Philosophy* (1847)
*The Communist Manifesto* (1848)
*The Eighteenth Brumaire of Louis Bonaparte* (1852)
*Grundrisse (Outline of a Critique of Political Economy)* (1857)
*Preface to a Contribution to the Critique of Political Economy* (1859)
*Theories of Surplus Value* (1862–3)
*Capital*, volumes 1–3 (1863–7)
*Critique of the Gotha Programme* (1875)

## Introduction

*'Men make history but not under conditions of their own choosing.'*

Marx is an important transitional figure between those writing in the aftermath of the French Revolution of 1789 and the writings of Durkheim and Weber. Whilst Marx sought to further the radical political changes initiated by the 1789 Revolution, Durkheim and Weber's sociologies were in part shaped by their attempts to take stock of its legacy in the politics and culture of early twentieth-century France and Germany respectively.

Marx's ideas developed initially from his criticisms of German Idealist philosophy, particularly the work of Immanuel Kant, (1724–1804), G. W. F. **Hegel** (1770–1831), and Ludwig **Feuerbach** (1804–72). Kant and Hegel were inspired by the Revolutionary ideals of democracy, equality and freedom and yet critical of the practices employed to attain them. Each, in different ways, sought to use philosophy to understand more systematically how peaceful progress towards equality and freedom can be sustained. For this generation of German Idealist philosophers then, the French Revolution was in important senses unfinished, and Marx, beginning in the early 1840s, took up their project to work out how its promise could be delivered.

Marx was one of a series of critics who argued that, despite their best efforts to find a secure rational basis for political progress, the problem with the German Idealists was that their ideas remained just that: *ideas* about how to proceed which left the real world untouched. Marx, in contrast, wanted to bring intellectual analysis and practical political action together to change society. Therefore, he turned to the political economists, Adam Smith (1723–90) and David Ricardo (1772–1823), as well as to French socialists, to develop an overall theory of the history, politics and economy of modern capitalist societies. We can see here, then, a clear example of the **Enlightenment**-inspired belief that humans can, by understanding their world, thereby also change it.

Looking at Marx's work from the perspective of the early twenty-first century, it is easy to dismiss his ideas as quite simply both wrong in their analysis of **capitalism** and disastrous in their predictions about the promise of the communist society that he believed would replace it. However, while it is important to expose the failures of Marx's predictions for the future of capitalism, this does not exhaust his significance within social theory. It is this latter aspect of his work which we will discuss in more detail in this chapter.

Marx's was one of the most significant attempts to develop a multi-dimensional analysis of modern society; one which would not just describe the ways things appear to be but would penetrate beneath accepted views and offer a decisive challenge to the most powerful beliefs and values of early capitalist society. This ambition led him to develop an historical analysis of modern society which focused on what was often overlooked in other kinds of history. Rather than looking at monarchs and battles, he argued that historians should look at the work of ordinary people, because this is the activity that really makes and changes history. Perhaps more importantly for his significance as a social theorist, however, Marx returns repeatedly to the failure of the leading economists of his time to recognize the social relationships between real people that are necessary to create the commodities on which capitalism relies. As Giddens puts it, for Marx, 'any and every "economic" phenomenon is at the same time always a social phenomenon, and the existence of a particular kind of "economy" presupposes a definite kind of society' (Giddens 1971: 10).

For Marx, 'economic activity' always includes work or labour as a set of social relationships. This is what he is trying to draw attention to with his argument that the crucial feature distinguishing humans from animals is that humans have to transform the natural world in order to survive in it. Whereas animals can survive by consuming what they need, humans need to *make* everything they need – from clothing to shelter to food – out of materials from their natural environment. Without burrows, lacking fur or claws, in this vulnerable state humans need to work together to survive, hence they need to develop social relationships: 'By social we understand the co-operation of several individuals, no matter under what conditions, in what manner, and to what end' (Marx and Engels 1969: 291–2).

Here, then, Marx is developing a sociological analysis of economic production. It is not only that, for example, we build homes or sow crops, but that we do so as 'praxis'; by this term Marx refers to all the practical know-how, theoretical knowledge and other social resources available to any particular historical society or group within it. This is what he means by referring to his method of social, economic and political analysis as '**historical materialism**' – nature, both 'out there' and our own biological possibilities, is 'the raw material' which we work on and transform in order to produce what we need to survive. The tools and actions we put in place to fulfil basic needs also change nature, and the resulting new product in turn changes our future needs. For example, a particular society may learn that certain crops grow better than others and so focus on these; they then become staples for that society and scarcity will come to mean an absence of this particular crop rather than of any food at all. In a very real sense then, humans are social products too. We create ourselves anew in creating what we need to survive, as 'universal producers' we are also historical products.

Marx's strategy of making explicit the social relationships embedded in all aspects of human society offers a powerful way of making the familiar world strange and inviting us to reexamine it. Consider everything in a particular society, Marx suggests – from fabulous palaces and galleries to factories, roads, beds and beer glasses – as fossil-like renditions of layers of human imagination, labour, know-how and communication. He then invites us to question how it is that we are led to experience the social world as an alien force, even though we all help to create it. This point goes to the heart of Marx's work and its distinctiveness within social thought. We will return to it at the end of the chapter after we have looked at some of his ideas in detail.

## Marx and historical materialism

For Marx, then, **social structures** are not randomly created. He argues that there is a quite definite pattern to the way societies in different parts of the world, and at different times in history, have organized the production of material goods. This theory of history and society is, as we mentioned above, called historical materialism. For our purposes we can identify the following elements.

Looking back over the history of human societies, Marx claims, we can with the benefit of hindsight identify a pattern to the process of economic and societal development and change. Societies that have existed or do exist today exhibit one of five different ways of organizing production. These different ways of producing goods Marx called **modes of production**. The five are (in chronological order): the primitive communist, ancient, feudal, capitalist and communist modes.

Apart from the first and last modes of production – the primitive communist and communist – each mode has one crucial characteristic in common. Each is a way of producing goods based on classes. Though the term 'class' has different uses elsewhere in sociology (and all sorts of uses in speech) the Marxist usage is a quite specific one. According to Marx, in all non-communist societies – in the ancient, feudal and capitalist modes – there are just two classes that matter. These are the class that owns the means of production    it is their property – and the class that does not own it.

In systems of production based on classes, goods are produced in the following way. The majority of people, who do not own the means of production, do the productive work for the benefit of those – the minority – who do own it. In Marxist theory, this is the key feature of non-communist societies existing throughout history. The production of material goods always takes place by means of the exploitation of the labour of the majority, non-property-owning class by the minority class, which owns the means of production and does not work. In other words, whatever degree of cooperation or even friendliness might exist between individuals from each class, their interests objectively conflict. Those belonging to the dominant economic class are by definition engaged in an exploitative relationship with those in the subordinate class.

There are no classes in either of the communist modes. In primitive communist societies people cannot produce a surplus. This is usually because of an inhospitable environment, or a lack of technological know-how, or a combination of the two. Because such peoples only produce enough to allow them to exist at subsistence level, everyone has to work. There is no surplus property, and so therefore no opportunity for classes to emerge to exploit it. In the communist mode there are no classes because private property has been abolished – individuals are not able to own the means of production. Because in any class-based mode of production goods are produced in this exploitative way, in Marxist theory the owners of the means of production are usually referred to as the dominant class, while the non-owning, exploited class which performs the productive work is called the subordinate class.

According to Marx, the history of human society is the history of different kinds of productive systems based on class exploitation. He says we can divide up the history of any society into different epochs or ages, each of which is dominated by one particular mode of production, with its own characteristic class relationships. All societies will eventually pass through all these stages in history and all will eventually become communist. However, not all societies evolve at the same rate. This is why at any particular time in history different societies exhibit different modes of production – they are at different stages of historical development.

All non-communist modes have in common the production of goods by means of the domination and exploitation of one class by another. What distinguishes different modes of production from one another? Each non-communist mode of production has a different, dominant, property-owning class and a different subordinate, exploited, non-property-owning class. Furthermore, each mode grows out of the previous one.

## The ancient mode of production

The oldest form of class production – hence its name – is the ancient mode of production. This mode grew out of the subsistence or primitive communist mode primarily because of technological improvements. For example, in the Iron Age humans developed productive techniques that allowed for specialist animal farming and settled agricultural production. This in turn enabled the production of a surplus, and required a more complex **division of labour** than was necessary in a purely sub-sistence economy. In effect, a dominant class of *non-producers* could emerge.

The distinguishing feature of this mode of production is that people are owned as productive property by other, more powerful people. That is, it is production based on slavery. Here, then, there is a domin-ant class of *masters* and a subordinate class of *slaves*. Production takes place by means of the involuntary labour of people who are owned as property by others. Ancient Greece and Rome provide the classic examples of slavery as a mode of production. In the Greek and Roman empires about a third of the population was enslaved. Most had entered into slavery as prisoners-of-war, following battles undertaken as part of the imperialist (empire-building) policies of the Greek and Roman states. One of the main reasons why the ancient mode of production disintegrated was that the state power upon which it depended became eroded. As it became more and more difficult for the ancient states to control and coerce people living in distant parts of their empires, so did the possibility of sustaining slavery as a mode of production.

## The feudal mode of production

In place of the ancient mode of production emerged a new mode with a much more local character, called feudalism. Feudal production was based upon the ability of warriors or nobles controlling small local ter-ritories by force of arms to coerce and exploit an agricultural labour force. In feudalism the dominant class controls the land, and comprises the *lords*. The subordinate class is made up of *serfs*. Production takes place by means of the labour of those who have to work the land in order to survive. Since these labourers do not own the land, but are merely tenants on it, they are obliged to give up much of the product of their labour as rent (in the form of a 'fee' called a *tithe*) to the landlords.

Feudalism dominated Europe from the Dark Ages until early modern times. Two factors in particular heralded its death and helped to usher in a new mode of production, based on a new form of class exploitation. First, strongly centralized political power was re-established in Europe not in the form of large, unwieldy empires, but in the form of absolutist monarchies. This allowed sufficient state control to be exercised within national territories in European coun-tries for proper legal systems to be devised and enforced. This, in turn, provided an opportunity for economic activity to extend beyond local feudal boundaries, and for widespread trade to become possible, for example, through the gradual unification of tax and currency systems within major trading areas, and along major trading routes such as the Rhine.

Second, as a result of the changes brought about by the agricultural revolution, agricultural production became rationalized and more efficient. One of the most significant consequences of this was the Enclosures Acts. These Acts denied the bulk of the agricultural labour force the subsistence rights over the strips of land they had been entitled to under feudalism. Replaced by sheep, and by non-labour-intensive farming using machines, these labourers were made landless. As Marx described it in *Capital*, 'Sheep ate men' (Marx 2008). Thrown off the land, and with no other means of subsistence than their labour power, workers were forced to sell their labour to employers for a wage. A *labour market* thus emerged for the first time.

## The capitalist mode of production

Production now took on a new class character. The labour power of a class of landless labourers – the **proletariat**, as Marxists call them – could now be purchased for a wage by a class of property-owning employers, for whom the Marxist term is the **bourgeoisie**.

So capitalism developed in Britain before industrialization: agricultural goods were produced first of all in a capitalistic way. It was only later, when factories were built and industrial machines were developed, that industrial capitalism became established and an urban proletariat emerged. In capitalist society, the bourgeoisie are the dominant class because, like the masters in slave societies and the lords in feudal societies, they own the productive wealth – the means of production.

During the development of capitalism, the character of the property in which capitalists have invested their wealth has, of course, altered. In the early stages of capitalism, as we have just noted, productive property primarily took the form of land, with the proletariat earning wages as agricultural labourers. Later, industrial production gave rise to capitalist investment in factories and machines, with the proletariat earning wages as industrial manual labourers. Still later, capitalism took on the form typical of contemporary industrial capitalism. Today, instead of actually owning and controlling industrial production themselves, the ownership of productive property usually takes the form of capital investment in stocks and shares. (Though of course, capitalist landowners, and owners and controllers of their own enterprises – especially the smaller ones – still exist in plenty today.)

Despite these alterations to the nature of productive property in capitalist society, for Marxists the character of class relations between owners of property and non-owners of property is essentially the same as in the earlier class-based modes of production. Though the bourgeoisie do not make goods themselves, they nevertheless own the means of production. For this reason, they will always profit from the difference between the cost to them of the labour of the proletariat, and the value of the goods produced by the proletariat's labour power. The important fact is that workers will always be paid less than the value of the goods they produce. If this did not happen, the system could not work; without profit, reinvestment of this surplus into the productive power of capitalism would not take place, and enterprises would wither and die in the face of competition. This *surplus value* costs the capitalist nothing, and is a tangible symbol of the exploitation of wage-earners' labour power by employers. Though not as obvious as the exaction of tithes by feudal lords, or the ownership of people by slave-owners, the relationship between the capitalist and the wage-earner is of exactly the same kind. In Marx's words, 'The history of all hitherto existing society is the history of class struggles' (Marx and Engels 1976 [1848]).

## The role of the superstructure

So far, our account of Marxist theory has concentrated on production – on economic relationships. But what about the cultural, political and legal dimensions of social life? As we have seen, in developing his critique of capitalism Marx is concerned to show that economic relationships are also social relationships in that they presuppose a definite social, political, cultural and legal context. This other side of Marx's analysis also needs to be examined now: how does he understand the relationship between economic production and the cultural, political and artistic dimensions of a society?

Marxism is often understood as claiming that those aspects of society placed under the broad heading of 'culture' are really ideas in our heads, individually or collectively, which like mirrors 'reflect' economic relationships. But perhaps it makes more sense to distinguish between dominant systems of belief and the ideas we have as individuals. Marx allows the possibility that there will be individuals and groups within a society who have ideas that differ from or challenge dominant views, and indeed he would have to allow this or else rule out the possibility of his own ideas! However, his argument is that, in a class society, the more dominant beliefs and values will tend to support the interests of the dominant class. In order to convey this, Marx calls the way a society organizes production its **infrastructure** or **economic base**. The rest of its social organization – its non-economic activities and its ideas, beliefs and philosophies – he calls its **superstructure**. The use of these terms is important, since it stresses the way in which a society's superstructure is created by its base; that is, one set of activities is built upon the other.

## Institutions

First, at the level of social structure, the non-economic institutions in any epoch are always organized in such a way as to benefit the mode of production. For Marxist sociologists writing in the twentieth century, the task then became that of analysing how specific institutions which appear to be divorced from economic considerations are in fact structured so as to support the values and activities of capitalist economic activity. Below are two such accounts of key institutions – the family and the education system – in capitalist society:

## The family

Most Marxist analyses draw attention to the way in which families tend to encourage and reproduce hierarchical, in-egalitarian relationships, and to act as a safety-valve for the work-force of capitalist societies, dampening down their discontent so that it is robbed of revolutionary content. In providing a place where children can be conceived, born and reared in relative safety, the family is providing tomorrow's labour force. At the same time, by offering a centre for relaxation, recreation, refreshment and rest, the family helps to ensure that members of today's labour force are returned to work each day with their capacity to work renewed and strengthened. This is what is meant when it is said that the family reproduces labour power on a generational as well as a daily basis.

## Education

Bowles and Gintis argue that schooling operates within the 'long shadow of work': that is, the education system reflects the organization of production in capitalist society. For example, the fragmentation of most work processes is mirrored in the breaking up of the curriculum into tiny 'packages' of knowledge, so that each subject is divorced from all others; lack of control over work processes is reflected in the powerlessness of pupils with regard to what they will learn in school or how they will learn it; and the necessity of working for pay when jobs seem pointless and unfulfilling in themselves is paralleled by the emphasis in schools on learning in order to gain good grades, rather than learning for its own sake. Therefore, Bowles and Gintis claim there is a correspondence between the nature of work in capitalist societies, and the nature of schooling. (Bilton et al. 1981: 292–3; 387)

Each institution betrays the imprint of capitalism and the outcome is the same – the reproduction of capitalist relationships regardless of what might be intended by the individuals involved. In this light, twentieth-century Marxist sociology closely parallels the structural-functionalist theories we shall discuss in the following chapter. For such sociology, as for **functionalism**, the analysis of an institution takes the form of identifying its positive role in the **social system**. Indeed, the above accounts of the benefits for capitalism of family life and schooling could quite legitimately be said to identify the 'function' that these institutions perform in meeting the needs of capitalism. Though both Marxism and functionalism are 'systemic' theories, the crucial difference concerns the way they each characterize both the system and those whose needs are being met by it.

## Ideologies

The relationship between the base and the superstructure is apparent in the way the prevailing beliefs in any epoch also support the organization of production. This is especially important in societies where the activity of producing goods involves the exploitation of the bulk of the population, rendering them severely disadvantaged and the society grossly unequal. While the compliance of the subordinate class in this arrangement can be secured by physical force, in the Marxist view the most effective way of ensuring that compliance is via prevalent beliefs and values. As we said earlier, for Marxists, **ideologies** are systems of belief which:

- legitimate the class-based system of production by making it appear right and just, and/or
- obscure the reality of its consequences for those involved.

According to Marxists, the dominant ideas, beliefs and values in a class society (which are the ideas about which there is most agreement) are not there by chance. They act as ideologies, propping up a structure which, without such ideological support, would risk serious challenge from the subordinate class. Marxists argue that although from time to time dominant classes *do* have to resort to naked force to maintain their power and supremacy, the absence of such obvious coercion should not be taken to signify an absence of exploitation. On the contrary, they suggest, all a lack of naked oppression can ever indicate is a lack of effective opposition, and the lack of any need to use force. It does not mean that domination is not taking place – only that the dominated are insufficiently aware of their condition or else lack the power to have their resistance registered.

How do such dominant ideas become established? Like functionalists, Marxists argue that particular ideas are transmitted through various key agencies of socialization. In contemporary society, for example, both Marxists and functionalists would point to the important role played by institutions like the family, the education system and the mass media in promoting generally held beliefs and values. The essential difference between functionalists and Marxists concerns their interpretations of the role of the socialization process that such institutions try to ensure. For functionalists, socialization is the way we learn ideas that we need to know in order to think and behave in the ways required of us by the social system. For Marxists, it is the way we learn those ideas which serves to justify the real character of a class society. For both theories there is a prevailing culture which people are expected to learn through socialization. The difference between them concerns the job this culture is taken to perform. For functionalists, it ensures social integration. For Marxists, it is intended to ensure social inequality and domination.

## Ideologies in contemporary Britain

We can look at some prevailing ideas in contemporary capitalist Britain to see how a Marxist would explain their superstructural significance. From the Marxist viewpoint, the type of ideas in Britain which help to perpetuate capitalism in this society are ones that attempt to:

- divert people's attention away from the reality of class inequality
- reproduce demand for goods by encouraging consumerism
- encourage the wage-earning class to accept their subordinate role
- justify the inequality between the classes.

How is this done? How do such ideas come to prevail? A Marxist approach to the superstructure of contemporary Britain might include the following.

## Diversionary institutions

Capitalist production is exploitative, according to Marxists. A major reason for its survival is that institutions exist to divert the attention of the exploited away from the reality of their condition. One important vehicle for doing this is the entertainment industry. For example, much popular music, with its characteristic emphasis on the attractions of romantic love and/or sexual satisfaction as the pinnacle of human fulfilment hardly aims to shed light on the reality of class exploitation! And the same can be said of much popular literature. Escapism of other kinds also abounds: the never-ending production of crime novels, war novels, science fiction, and so on, bears testimony to this escapism. A substantial proportion of television and radio programmes has similar consequences. From situation comedies to quiz shows, from soap operas to cops and robbers films, such entertainment promotes a trivialization of reality. Programmes like these create 'pretend' worlds to distract and divert us from the facts of life in a class society.

The family can also perform a similar task. A dominant belief in contemporary society is that individual emotional satisfaction can only be found in marriage and child-rearing. However pleasant or otherwise the successful accomplishment of such goals may be, we must realize that the pursuit of such an achievement renders a desire for fulfilment through other activities, like work, less likely. The result is that exploited, meaningless work is tolerated. Life becomes about the achievement of marital and parental satisfaction, in order to compensate. As a Ford car worker told Huw Beynon: 'I just close my eyes, stick it out, and think of the wife and kids' (Beynon 1973).

Much of the news media perform an important diversionary role in capitalist society too. For example, in Britain, tabloid newspapers like the *Sun*, the *Star*, the *Daily Mirror*, the *Daily Mail* and the *Daily Express* traditionally concentrate on the trivial, the sensational and the titillating rather than on a serious reporting of events. This deliberate suppression and distortion of reality can only further encourage people living in a capitalist society to divert their gaze away from inequality, deprivation and exploitation. Indeed, since it is only through mass media that we gain most of our information about reality, a failure to provide such information is not only diversionary. It also means we are being provided with a picture of the world that is false.

## Consumerism: the reproduction of demand

Capitalism depends on the reproduction of demand. Any social institution that promotes the purchase of goods perpetuates their production by capitalist means. Clearly, the main way in which we are encouraged to consume is by means of advertising. Whether on television or radio, in the cinema, in newspapers and magazines or on billboards, advertisements glorify the possession of material goods and thereby promote their acquisition. The family helps reproduce demand too. In Western societies, many people live in nuclear families – the smallest kind of family unit. Each family is economically independent, purchasing its own goods. This ensures that demand is maximized. In larger households, demand for consumer goods would decrease.

## The acquiescence of wage-earners in their subordination

Capitalism depends on the bulk of the population being socialized into accepting a subordinate role. Once again, the family plays an important part. It is in the family that we first learn the meaning of authority and obedience. Learning to submit to the wishes of parents provides just the training necessary to cope with being a wage-earner and under the authority of an employer. Education obviously reinforces this training.

## The justification of inequality

Capitalism depends on its inherent inequalities, if they are recognized at all, being accepted as just. It is in the classroom that we first encounter the inevitability of inequality. Here we learn that people do not only possess *different* abilities. They possess *better* or *worse* abilities. 'Clever' children succeed and are rewarded with good grades and exam results. 'Less able' children deserve poorer rewards. What better training for life in a society where different abilities are also deemed superior or inferior, and judged accordingly? Experiences in school can only encourage people to believe that inequality of reward is just. Such beliefs are expressed in such commonly held views as these: 'Of course doctors should be paid more than refuse collectors. They do a much more important job.' The unequal distribution of rewards among different occupations reflects their importance. Or again, 'Anyone could collect rubbish. Only able/intelligent/skilled people can become doctors.' Achievement within an unequal world reflects merit. In a fundamental way, then, education, with its intrinsic emphasis on competition and selection, on success and failure, on merit and de-merit, teaches members of a capitalist society the justice of inequality. In particular, it teaches the 'less able' – the 'failures' – to expect, and accept, low rewards in their lives.

Marxists argue that such an analysis of the relationship between the infrastructure and the superstructure tells us a great deal about power in a class society. The dominant class rules, but not necessarily by being the actual office-holders who make decisions. It rules because its interests are more or less successfully passed off as universal, as common sense, In Marx and Engels' words: 'The ideas of the ruling class are, in every age, the ruling ideas' (McLellan 1977: 176).

## Class consciousness

It is for these reasons that the concept of **class consciousness** is of such importance in Marxist theory. However, Marx is clear that the sub-jective conditions or the state of political awareness of the working class is not the determining factor in bringing about social trans-formation. According to Marx, the impetus for revolution does not arise randomly, or by chance. Ideas about how a society ought to be restructured can only become influential under certain circumstances. In particular, pressure for change builds up when institutional arrange-ments (which have come into being to support a particular mode of production) no longer suit productive relationships, because of the alterations these have undergone over time. Marx identifies a series of processes that he believes will happen within the realm of production and will place increasing strain on ideologies intended to contain oppo-sition to capitalism. These objective conditions will foster heightened political awareness among the working class so that full advantage can be taken of the weakened state of the bourgeoisie and collective oppo-sition to their political and economic power can be sustained.

# Social change

## Feudalism to capitalism

In feudal society, the landowners were the dominant class, owning the dominant means of production. The superstructure supported their dominance, and ideas that reflected their class interests were the ruling ideas. For example, feudal law bound serfs to the land, and polit-ical power was in the hands of landlords and nobles. Feudal religion legitimated these arrangements. As one Victorian hymn puts it, three hundred years later:

> The rich man at his castle,
> The poor man at his gate:
> God made them high or lowly,
> And ordered their estate.

As capitalist production replaced feudalism, the superstructure changed and came to support and justify the new economic arrangements. Technological innovations began to transform the nature of production, from labour-intensive agriculture to mechanized agriculture, and ultimately to industrial production. As these agricultural and industrial revolutions unfolded, so the new capitalist class emerged as the owners of the foundation of the new and growing means of production – capital.

For a time, however, the superstructure lagged behind these changes, its character still reflecting and legitimating the old economic arrangements. For example, though capitalist production required a mobile labour force and land to be freely available for buying and selling, the old legal and political arrangements prevented this.

Eventually, the strain or contradiction between the interests of the new bourgeoisie and the power and practices of the old landowning class became too great, and the landlord class was overthrown. Though this happened quite quickly and violently in other European societies, the change began earlier, and was more gradual, in Britain. By means of various political alterations which took place over a few centuries, the landlord class came to share political power, first with the capitalist landowners, and then with the new industrialists. Eventually the control of political decision-making passed irrevocably into capitalist hands, though a residue of influence has remained with the landlords up to today.

## Capitalism to communism

Marx predicted that the same kind of process would be apparent in the revolutionary transformation of the capitalist mode of production into the communist one. Again, the practical transformative actions of the people – their 'praxis' – would be the motor of this change. However, these revolutionary practices could only gain momentum and spread in tandem with certain weaknesses in the economic system becoming more evident. This would happen as capitalism developed as a mode of production. According to Marx, the evolution of capitalism can only occur by means of the continual exploitation of the working class. That is, since capitalism survives only by exploiting the wage-earning class to a greater and greater extent, the increase in such exploitation will do much to radicalize the working class and encourage the development of revolutionary class consciousness. In other words, the very steps taken to ensure capitalism's 'progress' as a productive system will, at the same time, guarantee the sowing of the seeds of its own destruction. This is how Marx believed the transition to communism would come about.

As we said earlier, capitalism was established prior to the development of industry. But it was only with the Industrial Revolution, representing progress for capital, that the reality of capitalist society could start to become visible to its members. Industrial production created large urban settlements of workers who found themselves in similar positions for the first time. Living in the same overcrowded conditions of poverty and squalor, and working in the same factories, the urban proletariat could together begin to recognize their common exploited state. Thus, as capitalism develops as a mode of production, exploitation increases, and, as this happens, class consciousness begins to become more revolutionary.

Capitalist production depends on capital accumulation. Capitalists accumulate capital by increasing the return from the sale of their goods while at the same time lowering the costs of production. One major way of lowering costs is to reduce the size of the labour force by increasing the mechanization of production. This has two effects. First, smaller capitalist businesses, lacking the capital to invest in new machinery, are unable to compete successfully. They go to the wall, and join the proletariat class. Second, unemployment increases among the proletariat. Since wage-earners are also consumers, an increase in the impoverishment of some of them reduces demand for goods. Faced with this loss in demand, capitalists have to cut costs still further in order to retain profit levels and remain solvent. This is done by either decreasing their labour forces still further or by reducing wage levels. This can be done in two ways. Wages can be actually reduced. (The 1926 General Strike took place when miners' wages were reduced). More typically, wages can be 'increased' at a slower rate than the rate of inflation. As a result of either of these methods, demand decreases still further and this further affects supply. As this process continues, the gap in reward between the contracting bourgeoisie and the ever-growing proletariat increases. As the proletariat becomes increasingly impoverished in this way, the conditions emerge for the development of a fully fledged revolutionary class consciousness. The proletariat is thus transformed from being merely an *objective* class, a class 'in fact', to being a *subjective* class – a class in their political actions – as well. It changes from being just a class *in* itself to being a class *for* itself. When this class consciousness reaches its fullest extent, the proletariat is in a position to rise up and overthrow capitalism, taking over the means of production and the state apparatus, as the capitalists did before them.

According to Marx, this is the final revolution in a society. Unlike in earlier revolutions, there will be no new exploiting class. Rule by the proletariat means self-government by the vast majority, by the workers. Over time the signal feature of class society – private ownership of the means of production – is abolished and all productive means are collectively owned. This, Marx argues, also brings about the end of **alienation** and the beginnings of a social order which can utilize the productive power of the capitalist infrastructure to support the full development and enjoyment of those aspects of social relationships previously distorted by the endless pursuit of private profit for the bourgeoisie. The productive efficiency of capitalism can now be directed to supporting all members of society. The promise of communism for Marx lies in its enabling people to control their own destiny and 'make their own history' in a more conscious, 'rational' and genuinely collective manner than had been possible in previous class-based societies. Marx resists painting a detailed vision of communist society because this risks the fantasy or utopianism he is critical of in other socialist thinkers. He does however offer a glimpse of the transformation of the experience of 'work'. For Marx the rigid parcelling out of skills and talents is characteristic of class-dominated capitalism where the separation of mental and physical labour is deeply rooted in divisions within individuals and between classes and occupational groupings. Under communism, according to Marx and Engels, it will be 'possible for me to do one thing today and another tomorrow, to hunt in the morning, fish in the afternoon, rear cattle in the evening, criticise after dinner, just as I have a mind, without ever becoming hunter, fisherman, shepherd or critic' (McLellan 1977: 169).

So, only in communist society can human beings fulfil their social potential as individuals. In all other forms of society, the production of material wealth by the dominance of one class over the rest denies this possibility.

## Controversies within Marxism

Marx died before the influence of his ideas became widespread. Once Marxist politics became established in the late nineteenth and early twentieth centuries, and particularly after the Russian Revolution in 1917, such ideas were the subject of immense controversy both as revolutionary political theories and as analyses of capitalist society. As we shall see in the following chapters, Weber and Durkheim at least in part developed their own analyses of capitalist societies as criticisms if not of Marx's ideas then certainly of those of his later political and intellectual disciples. With reference to Marx's analysis of the problems of capitalist society, both Durkheim and Weber departed little from Marx's account of the social conflict and inequality created by capitalist **relations of production**, however neither of them saw this inequality as the core hallmark of **modernity** as Marx did. Moreover, they were both convinced that revolutionary socialism would be more likely to threaten liberal ideals of individual freedom and equality. For the purposes of this chapter, we will sketch in some of the most significant developments within those social theories that developed after Durkheim and Weber and that sought to update Marx for the twentieth century.

One issue which proved to be particularly fertile ground for the sociological debates around Marxism was that of the relationship between the economic base and the superstructure of society. At this time, critics of Marxism argued that it is guilty of **economic determinism**. According to this criticism, Marxists are arguing that 'all social, political and intellectual development is caused by economic changes and even that all human action is economically motivated' (Lee and Newby 1983: 116). Marxists have insisted that reading Marx this way is to 'vulgarize' Marxism (though they admit, as Marx did himself, that some of Marx's nineteenth-century followers did commit such an error; referring to such work, Marx complained, 'I am not a Marxist'). Marxists say that Marx certainly did not mean that at any particular time the whole of social life is economically determined, or that everyone is always guided by economic motives in their actions.

In part, the emphasis on the determining nature of the economic base within Marxist theory was a reaction to the approach to understanding contemporary capitalist societies offered by, for example, Ralf Dahrendorf and Daniel Bell, which presented inequality, exploitation and class domination as in some senses temporary problems soon to be erased from industrial societies. In this context Marxists wanted to stress the objective nature of class inequality in a capitalist system – it is not something that can be wished away or removed by the increasing prosperity of capitalism.

If we look to Marx for a set of prescriptions for political action then this debate over the power of 'the superstructure' to generate social change is of crucial importance. According to this view Marx is seen to be offering a blueprint for the creation of the good society, a vehicle for human emancipation via societal progress. For this kind of Marxist, the theory *has* to be right, because it is both a prediction of what will happen and a weapon of political transformation – the purpose of the theory is to destroy capitalism.

With this in mind, the fervour and intensity of the debate among twentieth-century Marxists and their critics is easily understood. If Marx is seen to have been offering a blueprint for social revolution or a crystal ball, then his work must be regarded as a failure. As Lee and Newby put it, modern Marxism has had to come to terms with the occurrence of a non-event:

> In *no* advanced capitalist society has a successful proletarian revolution taken place . . . moreover . . . the most advanced capitalist nation in the world, the United States, appears ostensibly to be almost a living testament to the falsity of some of Marx's predictions. Not only have the majority of American workers persistently increased their standard of living, there is no significant attachment to socialism among American workers and certainly no widespread revolutionary movement aimed at overthrowing capitalism. In Europe during the 1930s, furthermore, many of the conditions which Marx's writings would lead one to believe would prompt the growth of working class consciousness were present – the widespread immiseration and unemployment of workers in the midst of a severe economic crisis in advanced capitalist societies. The outcome, however, was not the growth of revolutionary socialism within the working class but, equally often, the growth of Fascism . . . the proletariat has persistently failed to act in the ways which Marx both predicted and desired. (Lee and Newby 1983: 134)

Living through such a consolidation of capitalism and confronted by a working class that was profoundly disinclined to emancipate itself cannot have been easy for those twentieth-century Marxists who hoped for a theory that would provide a much more accurate map of the future of capitalist society than Marx appeared to have offered. Indeed, living in the twenty-first century, we now have to add the calamitous events (for Marxists) in Eastern Europe in the 1990s. Not only did communist regimes collapse like cards, and not only did the Soviet Union self-destruct, but an ancient form of political ambition emerged to replace communism in Eastern Europe – nationalism. Furthermore, the new post-communist regimes are enthusiastically embracing capitalism, the free market and *laissez-faire* **individualism**.

None of this *necessarily* means that Marxist theory is a bad theory of capitalism, however. Just because it has been found wanting as a theory of political action does not mean it is therefore faulty as a theory of the political economy of capitalism. This was in fact the position taken by the majority of Western Marxists prior to the fall of Soviet communism – an insistence that the Soviet Union represented only one particularly deviant interpretation of Marxism and that Marx's ideas and analysis of capitalism were too valuable to be thrown away with the Stalinist bathwater. However, this common ground amongst Western Marxist theorists in rejecting Soviet state socialism did not give them a common vision of how to bring Marx into the late twentieth century. As we shall briefly set out below, one version of Marxist social theory sought to rehabilitate Marxism as a scientific analysis of the objective workings of the economy. Another school instead wanted to account for the persistence of capitalism by developing a much more diffuse Marxist analysis of the culture of late capitalism. One particularly bold attempt to add scientific certainty to twentieth-century Marxism as a political theory was initiated by Frenchman Louis Althusser (1918–90).

## Althusser and structuralist Marxism

For structuralist Marxists like Althusser, questions about the causal power of 'ideas' represent fundamental misreadings of Marx's work. Or rather, such questions pertain only to the early 'humanist' Marx. This early Marx was still searching for the appropriate scientific methodology he later applies in *Capital*, and so he presented his critique of capitalism in the language of the philosophy, or religion, of his time. The early Marx also presents his critique in terms of the subjective experience of capitalism rather than by analysis of its objective structures. Like the supporters of other forms of structuralism, Althusser completely rejects the relevance of the idea that humans can be 'subjects' – creative agents – in charge of their lives and worlds. Therefore what individuals may feel or experience is irrelevant. For him, human life is always entirely structured, and change can only ever come about at the level of a structure whose workings have nothing to do with human cognition, choice and purpose. Althusserian Marxism thus sees itself as the heir to the 'late' Marx.

Althusser is equally opposed to crude, economistic Marxism and to humanist Marxism. Concentrating on the base, on economic organization to the exclusion of the superstructure, is for him as faulty as concentrating on ideologies – the ideas believed by the working class. Althusser insists that it is only scientific Marxism, resting on a proper understanding of the complexity of the structure of capitalism, which can lead to the destruction of the latter.

According to Althusser there are three levels in the structure of a class society: *economic*, *political* and *ideological*. He defines these levels broadly, so that they embrace most aspects of human life. The 'economic' concerns all aspects of material production, the 'political' all forms of organization, and the 'ideological' all kinds of ideas and beliefs. The political level and the ideological level are not the simple creation of the economic. Although the economic level is ultimately the determining level – 'determinant in the last instance' as he puts it – Althusser defines the political and ideological levels as having 'relative autonomy'. They are thus independent and important in their own right, and the interplay between the three levels is complex and varied. Ian Craib uses a nice architectural analogy to explain this:

> We can look at the relationship between the floors of a multi-storey building: it would be nonsense to say that the first and second floors are caused by the ground floor, even though they rest upon it, have some sort of relationship to it. Each is separate from the floor above and below it, and what goes on on each floor is not determined by what goes on below it. The first floor might be a shop, the second floor offices and the third floor living quarters. Althusser's term for describing this relation where there is a causal connection but not complete dependence is 'relative autonomy'. The political and ideological levels are neither completely dependent on the economic nor completely independent. If we take this building as a single enterprise, the office work which goes on on the second floor obviously depends upon the sort of trading that goes on in the shop but there are various ways in which it might be organized, and the work relationships there may develop in ways not influenced by the economic activity going on below. Similarly if the owners live on the third floor their standard of living and way of life has its limits set by the nature of the business they run but there are choices within these limits and the development of a marriage and family life has its own dynamics.

Althusser's next step away from crude Marxism is to argue that the causal processes are two-way: the political and ideological levels affect the economic. Returning to the example, decisions based on administrative criteria in the offices may have an effect on the trading in the shop – a 'streamlining of the management structure' for example, might lead to increased turnover. Similarly if the business is jointly owned and the

marriage fails, the settlement between the partners might have an important effect on the nature of the business. (Craib 1992: 131–2)

As you might expect from this perception of the structure of class
society, Althusser argues that the study of history reveals periods when
one level dominates over the other two but that this is never a per-
manent state of affairs. Thus it could be argued that 'the structure in
dominance', as he calls it, in nineteenth-century capitalism was the economic, with the industrial bourgeoisie dominating not only economic
but eventually political life, too. The power of the ideological level,
mainly represented by the church, could be said to have dominated
feudal society, while today a strong case could be made for seeing the
structure in dominance in present-day Britain to be the political, via
the power of the state and its penetration into so many aspects of life.

Althusser is also well known for a conceptual separation of the
two elements by which the state exercises its power. He refers to
organizations like the police, the army, the legal system and so on
as constituting a *repressive state apparatus*. Alongside this political
apparatus is another – the *ideological state apparatus* – made up of
educational, media, religious and cultural institutions. Althusser's
conception of a layered, interconnected structure is apparent here too;
just as different structures in dominance prevail at different times in
history, so different elements of a particular level will dominate at different times. Thus in modern society, education has taken over from
religion as the principal ideological instrument of oppression; the work
of Bowles and Gintis (1976) referred to earlier – on the correspondence
between the needs of capitalism and the function of education – is an
example of Althusserian theory in practice.

Althusserian theory was particularly influential for Marxist sociology at least until the mid 1980s. However, it was not the only
neo-Marxist theory around at this time. For those neo-Marxists who
were not looking to Marx for a blueprint of the future, and for those
who were also suspicious of 'scientific' attempts to resolve political
problems, Marx's ideas were taken forward into a more nuanced
analysis of the culture of late capitalism. These Marxists – Antonio
Gramsci (1891–1937), and the early 'Frankfurt School' based in the
Frankfurt Institute for Social Research (founded in 1928), in particular
– attempted to update Marx's ambition of producing a critical theory
of society. This would combine sociological analysis with social criticism and give support to the least powerful. Gramsci was imprisoned
by Italian Fascists during the Second World War, while the leading
figures of the early Frankfurt School were forced into exile from

Nazi Germany. In the face of evidence as to the scale of violence and destruction present within capitalist societies, they all, then, had good reason to be highly sceptical of the optimistic belief that capitalism was but a staging post en route to communism, or that the working class were by definition politically progressive.

In response to this the Frankfurt School sought to develop another core feature of Marx's thinking – the requirement to analyse the culture of capitalist societies. If, as Marx argued, capitalist relations of production filter through into all aspects of social relationships, then we can expect even the most trivial aspects of popular culture, as well as more 'high-brow' art and literature, to bear the marks of capitalist values. Looking at the totality of life under capitalism becomes important in this context because it helps us to understand why people 'buy into' these values as well as to identify more diffuse or indirect signs of critical opposition to capitalism. The Frankfurt School theorists and Gramsci share the belief that Marxist theory requires a more subtle and detailed account than that offered by Marx of how economic power translates into political and cultural domination. However, the Frankfurt School and Gramsci differed over the possibility of bringing about genuinely progressive social change. Whereas Gramsci was optimistic, the Critical Theorists ultimately lost all faith in the revolutionary potential of the working class.

## Gramsci

Gramsci is famous for his notion of *hegemony*. He uses this concept to summarize the all-consuming way in which ideologies work to distort a person's view of the world. More than merely referring to the dominance of certain ideas from which capitalism benefits, hegemony conveys the inability of believers even to acknowledge that their beliefs are, in principle, capable of being different, so natural do they take them to be. Describing beliefs as hegemonic, therefore, means indicating that those who subscribe to them take them so much for granted that it requires deliberate and sustained effort to point out their existence, let alone to change believers' minds.

Because of this theoretical view of the nature of belief under capitalism, Gramsci was led to insist on the political importance of directly challenging the hegemony of ruling ideas. Gramsci argued that of course Marx was right to say that social change depends on the proletariat seeing the world as it really is. However, he was wrong to assume that this would happen simply as the by-product of economic developments. Marxists have to become persuaders, preachers and teachers. Before political action can be undertaken to overturn the system, the battle for the *minds* of the soldiers has to be won – bourgeois hegemony has to be deliberately taken on and defeated.

The idea that ideologies have to be exposed before effective political action can be sustained is essential to Marxism. What is different with Gramsci is the account of how this will happen. He says it will not happen automatically through economic developments because of the strength of hegemonic beliefs; it has to be deliberately secured through education – by means of counter-socialization.

## Critical Theory: the Frankfurt School

The three main Frankfurt School thinkers were Herbert Marcuse (1898–1979), Theodor Adorno (1903–69) and Max Horkheimer (1895–1973). Forced to flee Hitler's Germany (in 1933, to the USA), they watched the rise and fall of the Nazi state and then the post-war entrenchment of the capitalist way of life with increasing disillusion. They eventually came to view the emancipation of the working class as a hopeless prospect, principally because of their belief in the immutability of certain superstructural forces which they saw as inexorably suffusing, and dominating, modern life under capitalism. For many thinkers today, the conceptual tools they used to explain the triumph of capitalism by means of these forces remain highly relevant for an understanding of contemporary life.

Just as Gramsci was concerned to emphasize the control of ideas as the principal source of the power of capital, so Critical Theory also focuses on instruments of cognitive and emotional domination as the key to capitalism's success. For Critical Theory, three features of the culture of capitalism in particular function as these instruments:

- the way of thinking called **instrumental reason**
- the role of mass, or popular, culture in stupefying the thought-processes of people and rendering them incapable of being critical of their world
- the prevalence of a type of personality that not only accepts domination, but actively desires it.

## Instrumental reason

The Frankfurt theorists' use of the concept of instrumental reason echoes Weber's focus on **rationalization** as the key feature of modern life (see Chapters 4 and 9). It is intended to convey the predominance of humans and things being seen as instruments – as means to ends – rather than as having value in themselves. Instrumental reason thus focuses on *how* things can achieve goals, rather than on whether the goals are worthwhile, or whether the instruments involved should be used for particular purposes.

The centrality of such reasoning in modern society is in many ways a consequence of capitalist activity, where a preoccupation with new and ever more efficient means of achieving productive ends becomes the be-all and end-all. In this, too, the key role of **positivist** science in modern life – characterized by a never-ending search for the causes of effects, for technical knowledge of how things produce other things – is crucial. Indeed, Marx's own dedication to science as the route to worthwhile knowledge itself eventually came under criticism from the Frankfurt theorists. In summary, for these theorists, the essence of being human lies in the ability to think critically about meaning and value and ultimate good. A preoccupation with instrumental reason means that criticisms of the existing social order are less likely to be effective.

## Mass culture

The rise of *mass culture* is another major instrument of mental domination identified by the Frankfurt writers. They insist that an examination of the role of cultural agencies such as popular music, the cinema and radio (writing today they would obviously have included television, the internet and computer games) is essential for understanding the disinclination of modern humans to do anything but passively acquiesce in their subordination. Indeed, Critical Theorists are famous for their contemptuous dismissal of popular entertainment as dehumanizing, debasing and worthless. This has led to charges of intellectual snobbery and cultural elitism, but the Frankfurt writers were convinced that the superficiality of low-brow art, and its apparent mission to trivialize reality, short-changes the mass audience by promising happiness and delivering an empty caricature of it. Indeed, the term 'Critical Theory' to describe their ideas stems from this view. For them, not even intellectuals or artists concerned about, and familiar with, serious and worthy cultural products can escape the shackles and impoverishment of a culture reliant on a system of economic production which treats the producers as commodities or things to be exchanged. This system will spread its poison even into the highest reaches of artistic and cultural life.

## Personality manipulation

The final element in Critical Theory is an interest in the sort of *personality* characteristics created by the modern world. Marcuse in particular developed this theme. He uses Freud's ideas to argue that all societies need to promote the repression or *sublimation* of the desires of their members in order to prevent the collapse of social order in an orgy of individual self-gratification. As a result, any proper analysis of modern society must include an examination of how such repression is achieved in our sort of world. According to Marcuse, in the early stages of capitalism a high degree of repression is necessary to ensure that people concentrate on work and production. In later, mature, capitalism, however, there is less need for such an exclusive focus, so that the retention of such repression becomes surplus to the system's requirements. In such circumstances, continuing to insist on such surplus repression might well lead to discontent, so psychological pressure is exerted – via what Marcuse calls *repressive de-sublimation* – to allow us to realize and pursue our desires, but in ways that are useful to the system. Thus, the routine use of sexual images to sell commodities in capitalist societies – cars, alcohol, coffee, clothes, or whatever – is not only sales technique (associating the commodity with an enviable sexual state or circumstance) but also a way of satisfying desires whose *dis*satisfaction would be potentially dangerous. As with other forms of human potential, then, for Marcuse, the use of sex in this way takes what for many is an integral and profoundly fulfilling part of human existence and turns it into an instrument of domination or manipulation.

# Conclusion

This chapter has tried to outline some of the core ideas to be found in Marx's work as well as map the somewhat bumpy routes along which they were carried in the politics and intellectual debates of the twentieth century.

As we suggested at the beginning of this chapter, Marx intended to apply to direct political ends his analysis of the real historical and social relationships in which humans engage. In this light we can recall his concept of praxis – that unique capacity of humans to collectively create and transform their material and social relationships. He claims that the creative possibilities involved in this concept of praxis remain hidden to us, disguised in ideologies and congealed in the apparently hostile world produced under capitalism. Within capitalist societies, humans are reduced to things, he claims, to packages of skills and labour time to be sold as any other commodity. The social and creative possibilities of praxis are reduced to the value created by labour and measured as profit. We might see this analysis of the paucity of what capitalism allows us as forming the backbone of his later arguments for the overthrow of capitalism. However, it is fair to say that the implications of this concept of praxis were not fully developed either by Marx or in any sustained form by the main currents in twentieth-century Marxism.

Many of Marx's writings contain the word 'critique', and this really means exposing the extent to which capitalism represents only a partial realization of its human promise. It is not that Marx is anti-capitalist in the sense of wanting to go back to an earlier, easier time, and, for him, communism is not a society in which people would live under a grey, enforced conformity, in fact for him the opposite is the case. Capitalism harbours the economic power to allow all to develop their full potential as individuals but within a set of social, legal and political relationships which leave the majority of the population unable to realize their true potential as universal producers and as social beings. As Giddens puts it 'the enormous productive power of capitalism generates possibilities for the future development of man which could not have been possible under prior forms of productive system. The organization of social relationships within which capitalist production is carried on in fact leads to the failure to realise these historically generated possibilities' (Giddens 1971: 15).

For Marx, and for his later followers, this core point is retained – the overthrow of capitalism is necessary to allow this potential to be fully realized. He resisted spelling out the details of what communism would look like, describing such an enterprise as 'writing recipes for the cookshops of the future' (Marx and Engels 1969: 183). But perhaps the contrastive value of what he does tell us about future communism is clear. Communism, he believed, would be able to harness the productive power of capitalist production in a new set of social relationships that would allow people to develop as fully rounded social beings, rather than as producers who, in being **alienated** from the things they produce, are also alienated from each other.

Debates about the scientific versus the humanist Marx or about the relative importance of base and superstructural features of capitalism can lose sight of what we might see as Marx's deeply-rooted sociological imagination. If we reduce his concept of 'economic activity' to 'work', and similarly reduce all we might say and do and make in relation to other humans to 'ideas', then we are in danger of recreating the division he criticized in the philosophy of his time between human thinking and doing. For him we are social and historical beings, created in and through our dealings with each other (whether via base or superstructural actions). We are social 'all the way down'. Suggesting this is not to ignore evident weaknesses and inconsistencies in his work, but instead to point to some of the ways in which this core identification of humans as their own social and historical products has been taken up by subsequent social theorists, minus the belief in the privileged position of the proletariat as the saviour of humanity from capitalism. We opened this chapter with Marx's comment that humans make history but not under conditions of their own choosing. The work of Giddens and of Habermas can be seen as attempts, outside of a Marxist framework, to consider in more detail both the potential of ordinary human actions to make and re-make the world and the potential of the latter to escape our conscious control. Giddens' **structuration theory** makes this point, as does Habermas in his analysis of the life-world and the system, as we shall see in Chapter 8.

In the following chapter we will look at Durkheim's work. He too can be seen to develop a deeply socialized concept of humans – to claim that we are as individuals dependent on collective practices for our survival. His work has also, like Marx's, exerted a powerful and controversial influence on later social theorists. But as we shall suggest, for a significant part of the twentieth century the emphasis given to the *political* differences between Marx and Durkheim tended to obscure the sociological richness of their respective works.

# Further reading

## General introductions

Harvey, David (2009): *Introduction to Marx's Capital*, Verso.
Harvey, David (2010): *A Companion to Marx's Capital*, Verso.
McLellan, David (2007): *Marxism after Marx*, 4th edn, Macmillan.

## Collections of extracts

Marx, Karl and Engels, Friedrich (1969): *Basic Writings on Politics and Philosophy*, Fontana.
McLellan, David (1988): *Marxism: essential writings*, Oxford University Press.
McLellan, David (1977): *Selected Writings of Karl Marx*, Oxford University Press.

## Critical commentaries on Marxism

Anderson, Perry (1976): *Considerations on Western Marxism*, New Left Books.
Callinicos, Alex (2010): *The Revolutionary Ideas of Karl Marx*, Bookmarks.
Giddens, Anthony (1971b): *Capitalism and Modern Social Theory: an analysis of the writings of Marx, Durkheim and Max Weber*, Cambridge University Press.
Held, David (1989): *Introduction to Critical Theory*, Polity.

# 3 EMILE DURKHEIM

**Emile Durkheim:** born Lorraine, France, 1858, died Paris, 1917

## Major works

*The Division of Labour in Society* (1893)
*Rules of Sociological Method* (1895)
*Suicide* (1897)
*The Elementary Forms of Religious Life* (1912)

## Introduction

For much of the twentieth century Marx and Durkheim were seen, particularly by theorists influenced by structural **functionalism**, to represent opposing approaches to theorizing modern society. According to such accounts, Marx is concerned with economic power and class conflict and has nothing much to say about culture; whereas Durkheim offers no account of power relationships but sees cultural analysis as a vital area of sociological study. More generally, while Marx intends his theories to support a worker's revolution, Durkheim would regard such a commitment as a betrayal of proper scientific neutrality.

Such readings of both thinkers can be seen as results of two main factors: significant parts of their work were only discovered or translated into English after they died, and when they were published it was within a political and intellectual climate that lent itself to such stark oppositions, particularly in America. However, more recent commentators have brought together the historical and political themes in Durkheim's work as a whole, in the light of which we can see that, although there are significant differences between Marx's and Durkheim's work, the latter's contribution to social theory is more than simply that of founding functionalist sociology. In fact, Durkheim is, like Marx, an historical thinker who attempts to analyse the moral, political and psychological impact of the modern **division of labour**.

Like Marx's, Durkheim's is a theory designed to promote the good society. Like Marxism, it is a *response* to modernity, and, like Marxism, it is a *part* of modernity – it is part of the modern belief that societies can be transformed for the better, that progress can be achieved in social organization through the application of human knowledge. Like Marx, Durkheim believes that social progress depends on finding ways to develop the potential for individual fulfilment and freedom to change within the structure of society as a whole. Durkheim and Marx also share the belief that the division of labour, the social relationships within which we coordinate how we produce what we need to survive, is part of the shared moral and political environment and should be treated as such. However, according to Marx, the opportunity to be free in modern society will only be possible when the class-based productive system characteristic of **capitalism** is abolished. In contrast, Durkheim sees the problems faced by modern societies to be moral rather than economic. He argues that 'a state of order or peace among men cannot follow of itself from any entirely material cause, from any blind mechanism however scientific it may be. It is a moral task' (Durkheim 1957: 12).

Durkheim's response to **modernity** has two main elements:

- he wanted to ensure that modern societies were harmonious
- he wanted to create a *science* of society to generate the knowledge necessary to show how this harmony could be achieved.

On one hand he maintained that shared moral beliefs act as a social 'glue' and create a sense of harmony in a society. On the other hand, dissatisfied as he was with philosophical guesswork and generalizations about what makes for a good life and a stable society, he sought to produce a *science* of morality. Durkheim was convinced that sociology could fulfil this need for an objective, verifiable and empirically grounded science of moral beliefs. He believed that such a science was desperately needed to point the way towards 'social peace'. More specifically, Durkheim argued that such a sociology of moral beliefs would be able to discover the most appropriate moral framework for the complex, socially differentiated and primarily secular societies of Europe, and specifically of France. As we saw in the previous chapter, Marx sought to fuse social analysis and criticism as a contribution to the radical transformation of capitalist society. Durkheim explicitly committed himself to values of scientific neutrality, but he did also get involved in some of the political and intellectual controversies of his day (see Lukes 1973). He is like Marx and their **Enlightenment** forebears in seeking to employ the critical faculties of reason to understand the laws of collective social life and – again like Marx – to analyse how the ideals of the French Revolution might be made a reality.

## A science of society

At the beginning of Durkheim's intellectual career, sociology was not yet taught in French universities and it was really only in the late 1890s that an established body of published sociological research began to be available. His ambition to establish sociology as a respected scientific discipline meant that it was necessary to develop specifically sociological theories – as distinct from historical or psychological ones, for example – and a clear set of methodological principles that would allow the theories to be tested via research.

Durkheim's ambitions to establish sociology as a science grew within the context of his concerns about the disunity and disillusionment of French society experienced intermittently since the 1789 revolution and heightened by France's defeat by Prussia in 1871. Without wanting to explain Durkheim's sociological project as simply a response to the issues which dominated French society during his lifetime, if we are to understand the nature of his ideas it is important that we briefly look at the context of their development. The question of how to rebuild France after the defeat by Prussia dominated political and intellectual life. Broadly speaking, Catholic and conservative opinion argued for a return to traditional values and the reigning in of republicans, socialists and other groups in favour of expanding democracy and workers' rights. Revolutionary socialists in contrast, sought to extend the campaign for **secularization**, equality, and support for unions and welfare programmes. Communists and revolutionaries sought to abolish private property altogether (see Thompson 2002; Lukes 1973; Giddens 1971b; Morrison 1995).

Durkheim, despite often being portrayed as a conservative, was actually concerned that the struggle between conservatives and radicals would drown out the liberal principles bequeathed by the French Revolution. He was not in favour of socialist revolution but, equally, he did not believe it was possible or desirable to go back to an earlier and largely imaginary period of harmony based on feudal forms of authority. Instead, Durkheim argued that the ideals of the French Revolution of liberty, respect for the individual, and equality had to be systematically and carefully incorporated into modern French society.

One of the reasons why Durkheim has been characterized as a conservative is that he was influenced by Comte, who first developed the project of a systematic science of society that could provide a guide for social and political reform. However, Durkheim was influenced not by Comte's conservatism but by his advocacy of **positivism** as the methodology for the new science of sociology. Durkheim criticized Comte's work for being over-reliant on philosophical speculation, whereas Durkheim wanted to develop a scientifically precise approach to the carefully controlled strengthening of the moral climate of France in a progressive direction. This was deemed necessary because France was experiencing not only the political and cultural crises mentioned above but also rapid industrialization. This latter had allowed capitalism to develop in an unregulated and unjust manner and led to class conflict, unregulated competition and routinized, degrading, meaningless work (Lukes 1973: 174). All of these issues cried out for the scientific study of society's collective moral beliefs as sources of social cohesion. Durkheim thus saw the role of sociology as similar to that of a medical physician who applies scientific techniques to distinguish between health and illness and to prescribe the appropriate remedy for the latter. The medicine required in this case was an answer to how the process of transition from traditional to modern collective values could be best achieved.

## Social structure

For Durkheim the crucial feature of **social structures** is that they are made up of *norms* and *values* – cultural definitions of behaviour considered appropriate and worthy in different settings. Since it is through socialization that we learn these normative definitions, it is only this process which makes people into members of a society and therefore makes social life possible.

It was Durkheim who first of all stressed the view that even the possibilities of thought and experience are *inherited*, and not invented anew by each generation. For example, people who attend a religious service may believe sincerely in their god. But the beliefs and practices of their religion were in existence before they were – they *learned* them. Like all other social activity, religious belief and practice is structured by society and by the positions of people in it. As Durkheim puts it:

> When I perform my duties as a brother, a husband or a citizen and carry out the commitments I have entered into, I fulfil obligations which are defined in law and custom and which are external to myself and my actions. Even when they conform to my own sentiments and when I feel their reality within me, that reality does not cease to be objective, for it is not I who have prescribed these duties; I have received them through education . . . Similarly the believer has discovered from birth, ready fashioned, the beliefs and practices of his religious life; if they existed before he did, it follows that they exist outside him. (Durkheim 1982 [1895]: 50–1)

For Durkheim, then, the achievement of social life among humans, and the existence of social order in society, which he calls '**social solidarity**', is ensured by socialization – the process whereby different individuals learn collectively held standards or rules of behaviour. Durkheim's phrase for these rules was 'social facts'. Although these are only *visible* through the conformity of individuals to them, they are, nevertheless, in Durkheim's words, 'external to, and constraining upon' these individuals. Though not capable of being seen, such structures of cultural rules are as real to the individuals who are motivated by them as the world's physical structure by which they are also constrained. Society, in a famous phrase of Durkheim's, is a reality '*sui generis*' – it has its own existence which cannot be analysed by historical, psychological or any other social science but sociology.

Durkheim was convinced that these social facts required a sociological analysis to address the central problem of how to sustain social solidarity in the process of transition from traditional to modern society. Different types of society achieve solidarity in different ways. In pre-modern, traditional societies, where people live very similar kinds of lives, solidarity is achieved more or less automatically. This form of **mechanical solidarity** is the result of a simple division of labour. There are so few roles to play or different ways of living available that the need for the society's members to see the world in the same way – to share a collectively held set of rules about how to behave – is satisfied without much difficulty.

Things are much more problematic in modernity however. By definition, a modern society has a highly complex division of labour. There are so many different roles to be played and so many different ways of living possible that social solidarity is much more difficult to achieve. For Durkheim, this is the main danger in modernity. The forces separating and dividing people are so profound that social disintegration is a real threat. Furthermore, Durkheim believed that human beings are not naturally consensual. He believed that if left to our own devices, we are *anti*-social. The natural, as opposed to structurally constrained, state for a human is to be self-centred, greedy, insatiable and overly competitive. Without norms constraining our behaviour, 'humans develop insatiable appetites, limitless desires and general feelings of irritation and dissatisfaction' (Durkheim 1974: 72). The problem of modernity is that it encourages such excessive, rampant **individualism**. So not only are our natural propensities dangerously individualistic, but the very institutions of modernity can, without strategic re-alignment and re-inforcement, encourage such anti-social individualism, a condition Durkheim termed **anomie**. This term can mean 'without law', but Durkheim uses it to refer to the lack of a sufficiently secure framework by which people are provided with a sense of moral regulation and social integration, rather than to a lack of formal legislature. According to Durkheim, unless such counter-balancing social structural forces promoting cohesion and integration can be strengthened, social solidarity and social order are seriously threatened. Durkheim argues that the extent of our mutual dependence needs to be much more clearly and explicitly brought into the public's consciousness. To use his phrase, modern societies need to achieve **organic solidarity**. But how can the moral cohesion of modern societies be strengthened and anomic tendencies reduced? Solving this problem is at the heart of Durkheim's theorizing. He wants to demonstrate the truth of his assertions that stable societies are interdependent societies and he wants to locate the potential basis for promoting organic solidarity within the existing stock of moral beliefs. On this basis Durkheim's work develops in three separate, but related, directions:

• first, he argues that only if sociology is a science can we acquire the evidence we need to understand social arrangements
• second, he shows how societies work as interdependent **social systems** by using functionalist theorizing
• third, he demonstrates the crucial role of collective belief in inhibiting anomie and guaranteeing social solidarity in human societies.

# The laws of society

It is his conception of his subject matter that leads Durkheim to advocate the use of science to explain social life. The scientific method he favoured is known as positivism. The guiding principle for the positivist scientist is that if something exists in nature, it has been caused by something else in nature. That is, natural phenomena cause other natural phenomena. For example, when water reaches a certain temperature (cause) it freezes (effect). Furthermore, this always happens. There are no circumstances (depending on atmospheric pressure) when water will not become ice at a particular temperature. Such invariable cause and effect relationships are called *laws*. Science sets out to discover the laws of nature. These laws are 'given' for us. Whether we like it or not, water will freeze at a certain temperature. Whether we like it or not, the temperature is higher in the summer than in the winter. Whether we like it or not, leaves will fall from deciduous trees in the autumn. We live in a natural world that is organized in a particular way and we are stuck with this world, whatever our views about it. Science therefore only reveals *why* nature is as it is. We can describe this 'given' character of nature by saying it is an *objective* world. It exists, as a matter of fact, independently of any subjective feelings we may have or judgements we may make about it.

For Durkheim, social structures are just as objective and given as nature. For him, structural features are as much a given for the inhabitants of a society who encounter them at birth as is the natural world for the phenomena, animate and inanimate, that make *it* up. Daffodils do not choose to be yellow; frogs do not choose to croak and have bulging eyes; water does not choose to freeze. They do so, nevertheless. Humans do not choose to have two eyes, a nose and a mouth. Nor do they choose to have two arms and two legs. These are simply biological facts of life.

In the same way, for Durkheim, a society consists of a similar realm of *social* facts 'external to and constraining upon' the individual. We do not choose to believe the things we believe or to act in the way we act. We *learn* to think or do these things. Pre-existing cultural rules determine our ideas and behaviour through socialization. Thus, in the same way as the characteristics of natural phenomena are the products of laws of nature, so people's ideas and acts are the product of external social forces that make up social structures. Consequently, sociology must be scientific in its method of enquiry. In Durkheim's words 'sociology can and must be objective, since it deals with realities as definite and substantial as those of . . . the biologist' (Durkheim 1970: 39).

For positivist science this method involves *empirical observation*: only if you can muster evidence of causal relationships identifiable by the senses can you claim to have demonstrated their existence. Thus, Durkheim argues for sociology to rely on empirical evidence too. Since behaviour and belief are determined by external structural forces, when we quantify the incidence of action or of thought among people, what we have is empirical evidence of the extent to which the forces that have produced this behaviour and belief exist. The attraction of such **empiricism** was that it seemed to offer the possibility of certainty – of demonstrable proof. For many of those engaged in a project dedicated to social reconstruction and societal progress – the sociology of the modern world – such a prospect was indeed enticing.

According to Durkheim, as we have seen, order flows from consensus – from the existence of shared norms and values. For him, the key cause of social and individual ill-health stems from anomie – a lack of regulating norms. He argues that a strong, ordered society and individual liberation are only guaranteed where beliefs and behaviour are properly regulated by socialization: 'The individual submits to society and this submission is the condition of his liberation. For man freedom consists in the deliverance from blind, unthinking physical forces; this he achieves by opposing against them the great and intelligent force which is society, under whose protection he shelters' (Durkheim 1974: 72).

But why are order, harmony and consensus the right state of affairs? To answer this question, Durkheim turned to functionalism.

## Functionalism

Durkheim was the first major sociological theorist to use functionalist ideas, which he developed under the influence of the work of Herbert Spencer (1820–1903). Spencer argued that we can best understand the existence and character of social structures by comparing them to the origins and workings of biological organisms. Just as natural bodies rely on the integrated functioning of their individual organs to survive, so societies also require for their survival the harmonious integration of the individuals and institutions that are their constituent parts.

### The organic analogy

The use of a biological analogy in social science then, begins with the fairly uncontroversial premise that an organism is a living entity whose existence and health depend on all the organs that make it up working properly together. In the human body, for instance, all the organs are interdependent. The workings of the brain depend on the workings of the lungs, which depend on the workings of the heart, and so on. Furthermore, all (or nearly all, in the case of the human body) of these organs are indispensable. Each exists because it satisfies a particular need of the human body which no other organ can. For example, the heart exists because of the need for an organ to pump blood round the body, the liver exists because of the need for the blood to be purified, the kidneys exist because of the need to dispose of waste matter and so on. In other words, the reason why each of the constituent parts of the body exists is because each performs a particular *function* for the overall bodily system. Furthermore, all these necessary parts have to function together in an integrated way for the system as a whole to work properly. According to this approach then, the difference between referring to integrated wholes as 'systems' rather than 'structures' can be understood as simply the difference between a static picture of the whole – its structure – and what this looks like when it is actually working, as a system. In functionalist sociology the terms are often used in association with each other for just this reason. A society both has a structure and works as a system.

Durkheim and later functionalists argue that a social system works like an organic system. Societies are made up of structures of cultural rules – established beliefs and practices – to which their members are expected to conform. Sociologists describe any established way of thinking or acting in a society into which its members are socialized as being institutionalized in that society. For functionalists, the institutions of a society – for example the kind of family form it has, its political arrangements, its educational arrangements, its religious arrangements, and so on – are analogous to the parts of an organism. Societies consist of parts that are integrated and interdependent. As with organs, the reason why an institutionalized way of thinking or acting exists in a society is that it plays an indispensable part – or, to use the functionalist phrase, *performs a necessary function* – in maintaining the society in a stable and satisfactory state. In the case of the human body, if any organ fails to perform properly, ill-health, or even loss of life, is the result. For functionalists, such a functional failure by an institution – if it malfunctions – also leads to a comparable state for the whole social system. Functionalists have various phrases to describe this: a 'loss of social solidarity', a 'lack of integration', or a 'loss of equilibrium' are three favourite ones.

Crucially, therefore, this account of the origins and workings of societies means that the existence of a social institution, of a part of the social structure, is not the result of the members of a society deciding to act or think this way. After all, people do not *decide* to have bowels or a liver or a pair of kidneys. These organs exist because the body needs them to perform necessary functions. In the same way, in functionalist theory, the institutional arrangements of a society exist not because of any choice on the part of its members. They are there because they are performing a necessary function for the social structure as a whole. Durkheim and other functionalists therefore argue that we should always explain the existence of social arrangements by looking for the *function* being performed by them – for the needs of the social system as a whole that they are satisfying.

Therefore, the job of sociology should be to use science to reveal the laws governing social organization. These laws help us to assess how effectively an institution is serving the needs of the social system and contributing to a healthy society. 'Institutions performing functions', or 'institutions serving the needs of the social system', is functionalist jargon for people living their lives in the right ways – from which society benefits. The corollary of this is that if a society is *un*healthy – and you can tell because it will be disordered, riven with conflict, division and disagreement – it is because socialization is deficient. In these circumstances political action is necessary in the light of the social scientific evidence to ensure that the correct cultural prescriptions are re-established. The end result is a harmonious society – integrated, stable, cohesive and healthy – and happy, normatively guided individuals. We will look at Durkheim's account of the role of religion in pre-modern human societies as a good example of this functionalist analysis.

## Religion and society

The following is a simple example of the application of functionalist theory taken from one of Durkheim's own works, called *The Elementary Forms of Religious Life* (Durkheim 1976 [1912]).

In Australia, there is an aborigine people called the Arunta. They are divided up into two kinds of group. *Bands* are their domestic groups who live together day to day, eking out a meagre survival by hunting and gathering in the Bush. The Arunta also belong to much larger groups, called *clans*. Much like the Scottish clans of great importance long ago, each Arunta clan consists of people who believe themselves to be descended from a distant common ancestor – that is, they consider themselves to be related. Each clan has a *totem* – an object in natural life which Arunta clan members believe to be special to them. In fact, the totem is so special that, according to Durkheim, they imbue it with a religious significance. On rare but important occasions the whole of the clan (including members of many different bands, of course) gathers to worship the totem. In addition, during their day-to-day life as band members, whenever they come across their particular totem they treat it with reverence – as a kind of *sacred* object.

How should we explain this? Employing the assumptions of functionalist theory, Durkheim is not interested in the intention of any particular Arunta individual to practice totemism in their society. After all, it was present among them before they were born, and will continue to be there after they die. He wants instead to identify the *function* that totemism performs for the Arunta social system. The answer he gives is this.

Living such a precarious life (without things we take for granted like hospitals or welfare institutions), the Arunta people above all need each other to survive. The groups to which the Arunta belong are their lifeline; the obligations others feel to help them, when they need it, are their only hope. In these circumstances, argues Durkheim, what is needed is some means of ensuring that the group *remains* important in the eyes of Arunta individuals. Furthermore, the recognition of obligations must extend beyond band members alone. If not, all that would happen (as it does so often between people who feel no obligation towards one another) would be that individual bands would compete, and fight for, the limited resources available in their world. They would soon wipe each other out.

In the Arunta social system the answer to this problem of need for integration of separate groups is *totemism*. The totem is, as Durkheim puts it, 'the flag of the clan'. It is a symbol of those people in Arunta society with whom band members do not live, but whom they look upon as relatives. They are special people who should be helped and supported whenever necessary. Because of the totem, the group's symbol, its members are reminded of the group's existence when they might otherwise forget it. On the ceremonial occasions when the whole group gathers to worship the totem, a collective reaffirmation of its importance to them takes place. As Durkheim puts it, by worshipping the totem, the Arunta are really worshipping the group.

The *function* of totemism, then, is to integrate the Arunta social system (to draw its parts together and sustain it as a whole). It is, in Durkheim's terms, an instrument of *social solidarity*. Clearly, totemism is here being explained not in terms of what it *is* – what the content of its doctrines or beliefs are – but of what it *does*, that is, the function it performs for the social system.

This analysis also shows us why Durkheim considered it so important in modern societies to promote a secular civic morality based on the mutual awareness of mutual dependency. This ethic would correct the one-sided selfish individualism that Durkheim believed was becoming widespread in modern societies. In modernity, we play very different roles in the division of labour and therefore live very different lives from each other. However, both our survival and the survival of our society depend on the fact that these roles are interdependent. The only way we can survive to live our particular lives is if others are living theirs. In a modern economy, for example, the main reason any particular task needs to be performed is because all the other tasks depend on it. That is, the roles are interdependent. To survive, we need each other; our existence and our futures depend on our interdependence. Durkheim did not believe that a religious **belief system** such as Christianity could provide a sufficiently powerful or flexible system of belief to address the complex patterns of social interaction and differentiation experienced by modern society. He believes the scientific resources of sociology can be used to identify and bolster the sense of social solidarity nascent in the individualist ethic. He argued that sociology should help to develop a new secular morality by showing how it could be promoted in schools, workplaces and other organizations in which people come together from different walks of life. The fully rounded ethic of individualism – an ethic which teaches us that to express our own individuality we need to respect and protect that of all social members – Durkheim saw as a vital instrument of social solidarity and an important bulwark against the lurking threat of anomie.

As well as arguing for the need to promote the moral values necessary to bolster organic solidarity, Durkheim also made the case for institutional and legal changes. He promoted the importance of developing joint corporations that would help establish social interaction between worker and employee and the state. Durkheim also advocated social reform to allow for greater fairness and transparency in the allocation of jobs – a more meritocratic framework that would encourage people to ascribe to the overall goals of society. As we can see then, Durkheim developed a comparative analysis of the sources of social cohesion in pre-industrial and in modern societies. He used this analysis as part of a wider analysis of social stability and social change. This was intended to clarify how individuals can be encouraged to develop their own talents and lifestyles whilst at the same time learning to value the collective as the bedrock on which they depended.

# Twentieth-century functionalism

As we suggested above, Durkheim is regarded as the founder of functionalist analysis within sociology. It was Talcott Parsons (1902–79) who first introduced Durkheim's work to American audiences, along with that of fellow Europeans Alfred Marshall (1842–1924), Vilfredo Pareto (1848–1923) and Weber. Parsons assimilated the work of these authors into his own project of producing a single theoretical framework which he called the 'voluntaristic theory of action'. This theory initially displays its Durkheimian credentials in that, as John Heritage suggests, it was primarily concerned to show how individuals are socialized into collective values that motivate them to uphold the values which promote social integration (Heritage 1994). However, as Giddens argues, although the concept of anomie was as central to Parsons' work as to Durkheim's, for Parsons the possible threat of anomie was identified only in terms of individuals' interests and purposes clashing with those of the society as a whole (Giddens 1976: 96–7). In this context then, Durkheim's attention to moral regeneration as well as to institutional reform, and his grounding of his analysis of anomie in a historical analysis of the transition from traditional to modern societies, disappears from view.

Along with Parsons, other US functionalists like R. K. Merton (1910–) and Kingsley Davis (1908–97) were also important. Other significant functionalists were to be found among the leading British social anthropologists in the years between 1920 and 1960. The work of anthropology's first two major figures, Bronislaw Malinowski (1884–1942) and A. R. Radcliffe-Brown (1881–1955), was of particular importance here. In addition, the later writings of anthropologists like E. E. Evans-Pritchard (1902–73), Meyer Fortes (1906–83) and Max Gluckman (1911–75) all helped to establish functionalist theory in British social science. Until the 1960s, America dominated sociology, while social anthropology dominated British social science. So, from the early 1920s to the late 1950s, other theoretical perspectives, though they had long been in existence, had little impact. The theoretical stage was dominated by the functionalist version of structural-consensus theory. According to this view, society is a system which, whilst constraining of the individuals within it, is to all intents and purposes beyond their knowledge and control. As we shall see below, these themes came to define much social theorizing and empirical research until the latter part of the twentieth century, particularly in America.

Some twentieth-century functionalist theorists extended Durkheim's analysis of religion as a source of social cohesion in pre-modern societies to all religions. For them, religion must always exist, since all social systems need integrating. They argue that what is interesting is not what is *different* about the beliefs and rituals characteristic of, say, totemism, Buddhism, Hinduism, Judaism, Protestantism or Catholicism. For them, what is interesting is what is *similar* about what they each *do* – about the *integrative functions* all these religions perform for their social systems.

In this manner, Robert Bellah (1927–) argues for the existence of a 'civil religion' in the USA, in which American history and institutions are utilized to ensure the reaffirmation of essential American values and sentiments. As Roy Wallis puts it:

> Bellah finds evidence for the existence of civil religion in such events as Presidential Inaugurations. Inaugural addresses tend to be couched in a religious idiom, referring to God in general terms and to the travails of America as a modern Israel led out of Egypt. This stylised rhetoric is taken as indicating a real commitment on the part of participants to symbols and values which unify and integrate the community and provide sacred legitimation for its affairs. Other more frequent ceremonials such as Thanksgiving Day and Memorial Day are similarly held to integrate families into the civil religion, or to unify the community around its values. (Wallis in Mann 1983: 44)

Here, what is very apparent is an interest in the effects of a religion, rather than its constituent beliefs. Many different kinds of religious belief systems are lumped together, because of the similar integrative function they all perform. Second, very different kinds of belief systems, without any reference to, for example, gods or spirits or an after-life, are nevertheless thought of as equivalent to religion. Again, this is because of the similar function they are seen as performing. This directs our attention to a principal characteristic of functionalist explanation. Clearly, the inhabitants of India, Ireland or Israel would argue that their religions are not similar at all, since their focus would be on the beliefs themselves, not their effects. For the functionalist, however, the explanation of a belief or a pattern of behaviour observable in a society held by the *members* of that society is not usually thought to be particularly relevant. For them, the often unintended consequences of people's actions and beliefs needs to be identified – those consequences which, though not necessarily apparent to the people concerned, nevertheless have a crucial functional effect for the social system. To distinguish between these two levels of analysis, functionalists generally refer to the '*manifest*' function of institutions (those of which people are aware) and their '*latent*' functions (those of which people are often *un*aware). These latent functions are even more important to identify in order to understand the functioning and persistence of social systems.

These, then, are the characteristic features of functionalist analysis:

- an interest in the effect of an activity or belief, rather than its constituent ingredients: what it *does*, rather than what it *is*
- a stress on the need to go beyond people's own explanations of their activities in order to reveal the true functional significance of institutionalized behaviour and belief.

We will be able to see the character and consequences of these core functionalist interests by looking at a famous example from twentieth-century anthropology.

## The kula

Bronislaw Malinowski was the first anthropologist to undertake a long-term piece of field research. For four years (between 1915 and 1918), he lived among the Trobriand islanders, who inhabit a group of tiny coral islands off the coast of New Guinea. He published a number of books describing and explaining various aspects of Trobriand life, but the most famous is *Argonauts of the Western Pacific* (1922). This is an account of an elaborate gift-exchange institution, called the *kula*, which is carried on by the Trobrianders among themselves and with the members of other tribal societies who live on surrounding islands. Malinowski described the kula as follows:

> The kula is a form of exchange, of extensive, inter-tribal character; it is carried on by communities inhabiting a wide ring of islands which form a closed circuit . . . along this route, articles of the two kinds, and these two kinds only, are constantly travelling in opposite directions. In the directions of the hands of a clock, moves constantly one of these kinds – long necklaces of red shell, called soulava. In the opposite direction moves the other kind – bracelets of white shell called mwali. Each of these two articles as it travels in its own direction on the closed circuit, meets on its way articles of the other class and is constantly being exchanged for them.
>
> On every island and in every village, a more or less limited number of men take part in the kula – that is to say, receive the goods, hold them for a short time, and then pass them on. Therefore every man who is in the kula, periodically though not regularly, receives one of several mwali (arm-shells), or a soulava necklace (necklace of red shell disks), and then has to hand it on to one of his partners, from whom he receives the opposite

commodity in exchange. Thus no man ever keeps any of the articles for any length of time in his possession. (Malinowski 1922: 82–3)

How is such an institution to be explained? Malinowski argues that from the point of view of those involved in it, the kula is a significant way of gaining prestige. In industrial society, objects are used in order to gain prestige too, of course. Thorstein Veblen (1998) coined the famous phrase 'conspicuous **consumption**' to describe the way people in Western societies do not simply own things for the practical uses they have – their *utility* value. He points out how we also seek to own things for the value they have for us as *symbols* of who we would like others to think we are. Though there might be a certain utility advantage for the Rolls Royce owner in terms of the extra comfort the car affords him or her, at least as important is its value as a status symbol. It symbolizes or expresses the resources, and, by implication, the importance, of its owner. The same goes for the possession of couture clothing, diamonds, enormous houses in particular residential areas, and so forth.

Kula valuables similarly enable Trobrianders and their neighbours to gain prestige. But they do so in a rather different way. In the kula there is no advantage or prestige attached to *keeping* a valuable. You receive the admiration of others for two reasons. First, because *you* were chosen by your partner to be the recipient of the valuable article, rather than any other of his partners. Second, because you can show yourself to be generous by giving it away again in turn. As Malinowski puts it:

> Ownership . . . in [the] kula, is quite a special economic relation. A man who is in the kula never keeps any article for longer than, say, a year or two. Even this exposes him to the reproach of being niggardly . . . on the other hand, each man has an enormous number of articles passing through his hands during his lifetime, of which he enjoys a temporary possession, and which he keeps in trust for a time. The possession hardly ever makes him use the articles, and he remains under the obligation soon again to hand them on to one of his partners. But the temporary ownership allows him to draw a great deal of renown, to exhibit his article, to tell how he obtained it, and to plan to whom he is going to give it. (Malinowski 1922: 94)

Here then, social honour is not attached to the acquisition in order to possess. The purpose of wanting to acquire is not to own, but to give away again. In Malinowski's words: 'a man who owns a thing is naturally expected to share it, to distribute it, to be its trustee and dispenser

. . . the main symptom of being powerful is to be wealthy and of wealth is to be generous . . . the more important he is, the more will he desire to shine by his generosity' (Malinowski 1922: 97).

It would appear that here we have the answer to the kula. It is a system of 'conspicuous generosity', to parody Veblen. It is a way of allowing people to gain importance and to be seen to be important. Status-seeking is not the prerogative of the materialist West. The Trobrianders wish to be thought of as important and powerful too – they just use different ways to do it. From the point of view of individual Trobrianders this is almost certainly the whole story. For them, the kula is an institution geared to the pursuit of status. But is their story the only one about the kula that needs to be told? After all, they learned to kula; it existed before they did. Since they did not invent it, can we rely only on their views of what it is about? The functionalist in Malinowski will not allow him to stop here. He also wants to know why the kula is necessary for the Trobriand social system. He wants to know what the kula *does* – what its function is.

The answers that Malinowski and later functionalist analysts of his material give run along these lines: because many kula exchanges take place between partners who live on islands many miles apart, its existence allows economic and political relationships to take place between people who would otherwise never meet. The result is a greater economic and political integration of the whole of Trobriand society, and of different societies with each other, than would otherwise have been possible.

## The economic function of the kula

Though kula partners are not allowed to engage in ordinary trading with one another, non-partners are. Thus an expedition of a large number of members from one island to another will not simply result in kula exchanges. Between men who are not kula partners, bartering for non-kula goods is quite normal. According to Malinowski, this is an important *latent* function of the kula. It makes trading relations possible between people who would otherwise never come into contact with one another, for their mutual economic benefit. 'Side by side with the ritual exchange of arm-shells and necklaces, the natives carry on ordinary trade, bartering from one island to another a great number of utilities, often improcurable in the district to which they are imported and indispensable there' (Malinowski 1922: 83).

Here, then, is an economic function of the kula of which members would either be unaware, or certainly consider of secondary importance to the kula exchanges. In contrast, for functionalists it is such *unintended* consequences of people's activities that are usually of the greatest importance to identify.

## The political function of the kula

It is the fact that the kula makes possible such long-distance social interaction, embracing the whole of Trobriand society and linking the Trobrianders with more distant tribal societies, that functionalists have usually pounced on as its key. Two excerpts from *Argonauts of the Western Pacific* give a flavour of the kula's political function which is identified by Malinowski himself:

> An average man has a few partners near by . . . and with these partners he is generally on very friendly terms . . . the overseas partner is, on the other hand, a host, patron and ally in a land of danger and insecurity. (Malinowski 1922: 91–2)

> The kula is thus an extremely big and complex institution . . . It welds together a considerable number of tribes, and it embraces a vast complex of activities, inter-connected and playing into one another, so as to form one organic whole. (Malinowski 1922: 83)

Malinowski's functionalism and the integrative consequences of the kula which he sees as so central to its significance are clearly apparent here. In a later study of Malinowski's data, J. Singh Uberoi (1962) argued that the integrative function of the kula is even more fundamental than Malinowski himself acknowledged. His thesis is this. Among valuable things, only kula objects are owned by individuals, rather than by groups of kin. Only in the kula do people enter into relations as individuals rather than as representatives of their kin groups. Only in the kula is self-interest, rather than group-interest, the motivating force.

How does this reduction in the importance of kinship relations in the kula allow it to enable a great political integration of the whole community? Uberoi argues that because the kula enables people to be released from obligations to their kin groups, they are better able to perceive Trobriand society as a wider whole. Rather in the way that the totem tells the Arunta about the wider society on which they ultimately depend, the kula encourages the Trobrianders to think of their society as a whole, rather than as a collection of competing kin groups. This is how Uberoi puts it:

The kula extends the political society beyond the district by periodically depreciating the ties which bind an individual to the other members of his own local lineage or district, and re-emphasising his obligations towards his kula partner, who belongs to an otherwise opposed district . . . on a kula expedition . . . each individual . . . stands by and for himself, released from the normal restraints of group solidarity; but because he pursues his individual self-interest through wooing his kula partner, he stands not only for himself, but also for the whole chain of partners which goes to make up the kula ring . . . [The kula valuables symbolize to] the normally kin-bound individuals . . . the highest point of their individual self-interest [and also] the interest of the widest political association of which they all partake [the kula]. (Uberoi 1962: 159–60)

This is a typical functionalist analysis. The accounts of activities by the people involved in them are forgotten. The interest is in what *good* an institutionalized activity does, or has done, for the society as a whole. The assumption is that an institution would not exist unless it was necessary. The observer's job is to see *why* it is necessary, what *function* it is performing. The Trobriander sails to distant islands to pursue his self-interest and to maximize his prestige. Unknown to him, but perfectly apparent to the perceptive functionalist, is the fact that he is really integrating his society, both economically and politically.

## Social change

If we now return to the structural-functionalist perspective on modern society, we can see that in arguing that the causes of societal cohesion exist above and beyond the knowledge and purposes of social members, they need to address the problem of how social change happens:

- not only do functionalists have to take account of the fact that change *does* occur in societies, but also
- the idea of modernity – the modern ideal – is that knowledge is supposed to provide humans with the chance to create a *good* society and that change can represent progress, a good thing.

The functionalist is faced with a problem here, though. The functionalist model of the individual is the structural-consensus one of a determined, constrained, regulated social actor, whose choices are created for him or her by socialization. To be **modernist**, and allow that social change and social reconstruction can be actively promoted, and achieved, by social actors – that people can create society – turns the relationship between the individual and society on its head. The functionalist way around this is to use the organic analogy again, and to say that social progress occurs as it does with organisms – as *evolutionary* change.

Change takes the form of *structural differentiation*. This means that societies gradually develop a range of more specialized institutions which can deal more adequately with the new needs of the social whole. This emphasis on differentiation is apparent in the work of Parsons. Institutions change, says Parsons, if the needs of the system change. The rise of industrialization in modern societies has proved the major impetus to family change, for a new industrial economy requires a new form of family to perform new, specialist functions. A process of differentiation, thus ensuring evolution and progress, meets this need. In Parsons' own words:

> The kinship-organised household in predominantly [traditional, non-industrial] society is both the unit of residence and the primary unit of agricultural production. In [industrial] societies, however, most productive work is performed in specialised units, such as workshops, factories or offices manned by people who are also members of family households. Thus two sets of roles and collectives have become differentiated and their functions separated. (Parsons 1966: 327).

This splitting-off of the nuclear family household from production does not mean the family has lost significance however. After all, it is evolution – progress and improvement. The loss of the economic function to specialized workplaces means the new, non-productive household can concentrate on performing non-economic functions better than the dual-purpose, peasant household could. The removal of economic activity from the home means family members can give more time and attention to each other: thus the emotional quality of the relationship between adult family members is enhanced, and more effort is put into the socialization of children. The social system benefits: these developments improve the ability of the family to provide a secure emotional base for its members' participation in society (Parsons 1971). At the same time, now that production takes place in locations specifically designed for this alone, the performance of this economic function is also superior. Once again, the social system benefits; through evolution, then, modern societies forge ahead.

So, just as social structures have the character they do – not because of the purposive intentions of individuals, but because of system needs – so social change occurs, not because people want it, but because of evolution. The analogy with the organism therefore explains both social structure and social change; functionalism can be a theory extolling the virtues of modernity, while still seeing the individual as a societal creation.

## Criticisms of functionalism

As we can see then, those aspects of Durkheim's work which have remained influential within twentieth-century sociology and anthropology largely concern his holistic perspective. Functionalist anthropology and structural functionalism focus on studying how particular forms of social behaviour must be regarded as expressive of the total moral order of the society within which they take place. Within anthropology such a concern did much to promote the importance of detailed fieldwork rather than abstract guesswork as to why people acted as they did. Within American structural functionalism Durkheim's emphasis on the importance of analysing the underlying structures of a society, structures of which individual social members may be unaware, established an important principle of sociological investigation – the need to look at the unintended consequences of social action (as we discuss further below).

Both of these aspects of Durkheim's legacy remain significant in distinguishing the study of society from many kinds of philosophical accounts of social interaction as well as from common-sense beliefs about society. Durkheim's ambitions for a positivistic science of society have not fared so well. We will examine in more detail why this is the case in Chapter 7.

When we look at functionalism more generally, it is clear that it has exerted a tremendous influence on sociology. As we noted at the beginning of the chapter, for much of the first half of the last century it occupied a largely unchallenged theoretical position in the discipline. Through the influence of anthropology in Britain, and of Talcott Parsons and his supporters in America, by the middle of the century sociology came to be more or less synonymous with functionalist sociology. Other theoretical approaches were kept well in the background. The sociological enterprise was seen as principally concerned with a search for the 'real' significance of social institutions – the contribution they make to the maintenance of the social systems in which they are found. Because its influence has substantially waned today, it is easy to be over-critical of the rather narrow vision of functionalism's adherents. Now it seems rather strange that, during functionalism's ascendancy, so little attention should have been paid to relations of dominance and subordination, advantage and disadvantage in society. It also seems self-evident that humans must be recognized as being more than just 'cultural dopes', obediently learning sets of cultural prescriptions for action so that their social systems can persist. Today it seems clear that sociology must take account of people's **agency** in order to properly understand their actions.

However, in our eagerness to demonstrate the errors and partialities in functionalism/structural-consensus theory, we must not forget to acknowledge the contribution this kind of theory has made to sociology. It *is* important to recognize the unintended social consequences of people's beliefs and actions; sociology *does* have an important revelatory task; and it *is* necessary sometimes to go beyond people's own explanations for their actions in order to properly understand social behaviour. This is undoubtedly functionalism's contribution. Nevertheless, we would also be quite wrong to deny functionalism's weaknesses. Three main ones are usually identified. It is argued that functionalism:

• has an inherent tendency to 'reify' society
• is not able to explain social conflict and social change adequately
• is based upon an over-socialized view of human beings.

## Functionalism and the reification of society

Functionalists explain the existence of institutionalized patterns of behaviour and belief in terms of the good effects these have for the social system in which they are found. Institutions are not the product of decisions made by individuals, since they exist prior to these individuals. The problem of social order is not how human beings can create an ordered society. It is how social systems can create social beings, socialized into conforming to institutionalized rules of behaviour necessary for their existence. The insistence that societies acquire their functioning characteristics prior to the existence of their members leaves a rather awkward question, however. If *people* do not decide what is functional for their society, then who does decide? The functionalist seems to be left with the proposition that the social system itself decides what is good for it. Yet this is clearly absurd. Societies cannot think; only people can. This is known as the problem of '**reification**'. Functionalists seem to 'reify' society – to treat it as a thing – by endowing it with the ability to think and act intentionally that only humans have.

## Functionalism, conflict and social change

Whilst twentieth-century functionalism carries forward Durkheim's attempt to address how tensions and conflicts in society can be understood and addressed, it does so within a very limited remit. As we suggested above, Giddens (1976) argues, for the functionalist, conflict arises because the individual has not been properly integrated into the social order. If conflict is seen to equal a failure of individual integration, this seems to come remarkably close to *automatically* justifying whatever the status quo in a particular society happens to be; it seems to imply that all persisting social arrangements in a society must be beneficial, otherwise they would not remain in existence. In this light the question becomes that of how to control or re-integrate those who do not subscribe to the dominant values. When the problem of social change *is* addressed, it is seen as evolutionary, benign and adaptive; as a slow process, whereby the social system accommodates new circumstances. This leaves the theory unable to explain rapid, disruptive change – politically inspired innovation that dramatically overturns existing structures. The revolutionary overthrow of communist regimes in Eastern Europe in the late 1980s and early 1990s could hardly be understood by using the functionalist notion of change as organic adaptation.

## Functionalism and socialization

As we said in Chapter 1, *action* theories have crucial objections to the functionalist/structural-consensus model. For them, the real criticism of functionalism is that it over-emphasizes socialization as an explanation of social behaviour. The interpretive emphasis of action theory is that people are not passive recipients of cultural recipes for social action. Among living things, humans alone are able to *choose* how to act. Far from being a simple reflection of cultural prescription, such choices are made in the light of how people see the world – particularly how they interpret the actions of others. According to action theory, then, we cannot ignore the fact that actors act in the light of their interpretation of their situation.

## Conclusion

It was not until the 1960s that these sorts of criticisms caused functionalism to lose its influence. Alternative theoretical approaches came to be considered attractive and, indeed, superior. It was at this time that changes in their experiences altered people's perceptions of modern society, and sociologists were no exception. This was the decade of social reappraisal. The complacency encouraged by the economic prosperity of the 1950s, when Prime Minister Harold Macmillan confidently proclaimed that his British constituents had 'never had it so good', was replaced in the 1960s by a genuine concern for social justice and a real awareness of inequality and deprivation. Poverty had been 'rediscovered', in both Britain and the USA.

The Civil Rights movement in America began to demand equality for blacks. The feminist movement began to demand equality for women. US imperialism – most notoriously in Vietnam – was denounced by many in the Western world. In such a context, where social change was being demanded and conflict between different groups in society was clearly apparent, functionalism began to be seen as increasingly remote from the real world.

As we shall see in the following chapter, the work of Max Weber offered more promising material with which to develop an account of actors' meanings and their importance to wider social and historical processes of change.

## Further reading

Giddens, Anthony (1971b): *Capitalism and Modern Social Theory: an analysis of the writings of Marx, Durkheim and Max Weber*, Cambridge University Press.
Giddens, Anthony (1972a): *Emile Durkheim: selected writings*, Cambridge University Press.
Lukes, Steven (1973): *Emile Durkheim: his life and work*, Penguin.
Morrison, Kenneth (1995): *Marx, Weber, Durkheim: Formations of Modern Social Thought*, Sage.
Thompson, Kenneth (2002): *Emile Durkheim*, 2nd edn, Key Sociologists, Routledge.

# 4 MAX WEBER

**Max Weber:** born Erfurt, Thuringia, 1864, died Munich, 1920

## Major works

*Methodological Essays* (1902)
*The Protestant Ethic and the Spirit of Capitalism* (1902–4)
*Economy and Society* (1910–14)
*Sociology of Religion* (1916)

## Introduction

As we have seen, **functionalism** and Marxism, while giving very different accounts of modern social life, are nonetheless similar types of theory. For both, the world is as it is because of the characteristics of the **social structure**; change occurs because of the dynamics of the system and these theories of the system show how it works and how change takes place.

Of course, people living in different societies have their own theories about their own worlds, but these mental states usually do not correspond with structural reality, and usually have no influence on the way the social world is. This is why functionalists talk of 'latent' and 'manifest' functions and why Marxists talk of '**ideology**'. The idea that people should see how the world really is is unimportant in functionalism. While it is ultimately crucial for Marxism (other than in Althusserian Marxism), it only comes about when economic developments via the workings of the system encourage it, or when it is deliberately promoted by political activism or education. For functionalism all of the time, and for Marxism most of the time, then, mental states have no consequence for the structure of society. Weber's sociology is opposed to this kind of theory. For him, sociology 'is a science which attempts the interpretive understanding of social action in order thereby to arrive at a causal explanation of its course and effects' (Weber 1947: 89).

For Weber, the world is as it is because of social action. People do things because they decide to do so in order to achieve the ends they desire. Having selected their goals, and taken account of the circumstances they find themselves in, they *choose* to act. Social structures are the outcome of such action; ways of living are the product of motivated choice. Existing action-created social circumstances exercise constraint as structural forces, of course, but action is nonetheless still mental in origin – chosen in the light of the actor's perception of these structural constraints. Understanding social, action-produced reality involves explaining why people make the choices they do. Sociological theories are not theories of **social** *systems*, which have their own dynamics, but of the meanings behind actions – they are theories of the theories of actors.

## Social action theory

Weber called the method by which sociologists try to discover the meanings behind social actions *verstehen* or interpretive understanding. Because sociologists are human too, we can put ourselves in the place of others, appreciate the structural circumstances in which they find themselves, take account of their goals and thereby understand their actions. This is what distinguishes a social science from a natural science. Daffodils do not choose to open their leaves; apples do not decide to fall from trees. Natural scientists therefore do not have to be like daffodils or apples to explain their behaviour.

Unlike most action sociology, however (see Chapter 5), Weber's interest in actors' theories, in motivated, goal-oriented action, does not mean that he is only interested in the small-scale, in the meaning of specific interaction between individuals. Like Marx, Weber is interested in the broad sweep of history and social change, and believes that the best way of understanding different societies is to appreciate the typical forms of action that characterize them. But unlike Marx and Durkheim, who saw their task as uncovering *universal* tendencies in human social life, Weber rejects such a project. Weber reconstructs the meaning behind historical events producing social structures and formations, but at the same time sees all such historical configurations of circumstances as unique. The social world cannot be understood as governed by causal laws which sociologists can uncover in the ways that natural scientists attempt to do.

Weber argues that you can compare the structure of societies by understanding the reasons for the respective historical actions and events which have influenced their character, and by understanding the actions of actors living in them now, but that it is not possible to generalize about all societies or all social structures. To assist this kind of comparison, Weber argues that sociology should use as wide a range of concepts as possible.

## Types of action

Weber uses a classification of four types of action, differentiated in terms of the motives of actors:

| | |
|---|---|
| Traditional action | 'I do this because I always have.' |
| Affective action | 'I can't help doing this.' |
| Value-oriented action, or the use of **value rationality** | 'All I care about is this.' |
| Goal-oriented action, or the use of **instrumental rationality** | 'This is the most efficient means to achieve *this*', but '*this* is the best way to do *that*.' |

## Types of inequality

Though, like Marx, Weber saw relations of inequality as central to social life, he rejects the Marxist notion that class inequality is always the most important. For him, comparative and historical analysis testifies that *status groups*, possessing certain amounts of prestige, and *parties*, possessing certain amounts of political influence, can be just as significant sources of advantage as *class* membership. Furthermore, Weber defined class not simply as the possession of productive property, as Marx did, but as the possession of all of the kinds of life-chances generated by 'market power' in a society. That is, he defines class in terms of the individual's capacity to solicit rewards for the sale of his or her skills in society's marketplace.

## Types of power

Similarly, Weber rejects the Marxist notion that power is always tied to class membership, although an interest in power and force suffuses his work. As he puts it: 'Domination . . . is one of the most important elements of social action . . . in most of the varieties of social action domination plays a considerable role . . . without exception every sphere of social action is profoundly influenced by structures of dominancy' (Weber 1968: 141). Parkin (1982: 77) shows how Weber's typology of power identifies different appeals for legitimacy by the powerful:

| *Type of domination* | *Grounds for claiming obedience* |
| --- | --- |
| Traditional | 'Obey me because this is what our people have always done.' |
| Charismatic | 'Obey me because I can transform your life.' |
| Legal-rational | 'Obey me because I am your lawfully appointed superior.' |

By developing his conceptual apparatus in this way, without the sort of reliance on economic factors that characterizes Marx's work, Weber has often been portrayed as engaging in a major attempt to refute the **economic determinism** of Marxism. Since he sees ideas and motives as the driving force in social life, he certainly wants to refute economic determinism. His sociology is quite clearly wholly antagonistic to the view that all social behaviour can be understood as being economically caused.

A significant factor in Weber's antagonism to this view arises from his concerns about the state of German society at the time, and particularly its political climate. It is worth briefly outlining these concerns because they not only shaped Weber's criticisms of Marxism but are also believed to have led him to offer the deeply pessimistic account of the spread of **rationalization** that we will examine later in this chapter. As Marx's ideas developed, some sixty years before Weber was writing, they were fuelled in part by his desire to analyse why Germany, at that time still un-unified, was both economically and politically less advanced than France and Britain. It was the specificity of Germany's backwardness in these areas that led Marx to focus on the need to develop the revolutionary consciousness of the **proletariat** in the hope that this class would, through revolution, be able to secure and exceed the economic and social progress which Britain and France had already established over a longer period. Weber, writing after Bismarck had established a unified Germany, was still concerned by the relatively under-developed state of Germany's economy and of its political culture. He believed that Germany must develop in a liberal rather than an extreme left- or right-wing direction. Like Durkheim in France, then, Weber was trying to steer a liberal and progressive way through a political landscape shaped by the legacy of both feudalism and of Marx; a landscape riven by political extremes. As Weber saw it, the particular danger Germany faced was due to its failure to foster a political and economic climate that would allow strong political leaders to emerge, both from the working and middle classes. In this, Germany compared poorly to both France and particularly Britain. The earlier revolutions in France and, before that, in England had helped to strengthen the position of their **bourgeoisie** but German unification had occurred without such a maturing process on the part of the bourgeoisie. Without such strong leaders, and the vigorous climate of public discussion and political debate they would help to foster, he believed that the uniqueness of Germany's cultural heritage would wither away. Charismatic leaders like Bismarck were needed to put the Germany of Weber's time into a strong negotiating position in relation to the other states surrounding it and to help entrench the liberal values of individual freedom via democratic debate. All of these political concerns coloured Weber's reception of the socialist and Marxist parties that grew up in the wake of Marx's influence. Weber did not hold any of their leaders in high esteem and did not believe that the socialism and Marxism they espoused would do any more than increase bureaucratic control over the population.

Thus, for Weber, the Marxist focus on class and economic factors threatened further to prevent the flowering of more pluralistic and vibrant liberal values that he believed Germany most needed. However, as we have seen, while some of Marx's contemporaries who followed him were crudely economistic, it is not a charge that can be fairly levelled at Marx himself, as Weber in fact recognized in his comments on Marx's work. But there is another reason why it is wrong to see Weber's writings as a deliberate attempt to *disprove* Marx. This is because of the way he views the human activity of theorizing.

## Ideal types and sociological theorizing

According to Weber, the most obvious truth about thinking is that no human being can possibly grasp the whole of the reality he or she confronts – the 'meaningless infinity of the world process' as he describes it. Humans can only make sense of an aspect of reality – a selection from the infinite aggregate of events. Your theory represents your selection – your choice of what you think is worth looking at and your choice of what you think explains these things. But this does not make your personal, selected, partial account objectively correct – objective truth is unavailable to a human theorist. As Weber puts it, 'all knowledge of cultural reality . . . is always knowledge from *particular points of view*'. There can be no such thing as an 'absolutely "objective" scientific analysis of culture or . . . of "social phenomena" independent of special and "one-sided" viewpoints . . .' (Weber 1949: 72, 81). What we think exists depends upon what we think something's essence is. Thus, a functionalist might see a family as a system-integrating institution; a Marxist might see the same collection of people as a means of reproducing **capitalism**; while a feminist might see them as living lives which systematically oppress and subordinate the woman who is wife and mother. 'Seeing' therefore, is 'selecting'; 'seeing' is always theoretical. (It could be said that, in some ways, these ideas of Weber anticipate the *relativism* underpinning *postmodern* thought today. See Chapters 8 and 9.)

Since seeing from a particular point of view is an inevitable part of being human, says Weber, we should not try to ignore the fact, but make it explicit in our accounts of the world. We should describe and explain reality by highlighting and emphasizing our points of view to an extent which exaggerates the real world – by constructing **ideal types** of reality, as Weber calls them. To understand an aspect of social life, it is necessary to reduce it to what we think is its essence and then to highlight these features, so that others know exactly where we stand – what our point of view is. Our account of the world is then 'ideal' not in a judgemental sense, but in a 'larger-than-life' sense. We paint our picture of the world – selecting those aspects we consider significant or important – in bold strokes, so others can be left in no doubt.

Unlike Marx and Durkheim, then, Weber is not claiming to know the 'truth' about reality – only offering his version of it. Thus, in one of his most celebrated works (an account of the reasons for the emergence of modern capitalist society, and a portrayal of its principal features), Weber is not claiming that Marx is 'wrong' and he alone is 'right' in his theory. Weber regarded Marx's account as an ideal type and simply wanted to add his own account to Marx's, as an alternative, rather than claim to refute it. However, this alternative version can be seen to offer a direct challenge to the emphasis within Marxism on a single causal explanation of human behaviour – that of economic factors. Instead of seeing economic factors as causing changes in ideas and beliefs, Weber explains the rise of modern capitalist society as the result of a series of cultural, economic and political developments, each of which was influenced by and influenced the others. As Parkin summarizes it, Weber is 'concerned to show that early Protestant beliefs made an unparalleled impact upon the conduct of economic life' (Parkin 1982: 44), but he is not claiming that capitalism could only have arisen as a consequence of these religious ideas. Perhaps his key point is that economic interests are rarely purely economic, but are instead shaped by a wider range of meanings, beliefs and values. It is in this more complicated picture of human motivation that Weber examines the development of rational capitalism not simply as a means by which we produce what we need to survive but as a pattern of social behaviour sparked or motivated by the values of the early Protestants.

## Religion, capitalism and rationalization

Much of Weber's historical, comparative work is focused on the influence of religious beliefs on action. It is in this tradition that he sets out his account of the factors that encouraged the emergence of capitalism in those countries where it took root. This form of modern society, he argues, represents the institutionalization of *instrumental rationality* above all else. Whereas in other times and places other forms of action have prevailed, only in modern industrial capitalist societies has it become routine for actors to act for reasons of efficiency and calculability, rather than because of emotional or traditional reasons, or because of a single-minded dedication to an overriding goal. For Weber, **modernity** is best understood as the triumph of this way of thinking, this way of looking at the world, and this way of acting (though the last thing he wants to do is to join in the celebration). In *The Protestant Ethic and the Spirit of Capitalism* (PE), which he published as two articles in 1904 and 1905, Weber develops his analysis of modern capitalism as the end result of a rationalization process, rooted in the historical influence of specific intellectual traditions. The emergence of this way of living and acting is, for Weber, 'the central problem' in a universal history of civilization. As he states in the Introduction to this work, his investigations are guided by the question of why it was that

Western countries followed a path of scientific, artistic, political and economic development that culminated in a process of rationalization which is unique to the West. In Weber's account, the role of religious leaders in promoting differing kinds of ideas and orientations in different societies is crucial. As Bilton et al. summarize his argument: 'For example, the Buddhist monk withdrew from all worldly activity in order to achieve a spiritual elevation, while the Confucian Mandarin engaged in administration on the basis of highly traditionalistic and non-scientific literary knowledge. Only in the West did a cultural orientation emerge which favoured rationalisation' (Bilton et al. 2002: 485).

The part of Weber's argument that has become most famous concerns the role of Puritan Protestantism, and particularly Calvinism, in this process. In PE Weber outlines the affinity he sees between the kind of lives Calvinists were encouraged to lead by their religion and the kind of behaviour and attitudes necessary for capitalism to work effectively. He explains how, unlike in most religions, Calvinists are encouraged to concentrate on worldly work as the most virtuous activity and, at the same time, are exhorted to live ascetic – frugal, thrifty and austere – lives. Weber argues that this emphasis on the importance of industriousness and hard work coupled with a demand for an ascetic lifestyle is unique to Puritan religions, and that it was this combination of religious prescriptions that gave capitalism the chance to take root.

Weber's description of John Calvin's doctrines explains the psychologically troublesome situation that the adherence to the principle of predestination placed upon Calvinists. The doctrine of predestination holds that salvation is decided by God at birth and that there is nothing that an individual can do in his or her life to change this decision. For Calvinists, this led to an intolerable degree of uncertainty and, in response to this, to what Weber refers to as 'salvation anxiety'. This anxiety as to their eternal fate led Calvinists to look for earthly signs of being one of the chosen few who would enter the kingdom of heaven. Calvinists believed that although they could not *prove* for certain to themselves or to others that they had been called by God to salvation, evidence of their living dutiful, successful and productive lives would certainly help to alleviate the anxiety that they were destined for damnation. Their belief was that the Lord will only let the worthy prosper. Their lives therefore became dedicated to efficiency and rationality in order to maximize their productivity. But the symbols of their achievement – material riches accumulated through constant, ever-more-efficient labour – could not be consumed in any profligate, ostentatious or self-indulgent fashion, since this would contradict the other Calvinist virtue of asceticism. Thus, although wealth accumulation becomes the symbol of virtuous and efficient hard work for Calvinists, the consumption of the fruits of this labour is denied the believer because of the need to live an ascetic life.

Here, then, is the affinity between Protestantism and capitalism. Unlike other forms of economy, for capitalism to work, capital has to be accumulated – not to be consumed, but to be reinvested in the pursuit of ever-more-efficient, and profitable, techniques of production. The need is for the constant pursuit of rational means of production, by ploughing back the fruits of labour. The more wealth is made and the more successful the capitalist enterprise is, the more resources are available to improve the efficiency of production. Work is therefore an end in itself; profit to be reinvested is virtuous, and brings its own reward.

Weber's account is clear. Only Puritanism expects of its followers a way of thinking and a way of living that matches the peculiar demands made on capitalist producers. Without a population dedicated to worldly work for its own sake, prepared to eschew as sinful any sign of extravagance, capitalism could not have got off the ground. The creation of such a world thus represents the perfect example of the Weberian view of the role of beliefs and action in social change. According to Weber, capitalism is the child of a particular way of thinking and acting, not a **mode of production** spawned by economic forces.

But for Weber, this is a child that has grown into a monster. Incorporated within PE is a message that concerns not just the rise of capitalism but also its character and its relationship to the rationalization process. In his earlier writings Weber distinguished between two forms of institutional rationality: substantive and formal rationality. The definitions of these run parallel to his classification of rationality at the level of individual action, i.e. value rationality and instrumental rationality. Substantive rationality is always based upon an ethic or a **belief system**. Hence, Puritanism is a good example of substantive rationality: the ethic of salvation and of living a good life in order to obtain a goal dominated this religion and the members of its community. The pursuit of an industrious and productive life through toil and graft combined with the virtue of asceticism is quite rational when placed within the context of a particular religion.

However, substantive rationality contrasts sharply with Weber's notion of formal rationality which, like instrumental rationality, is based upon achieving an end goal without the substantive basis of a religion, ideology or belief system. In an important sense it represented, for Weber, a valueless pursuit. The threat to humanity posed by formal or instrumental rationality lies in its capacity to shape the institutions of modern societies so that they conduct activities that are essentially free of any ethical anchor. For Weber saw in capitalist business enterprise an example of formal rationality where the end goal – making a profit – drives action relentlessly and remorselessly towards the destruction of the human spirit. In the final few pages of PE Weber makes clear the irony of the story he has told. Calvinism was a necessary condition for the establishment of capitalism but its ethic (its value-driven substance) bears no resemblance to the face of capitalism today, instead, 'the idea of duty in one's calling prowls about in our lives like the ghost of dead religious beliefs'. The formal rationality has long since left its substantive roots behind. And there is one final twist in this tale, as Weber observes:

> The Puritan wanted to work in a calling; we are forced to do so. For when asceticism was carried out of monastic cells into everyday life, and began to dominate worldly morality, it did its part in building the tremendous cosmos of the modern economic order. In Baxter's view the care for external goods should only lie on the shoulders of the saint like a light cloak, which can be thrown aside at any moment. But fate decreed that the cloak should become an iron cage. (Weber 2001: 123).

## Bureaucracy and rationalization

The vividness with which Weber describes the fate and legacy of the Protestant ethic might lead us to suppose that he straightforwardly rejected modern economic and institutional structures and processes of organization. However, he does not allow himself to make life that simple. Weber wrote with conviction both of the deadening impact of the spread of formal rationality on our individual lives and of the need for such dry and informal processes to manage the **infrastructure** of complex modern societies. In order to work as smoothly and as predictably as possible, modern democratic capitalist societies require the systematic application of rationally devised rules and regulations.

As Morrison observes, 'with modern society comes the quantitative extension of administrative tasks, and these tend to increase to such an extent that there is a need for a large bureaucratic organization' (Morrison 1995: 295). As Morrison also points out, this form of legal-rational domination (see our discussion of types of power, above) is based upon technical criteria. These characteristics apply to the operations of both capitalism and bureaucracy and they define Weber's concept of formal rationality. They are:

1. Calculability – the calculation of the ends of action.
2. Efficiency – observations related to the best means of achieving the ends of action.
3. Predictability – an insurance of a given outcome.
4. Technology – the use of non-human technology in decision-making.
5. Control – safeguards against uncertainty.

With a little reflection we can recognize these traits in the bureaucracies that we frequently encounter in our daily lives, whether this involves trying to obtain a passport, a timetable at university, or customer service at a bank or other large organization. While these traits of formal rationality may often appear to be ineffective in dealing with the unique or the unexpected they are efficient as a method of securing end goals that are necessary for the management of large populations. In this respect Weber claims that formal rationality 'is superior to any other form in precision, in stability, in the stringency of its discipline, and in its reliability. It thus makes possible a particularly high degree of calculability of results. It is finally superior both in intensive efficiency and in the scope of its operations, and is formally capable of application to all kinds of administrative tasks' (Weber 1968: 337).

Here is a different commentary on modernity from those of Weber's two main nineteenth-century peers. Weber's story is one of the role of specific intellectual traditions in specific historical circumstances, rather than the unravelling of inexorable and universally applicable laws of societal development, as are those of Durkheim and Marx. It is also the story of the exile of the human spirit from modernity. Durkheim and Marx each constructed versions of a social theory that could specify the societal route to a future of progress and human emancipation. They both thought they had discovered the cure for social sickness and the recipe for societal, and thereby individual, health and happiness. For Durkheim, regulation through socialization is guaranteed to prevent **anomie**; for Marxists, **historical materialism** offers the prescribed medicine for the eradication of the modern disease of **alienation**.

But Weber is no doctor of social life; he has no cure for rationalization, which is, for him, the scourge of modern society. For Weber, the pursuit of technical efficiency, whatever the (non-material) cost, is inevitable and irreversible in modern industrial capitalism, and while in bureaucratic administration it reaches its zenith, it also represents humanity's nadir. Weber tells us that the rise of this form of society means it is now wholly illusory to hope to build the sort of utopia that, for so many thinkers, the birth of modernity seemed to promise. A world dominated by formal rationality – where efficiency, calculability and predictability are the dominant goals – means a world bereft of meaning, of mystery, or of a concern with spiritual fulfilment. Weber tells us instead to resign ourselves to the 'iron cage of bureaucracy' and the 'polar night of icy darkness' which modernity has created. For him, the triumph of capitalism or modernity as a form of life signals the end of the line for progress. The train bearing the hopes for humanity's spiritual welfare has run into the buffers of terminal instrumental rationality and the outcome is, in his words, 'a renunciation, a departure from an age of full and beautiful humanity, which can no more be repeated in the course of our cultural development than can the flower of the Athenian culture of antiquity' (Weber 2001: 123).

Before examining how Weber's work influenced subsequent social theorists it is worth returning briefly to our discussion of Weber's concerns about the future development of Germany. As we saw, he wanted Germany to develop a strong liberal democratic culture, and believed that this required an open and diverse public sphere that would encourage charismatic leaders to develop and compete with each other to steer Germany away from economic stagnation and political extremism. But he saw Germany as caught on the horns of a dilemma: on one hand mass democracy requires sophisticated processes of organization and administration to work properly and fairly. On the other hand, he noted that charismatic leaders are typically strong on 'ideas' rather than good at paperwork. He worried that potential leaders would not be recognized and brought on by a political culture which values structures and processes – means rather than ends. Without such charismatic leaders – who would inspire their publics to live according to ultimate values rather than get lost in instrumental reason and timid uniformity – Weber was convinced that Germany would be left languishing in the iron cage.

Giddens (1972b) suggests that Weber's analysis of the relationship between modernity and rationalization can be seen as his attempt to understand the nature of the bourgeoisie – the class of business and political leaders in his own country. It may be that in presenting the iron cage as the fate of modernity in this way Weber was trying to jolt them into action, to inspire the bourgeoisie to intervene and fight against the domination of instrumental thinking.

As we suggested earlier, when outlining the political context within which Marx and Durkheim developed their ideas, to look at that context is not to 'explain away' their ideas as expressions of circumstances entirely different to ours. Instead, knowing their context may in fact help us to become more aware of our own, as well better assess the usefulness of their work in our context. Weber has a strong tendency to present specific worries about Germany as if they were general problems with modernity, but we are under no obligation to follow the same line of argument. Weber's ideas have clearly left their mark. His melancholic if not utterly pessimistic portrayal of the modern predicament has proven to be immensely influential to future generations of social theorists. As such, it may be useful at this point to sketch briefly the different ways in which his ideas have been developed, because they offer a summary version of some of the key developments in modern social theory which will be discussed in subsequent chapters of this book.

## Rationalization after Weber

Weber's *Protestant Ethic* offers a particularly powerful account of the ways in which meaningful human action can produce *unintended consequences* at the level of social structures – consequences which we then appear powerless to control. In this disenchanted world, all ultimate values, including religious ones, have been pushed to the margins of culture. In his 1919 essay, 'Science as a Vocation' he suggests that the dominant belief is now in scientific progress, but science cannot give meaning to the world in the way that religion once did:

> Who – aside from certain big children who are indeed found in the natural sciences – still believes that the findings of astronomy, biology, physics, or chemistry could teach us anything about the *meaning* of the world. . . . If these natural sciences lead to anything in this way, they are apt to make the belief that there is such a thing as the 'meaning' of the universe die out at its very roots. (Weber 1991: 142)

In this context all we can do is to try to sustain our belief in our own values and hold on to them in the face of the **dehumanizing** grind of the bureaucratic machine. Indeed, bureaucracy 'develops the more perfectly . . . the more completely it succeeds in eliminating from official business love, hatred, and all purely personal, irrational, and emotional elements which escape calculation' (Weber 1968: 975).

Weber's account of the ways in which the administrative processes necessary to modern societies gradually push aside all human spontaneity and feeling has been taken up by later social theorists to draw attention to the extent to which scientific and bureaucratic rationalization generates a crisis of meaning and of morality. We briefly saw an example of such an approach in the work of the Frankfurt School in Chapter 2. Adorno and Horkheimer drew on the work of both Weber and Marx to argue that rationalizing processes combined with the spread of capitalist values meant that all forms of art and creativity had now been colonized by the commercial interests of the 'culture industry'. Arguably, Adorno and Horkheimer present their pessimistic case with the residual hope that other more socially critical forms of thinking and action could re-emerge from the isolated pockets of authentic forms of human contact still remaining.

However, as we shall see in Chapter 6, Foucault's portrayal of the 'surveillance society' reveals a further twist in this tale of triumphant rationalization. Foucault suggests that even those areas of social life in which we might think we are free from the demands of the social system, such as expressions of sexuality, are in fact examples of the most intense social surveillance and control. There appears to be no refuge left for authentic subjective meaning in the face of the expansion of bureaucratic control.

A more recent sociological elaboration of Weber's analysis of the ever-increasing spread of such control can be found in George Ritzer's description of the process of 'McDonaldization'. As we shall see below, on this account, McDonaldization is seen to destroy the enjoyment to be gained from experiencing the *uniqueness or individuality* of sources of sensuous pleasure and human contact.

## The McDonaldization of society

George Ritzer's (1940–) McDonaldization thesis relies on two main sources: Weber's account of the rationalization of modernity and F. W. Taylor's account of scientific management (commonly known as Taylorism). Ritzer takes from Weber the key characteristics of the rationalization process and collapses these into four categories: 'efficiency, predictability, calculability, and nonhuman technologies that control people' (Ritzer 2000: 23). He combines this with Taylor's managerial principles of 'time and motion'. Time and motion studies are aimed at producing goods and services in the most efficient way possible. More often than not this results in a fragmentation of production whereby a product is produced in stepped procedures that have been subjected to an analysis to produce what Taylor referred to as the 'one best way' of carrying out a task. Taylorism, as a method of capitalist production, lends itself to Weber's notion of rationalization neatly. By definition Taylorist production is efficient, but its methods are also consistent with capitalist organizations in general. And, as such, it yields reflexive control over production. Indeed, as noted earlier, Weber pointed out that capitalism always leans towards formal rationality. Its goal is to make as much profit as possible and this can only be achieved by rationalization. Ritzer's thesis demonstrates the ubiquity and character of formal rationality in contemporary society. He shares Weber's original concerns about the **disenchantment** of the social world. The fast-food outlet, he says, has become the model of a form of rationalization that represents a culmination of a series of processes that occurred throughout the twentieth century:

> What we have today is sufficiently more extreme than previous forms of rationalization to legitimate the use of a distinct label – McDonaldization – to describe the most contemporary aspects of the rationalization process . . . [and] . . . as Weber fretted over the emerging iron cage of rationality, I foresee a similar iron cage being created by the increasing ubiquity of the fast-food model. (Ritzer 2000: 39)

As the title of his text suggests, Ritzer's primary example is the McDonald's fast-food restaurant and in this section we will focus mainly on this company. McDonald's website claims that there are 'more than 31,000 local restaurants serving more than 58 million people in 118 countries each day' (www.aboutmcdonalds.com/mcd/our_company.html). The product and the service in each of these outlets is the same, as each franchise is obliged to follow the production process and rule-book of McDonald's. The manual informs the franchise what ingredients to use and what form these should take, how to prepare food, how to serve customers, and how to respond or speak to them. The way of doing things the McDonald's way is to follow the manual to the letter. Thus, every conceivable aspect of the business has been systematized to make burger production a methodical operation whether it is carried out in New York, London, Moscow or Kuala Lumpur.

Ritzer claims that McDonald's (and other fast-food franchises) operate according to the rationalist principles of efficiency, calculability, predictability and control. Aspects of the efficiency of the McDonald's organization that gave it a competitive advantage over its rivals can be traced back to the methods of its founders, the McDonald brothers Mac and Dick. McDonald's opened for business in Pasadena, California in 1937. Ritzer observes that from the start they 'based the restaurant on the principles of high speed, large volume, and low price' (Ritzer 2000: 36). The menu was extremely simple – hamburgers or cheeseburgers – and allowed the brothers to operate an assembly-line production system. The hamburger is a perfect item of consumption for this purpose. Unlike other fast-food there is only one way to cook it and its condiments are added rather than built in (Ritzer 2000: 42). The whole process can be broken down into parts. Hence, the McDonald brothers employed 'grill men', 'shake men', 'fry men', and 'dressers'.

However, it was not until Ray Kroc formed a partnership with the McDonald brothers in the late 1950s that McDonald's efficiency really took off. Until this time McDonald's had remained a small-scale operation. Reminiscent of F. W. Taylor and Henry Ford before him, Kroc studied in meticulous detail each component in making burgers. For example, experimentation with the bun found that sliced buns in a re-usable cardboard box could be handled quicker than partially sliced buns and that the paper between the burger patties required just the right amount of wax to enable them to slip off the paper and onto the lattice (Ritzer 2000: 42).

As the company grew, the other elements of rationalization developed. Calculability was essential to the franchised operation. Each burger must weigh exactly the same (1.6 ounces), be of the same diameter (3.875 inches), and contain the same amount of fat (19 per cent) to avoid shrinkage when cooking. The portions of French fries were equalized with the introduction of a 'fry scoop' (see Ritzer 2000: 79). Frozen chips were introduced to ensure consistency throughout the year and to avoid mess in the kitchen and they were made in a way that ensured an emphasis on the taste of salt and sugar rather than potato. Predictability and control follows from various aspects of efficiency and calculability. Indeed the concepts were at times indistinguishable. As Ritzer notes, to obtain predictability an organization or society 'emphasizes discipline, order, systematization, formalization, routine, consistency, and methodical operation' (Ritzer 2000: 83) . McDonald's has these traits in abundance. Its way of doing business is to handle every single detail of all of its outlets' operations and in so doing it ensures that each visit to any one its restaurants will be exactly the same as the last visit and the next. Routinization exists at every level of service right down to the scripted interactions between the counter person and the customer involving six choreographed steps: greet the customer; take the order; assemble the order; present the order; take payment; thank the customer and ask for repeat business (see Ritzer 2000: 90). To help ensure consistency McDonald's has its own

Hamburger University which all managers must attend and are taught by lecturers who follow a carefully constructed script. The aim of all of these measures, and an increased use of automated machinery in the kitchens, is to avoid human misjudgement (where misjudgement refers to any human action that is not consistent with what is prescribed in the McDonald's manual or guideline).

As noted at the start of this section, McDonald's represents a culmination of rationalization processes that developed throughout the twentieth century. But Ritzer's concern is not simply with McDonald's but with what he sees as a model for work elsewhere. Thus, the assembly-line method may be applied to the production of all kinds of goods and services, from motor cars to houses and holidays. It is, he says, even creeping into higher education. In each case the defining model of production is characterized by Weber's key features of rationalization or formal rationality.

Before looking at the main problems Ritzer associates with contemporary rationalization it may be worth pointing out that McDonaldization may be said to have some, albeit superficial, benefits. Ritzer willingly points out that aspects or consequences of rationalization can appear attractive. The recipient of rationalized services knows exactly what she will receive and may draw comfort from this predictability. For example, it is not unusual for an American or Briton abroad to seek out a McDonald's restaurant in a foreign city with confidence that the outlet can be relied upon to make a predictable and safe product. Ritzer also points to potential attractions to workers that rationalization brings. Casual labourers may appreciate a job that does not require much thought but helps them through, for example, their days as a student. And, following a set script may help waiters or servers to deal with difficult customers more easily. However, while McDonaldization provides some benefits, its consequences for society overall are, according to Ritzer, extremely negative.

For Ritzer, McDonaldization produces irrational, inefficient, de-humanizing, and unhealthy and dangerous outcomes. Take, for example, the apparent efficiencies of ATMs (automatic teller machines), or fast-food restaurants, or self-service tills in shops. There is a sense in which the workload for each of these systems is passed on to the consumer. The consumer now queues up to take money out of the 'hole in the wall', must clear away his own plates and debris (indeed take it away with him at drive-through restaurants), and must pass his own goods through a barcode machine. Hence, the efficiency gains tend towards one side. That is, towards those who push for rationalization: banks, fast-food restaurants and shops. Of course, efficiency gains can be passed on to consumers in terms of cheaper prices, but this too turns out to be double-edged, for the competitive advantages of rationalization encourage producers of indigenous goods to imitate such methods, e.g. the fast-food croissanterie. Thus, the outcome is the domination of the market by bland and homogenous goods and services. For Ritzer, the spirit of humanity withers in such circumstances as efficient systems leave no room for difference but systematically seek to root it out. Quite apart from considering the unhealthy ingredients of such food, Ritzer points to the disenchantment of experience such efficient processes of food production entail: 'Anything that is magical, mysterious, fantastic, dreamy, and so on is considered inefficient. Enchanted systems typically involve highly convoluted means to ends, and they may well have no obvious goals at all. Efficient systems do not permit such meanderings, and their designers and implementers will do whatever is necessary to eliminate them' (Ritzer 2000: 132).

And, while it is obvious that workers at McDonaldized companies must grin and bear the assembly-line methods of production, it is noted less often that consumers may also be subject to these conditions. The operating system of McDonald's, for example, is testimony to this. One main goal of the fast-food restaurant is to encourage customers to spend their money and leave quickly. The form of the food encourages the latter and it is further enhanced by the structure of the restaurant from its uncomfortable seats to the garish and clashing colours of the red and yellow décor. Every aspect of the restaurant says 'don't relax!' As Ritzer observes: '[t]he best that can usually be said is that the meal is efficient and is over quickly' (Ritzer 2000: 137).

Ritzer's account of McDonaldization is surely familiar to many of us in its depiction of the anonymous and curiously empty experience offered by contemporary consumer capitalism. But, perhaps like Adorno and Horkheimer's depiction of the culture industry, Ritzer gives a vivid account of the processes involved without considering what individual social actors make of such experiences. Are we all passively caught up in such processes, and as passively bovine as the food we are encouraged to eat, or do we perhaps bring to them differing degrees of scepticism and resistance, as well as outright rejection or complicity?

## The persistence of social action

For contemporary social theorists such as Bauman, Habermas and Giddens, such questions matter not simply in the context of Weber's emphasis on subjective meaning, or other issues relating only to us as individuals, but because what we each bring to such experiences tells us something important about shared or *intersubjective* stocks of meaning. For these theorists, shared meanings and values have not simply disappeared, driven out for ever by processes of rationalization. Social actors should not be reduced to passive carriers of instrumental or bureaucratic rationality. The mixture of fatalism and pessimism which can be seen in some of Weber's comments about the dehumanizing impact of rationalization can itself be potentially destructive because it can lead social theorists to lose contact with ordinary social actors' own accounts of their world. If this happens then social theory also loses the ability to understand how social actors in even their most routine daily actions help to sustain or to change larger scale social processes and structures. The point is that the ways in which social actors engage with bureaucratic systems, and with the demands made of them by those in authority, cannot simply be assumed but instead require empirical analysis and theoretical interpretation. Both Habermas' and Giddens' work can be approached as attempts to re-establish and refine sociological knowledge of the moral, ethical and practical skills we all employ in daily life and to look at how, for better or worse, these dealings contribute to the structural patterns of society as a whole.

Zygmunt Bauman's (1925–) analysis of modernity and the Holocaust offers the most compelling argument as to why such a sociological pursuit is necessary. Bauman argues that the Holocaust should be regarded as a 'test of the hidden possibilities of modern society which is crucial to our understanding of modern society' (Bauman 2000b: 12). He attempts to bring together an analysis of the processes of rationalization and of the actions of those who contributed to the Holocaust. He argues that the 'final solution' of physical extermination of European Jewry emerged 'inch by inch' in response to the obstacles that emerged in the Nazi's attempt to deliver Hitler's objective of removing the Jews from the Reich, without his specifying how this should be done. The idea of the Endlosung or 'final solution' of physical extermination was an outcome of the bureaucratic culture that is intrinsic to modern states. Such an unprecedented scale of mass murder depended on the skills and habits of a precise **division of labour**, of a smooth flow of command and information, 'on the skills and habits, in short, which best grow and thrive in the atmosphere of the office' (Bauman 1989: 15). Bauman claims that this reminds us of how ethically blind the bureaucratic pursuit of efficiency is, because it is intended only to make possible the rational coordination of the actions of a large number of individuals according to a set objective, 'free from interference of ethical norms or moral inhibitions' (Bauman 1989: 28). In this context, if the objective to be achieved is the removal of the Jews, then the use of violence to accomplish this objective appears simply as one means to be considered alongside a range of others. But Bauman importantly insists that such an outcome should not be seen as inevitable.

The perpetrators of the Holocaust were not simple cogs in the machine and these acts were not 'committed by born criminals, sadists, madmen, social miscreants or otherwise morally defective individuals' (Bauman 1989: 19). Instead Bauman details both the intersubjective processes of interpretation that were in play and those that were absent, which together created the context within which 'normal' moral agents interpreted and attempted to justify their actions. Bauman demonstrates how the evidence shows that the authorization and routinization of violence, and the dehumanization of the victims of violence, each contributed to reducing these social agents' moral inhibitions against violent atrocities. Thus we can see that the technical-administrative success of the Holocaust was due in part to the skilful utilization of '"moral sleeping pills" made available by modern bureaucracy and modern technology' (1989: 26). But Bauman's analysis also allows us to see that the process of mass extermination was built up through complex chains of interaction between normal moral agents. As he puts it, a 'multitude of minute acts and inconsequential actors' stands between the actor and the outcomes of their action, which creates a distance between 'intentions and practical accomplishments', and it is this distance which allows the agent to avoid direct knowledge of the consequences of their actions (1989: 25).

Bauman points to the failure of much post-war sociology to respond to the issues raised by the Holocaust. As we suggested above, the work of Habermas and of Giddens can help us in developing this response in so far as they each attempt to develop theoretical frameworks which allow us to analyse how what we all think, do and say in our everyday routines contributes to the creation (or the diminishment) of even the largest and most powerful structures of society. But before we look at their work in detail we will examine some of the American sociologies of action which, while they have influenced Giddens, Habermas and other European social theorists, were themselves developed much more in response to Parsons' theories about the nature of American society than to the crises generated in post-war Europe.

# Further reading

Giddens, Anthony (1971b): *Capitalism and Modern Social Theory: an analysis of the writings of Marx, Durkheim and Max Weber*, Cambridge University Press.

Poggi, Gianfranco (2006): *Weber: a short introduction*, Polity.

Radkau, Joachim (2009): *Max Weber: a biography*, Polity.

Whimster, Sam (2007): *Understanding Weber*, Routledge.

# 5 INTERPRETIVE SOCIOLOGY: ACTION THEORIES

## Introduction

In our earlier discussion of action theory in Chapter 1, we emphasized how the behaviour of human beings must be seen as the product of how they interpret the world around them. It is not that behaviour is *learned* or *determined*, as structural theories suggest. Rather, it is *chosen* as appropriate behaviour in the light of how people define the situations they encounter – what they take social settings to *mean*.

But a question we did not consider earlier is this: how far does this process of interpretation – which, according to action theorists, is always the origin of behaviour – affect other people involved in these meaningful encounters? This is clearly important. As we said in Chapter 1, most of the situations in which we find ourselves are inevitably *social* situations – they involve other people doing things. Nearly every time we interpret meaning in order to decide how to act we are interpreting the actions of other human beings.

## Symbolic interactionism

Symbolic interactionism (SI) is the name given to one of the best-known action theories. It is with symbolic interactionism that the phrases, 'definition of the situation', 'reality is in the eye of the beholder' and, 'if men define situations as real, they are real in their consequences' are most usually associated. Though rather cumbersome, the name given to this perspective does clearly indicate the kinds of human activity which its proponents consider essential to concentrate on in order to understand social life. According to SI theorists, social life literally is the 'interaction of humans via the use of symbols'. That is, they are interested in:

- the way in which humans employ symbols of what they mean in order to communicate with one another (an orthodox interpretive interest)
- the effects that the interpretations of these symbols have on the behaviour of parties during a social interaction.

SI stresses that *inter*action is a two-way interpretive process. We must understand not only that someone's action is a product of how he or she has interpreted the behaviour of someone else, but also that this interpretation will have an impact on the actor whose behaviour has been interpreted in certain ways too. One of the major contributions of symbolic interactionism to action theory has been to elaborate and explain the different kinds of effects that the interpretations of others can have on the social identities of the individuals who are the objects of these interpretations.

## The construction of self-image

The most common effect is that we use the interpretations of others – what they take our behaviour to mean – as evidence of who we think we are. That is, our self-image – our sense of identity – is a product of the way others think of us. In effect, it is a case of 'I am what I think you think I am.' For SI this is largely what socialization means. It is not, as structural theorists argue, a process whereby given, external, cultural rules are generally internalized by people. It is an outcome of the interpretive process – the allocation of meaning between people – that for action theorists is at the root of all social interaction. Our personalities are constructed by means of this interpreting process as follows.

During the course of our lives, we encounter a number of people, all of whom take our behaviour towards them to symbolize something about our selves. They interpret our behaviour in the light of the evidence they are provided with. They then act towards us in the light of this interpretation, indicating via the symbolic means available to them what kind of person they have decided we are. The image we have of ourselves is crucially influenced by the reactions of individuals we come into contact with. We cannot ignore what kind of person others are telling us we are; the image of our 'self' is seriously affected, if not created, by the image others have of us.

Take, for example, the relationship between a primary school teacher and his/her class. Being human, the teacher cannot help but make judgements about the children in the class, particularly about their ability. Equally, according to SI, since the children are human too, their view of themselves and their abilities will be influenced by the judgement of the teacher. So the little girl who sits attentively at the front of the class, behaves well and is keen and conscientious, is likely to be thought of as 'intelligent' or 'able'. In contrast, the boy sitting at the back of the class, who appears inattentive and lazy, is less favourably interpreted.

SI argues that often what matters is not whether the interpretations are correct, but the impact they can have on their recipients. In this case, even though the children are in fact of the same ability, the teacher has decided they are not, and as a result treats them differently. The little girl is encouraged to work, whereas the little boy is merely admonished for misbehaviour and kept under control. These different reactions of the teacher influence the way the children see themselves. Sustained by the support and encouragement of the teacher, the little girl works hard and fulfils her potential. Persuaded by the teacher that he has little academic ability, the boy concentrates on misbehaving. The teacher's judgements are thus confirmed; the prophecy about the children's abilities comes true. The justice of the interpretations matters less than the consequences of their application, particularly in the way the recipients are encouraged to see themselves.

The fortuity of the outcome of this process of interaction between interpreter and interpreted is plain to see. Our 'self' – the person we become – depends upon the particular people we happen to encounter in our journey through life. Other parents, friends, acquaintances and workmates could make us into very different people. In our example, a different teacher might have encouraged both children equally, with much more positive consequences for the little boy's self-image.

## Social acting: the presentation of self in everyday life

But the influence of the interpretations of others is only one half of the process of interaction emphasized by SI. Far from human personality being simply the passive construction of others, SI stresses the active role which humans play in the creation of their social selves. According to SI, since we soon come to learn that others will interpret our behaviour, our own interpretive abilities allow us to manipulate these interpretations to suit our vision of ourselves. We use our capacity to be self-reflexive in order to present the person we wish others to think we are. We play roles in a creative way to elicit from others the responses we desire. In effect, we manage, or orchestrate, the responses of others by presenting the image of our self that we wish them to hold. We become actors on the stage of life, writing our own lines.

The SI theorist most commonly associated with this emphasis on creative role-playing is Erving Goffman (1922–82). In *The Presentation of Self in Everyday Life* (1969), Goffman outlines his conception of social life as a stage upon which humans play themselves, and explains the social props that are pressed into service to present these selves to others. According to Goffman, very few human attributes, possessions or activities are not used in this theatrical way. The clothes we wear, the house we live in, the way we furnish it, the way we walk and talk, the work we do, and the way in which we spend our leisure time – in fact, everything that is public about ourselves can be, and is, used to tell others what kind of person we are. We thus 'manage' the information we provide for others. We control our dress, appearance and habits to encourage others to see us as the people we want them to see us as being.

For Goffman and his fellow interactionists then, socialization is usually about the triumph of the creative capacities of the individual over the reactions of others. Not all action theorists agree, however. *Labelling theory* is a perspective that has grown out of symbolic interactionism. Labelling theory is less interested in the ways in which people are able to influence others' interpretations of themselves than in the kinds of interaction where no such opportunities exist. Labelling theorists are mainly interested in the fact that sometimes people are victims, often helpless, of the interpretations, or *labels*, of others, to such an extent that their social identities can be imposed upon them, even against their will. Why should this happen? Why should we find ourselves in social situations where we cannot manipulate the interpretations of others?

## Labelling theory

### Labels which contradict the self-image

Sometimes we are in no position to protest against misinterpretation, because we are dead. For example, as already briefly discussed in Chapter 1, a verdict of suicide depends on the interpretations of a range of people – kin, friends, police officers and, in particular, coroners. Though bodies often indicate the truth, everything eventually depends on others' interpretations.

Sometimes we *can* protest against a wrong label, but this cuts no ice with our interpreters. For example, it is the public labelling of a person as a shoplifter in court, and later on in the local press, that will be the evidence others will go on, not our protestations of innocence. In any case, sometimes these protestations are merely seen as confirmation of the appropriateness of the label. For example, if you are diagnosed as being mentally ill even though you consider yourself perfectly sane, it is likely that you will make a considerable fuss about the prospect of being sent to a mental hospital. Normal though this reaction may be from your point of view, the danger is that your angry or excitable behaviour will be seen by others as confirmation that you are unbalanced. 'After all, no *normal* person would get into that state.' Finally, even if we rise above the interpretations of others and attempt to ignore what we consider a wrong label and act normally, it is perfectly possible that this can simply serve to confirm its justice to others as well. For example, when you are diagnosed as mentally ill, if you *don't* make a fuss and act as normally as possible in order to prove your sanity, this too may simply be interpreted as confirmation of your diagnosed condition. 'After all, no *normal* person would just *sit* there like that.'

Goffman's classic interactionist account of hoarding behaviour among mental patients in *Asylums* (1968) is a very good example of the confirmatory character of 'normal' behaviour once the 'abnormal' label has been applied. Hoarding is a very common feature of the behaviour of patients in mental hospitals. All sorts of apparently useless and trivial objects – like pieces of string, cigarette butts and toilet paper – are constantly in the possession of many of the inmates, who steadfastly refuse to let them out of their sight for a moment. The usual interpretation of this behaviour serves to confirm the label attached to the patient. It is argued that it is obviously abnormal to have such worthless items permanently about one's person and such hoarding can only be a reflection of considerable and deep-seated anxieties and emotional instability.

Goffman disputes this analysis, arguing that it only seems appropriate from the standpoint of life outside the mental hospital, where such 'useless' items are always available. Inside the institution, however, where, for the inmate, they are much more difficult to come by, it makes very good sense to look after them very carefully. Furthermore, since mental hospital patients tend to lack both privacy and storage facilities, an obvious place to keep them secure is about one's person.

Labelling theory argues that sometimes the process of labelling can be so overwhelming that even the victims of misinterpretation cannot resist its impact. Faced with a persistently applied label, the self-image of the labelled person can crumble. He or she comes to see himself or herself anew, embracing the alternative image others have applied. As in the earlier effects of labelling, the correctness, or 'truth', of the label has little to do with the power of its impact. Right or wrong in *fact*, its application and the reactions of others to its existence make it true. Once again, the prophecy is fulfilled, but in this case it becomes the reality for both the beholder and the beheld.

## The alteration of self-image

The identification of this process has been a feature of the application of labelling theory to deviance – the area where it has probably been most influential. One of its most significant contributions to the study of deviant behaviour has been to show that the identification of deviance is a product of the interpretation of a particular individual in a particular social setting (as is all labelling). It has also shown that the reactions of others to a labelled deviant are sometimes so severe that they can produce a dramatic alteration in an already established self-image.

Edwin Lemert (1912–96) has provided a famous account of the social construction of paranoia that demonstrates both these aspects of labelling very clearly (Lemert 1967). Paranoia is a mental condition in which the sufferer imagines he or she is being persecuted by a conspiracy. However, as Lemert points out, if paranoia is suspected in somebody then such a conspiracy actually does come into being. The 'ill' person is observed secretly. Since mentally disturbed people do not know what is good for them and can act irrationally, attempts to organize treatment will also be clandestine. For example, visits to doctors and psychiatric hospitals will be organized behind the patient's back. Any suspicion on the part of the suspected paranoid that this sort of thing is going on will, naturally enough, lead him or her to complain about it. Normal though such resentment may be from the labelled person's standpoint, in the eyes of its applicators this will merely serve to confirm the justice of the label. Clearly, here *is* someone who believes he or she is being conspired against by others. The fact that this is actually what *is* happening won't deter the labellers from having their judgement confirmed.

Such confirmation may lead to a stay in a mental hospital for treatment. It is at this stage in the construction of paranoia that persons so labelled experience the most sustained pressure on their self-images. Lemert argues that however certain they are of their sanity prior to institutionalization, organizational confirmation of the 'insane' label, particularly by means of deliberate attempts to change behaviour, might well seriously damage the inmates' previously held self-images. The suspicion may grow that perhaps everyone else was right all along and that they *were* too ill to appreciate their condition. After all, why else would they be in hospital? For the labellers of such people, particularly the psychiatric staff, this stage of self-image alteration – an acknowledgement of the need for treatment – is the first major step en route to a cure. The fact that it might simply be the *last* stage in the *social* construction of a mental condition, which began not with any real illness, but with an initial labelling by others is, of course, not considered. The impact which organizational labelling is designed to have on the construction of social personality and, particularly, on the creation of a new self-image, has been powerfully articulated by Goffman.

## Goffman and institutionalization

According to Goffman the official treatment of many kinds of deviant behaviour in organizations set up for the purpose is, as in the case of mental illness, a quite self-conscious attempt to alter the deviant's self-image, so that he or she may become more amenable to 'cure'. In a celebrated account of what he calls *'total institutions'* Goffman advances the view that establishments like prisons, concentration camps and mental hospitals, where labelled deviants are completely incarcerated for considerable periods of time, are essentially agencies of resocialization (Goffman 1968). His argument is not confined to the treatment of deviants, since he claims that the same principles underpin the rigorous training undergone by, for example, soldiers and the members of some religious orders. However, the involuntary nature of the deviants' membership of such institutions makes any successful alteration to their self-images particularly noteworthy.

Goffman defines total institutions as: 'places of residence and work where a large number of like-situated individuals cut off from the wider society for an appreciable period of time, together lead an enforced, formally administered round of life' (Goffman 1968: 11). He argues that in such establishments, the organization of life is deliberately designed to strip the inmate of his or her self-image and replace it with one more acceptable to the ethos of the institution. He calls this process '**institutionalization**'. For example, he says, admission procedures are often designed to remove all visible symbols of the inmate's former self and replace them with indications of the new person he or she is to be trained to be. Thus, names are often replaced by numbers (as in prisons, concentration camps and military establishments), or by new names (as in religious orders). The inmate's physical appearance is sometimes altered as visibly as possible; clothing is often removed on entry and replaced with institutional uniforms, and hair is cut in a severe fashion. Since the acquisition of possessions may be frowned upon and made difficult, all or most personal property is often confiscated on entry. Personal space may be denied, even for the most private of activities. In these ways, and in others, says Goffman, inmates are stripped of the props by which they retained a sense of their former selves and were able to communicate this to others.

Furthermore, attempts to alter the self-image of the inmate can be reinforced by its debasement, in ritual and other ways – a process Goffman calls the **'mortification of the self'** (Glossary, see: **depersonalization**). For example, new inmates may have to undergo humiliation upon entry, such as strip-searching (in prison) or ritual ablution (in mental hospital). During their incarceration inmates are often obliged to behave in the most obsequious and obedient manner towards the institution's staff, sometimes in the face of provocation. Such degradations, often in public, are designed, argues Goffman, to kill off the former self of the inmate, to render it soiled and thereafter unusable, and to encourage its replacement by a new identity, more suitable to meet the demands of the institution.

Though labelling theorists would normally expect such processes to prove irresistible to their recipients, Goffman is true to his interactionist principles. Believing that social identities are not just imposed on people but are created and recreated as a two-way interpretive process, Goffman stresses not only the impact of institutionalization but the capacity of inmates to resist or adjust to the processes to which they are subjected to a greater or lesser degree. He talks of those who do become 'colonized', or institutionalized, preferring life in the institution to life outside, or of those who become 'converted', acquiescing to the staff's view of the model inmate and acting out the role to the limit. He also talks of inmates who protect their selves by withdrawing from interaction with others, or who do so by actively rebelling against the institution, as well as of those (the majority, in Goffman's view) who 'play it cool' – who stay out of trouble and maintain their self-image by playing whatever reactive role circumstances demand.

If some labelling involves victimization of the kind we have been discussing, then labelling theory argues that we have to ask a further, final question – where do these victims come from? For example, why do some people come to be labelled as mentally ill and not others? Why do certain children come to be labelled as uneducable, and not others?

For labelling theorists the answer lies not in any reality of different mental conditions or levels of intelligence. Rather, it lies in the origin of the perception of these attributes by others. The focus is on the reasons for these kinds of labels being attached to certain kinds of people, rather than on any characteristics the victims of these labels may or may not possess. The interesting question is therefore not 'How did these people get like this?' but 'Why did *these* people come to be labelled like this, and not others?

The usual labelling theory answer to these questions is that the application of such labels is ultimately about the exercise of power. According to labelling theory the most damaging labels in social life – those of *deviant* – usually become attached to the most helpless and least powerful members of society, those least capable of fighting back and resisting the process. This analysis of deviant labelling as a reflection of the exercise of power is described by Howard Becker, one of its leading exponents, as a process where the 'underdogs' in a society become victims of its 'overdogs' (Becker 1967).

This is a feature of labelling approaches to deviant behaviour in general; deviants are generally seen as victims, not as wrongdoers. It is particularly evident in the typical labelling analysis of crime. Crime is seen exclusively as a product of labelling, and of the all-pervading impact that the allocation of such a label can have. Labelling theory sees the relationship between labellers and labelled in this area of social life as essentially one of power. Quite contrary to the conventional view, then, the victims are the underdogs who are made into criminals, whereas the wrongdoers are the more powerful overdogs who impel the powerless down a never-ending spiral of criminal deviance.

## Labelling theory and crime

Labelling theorists argue that there are two fundamental questions which have to be asked about crime:

- Why do some human activities come to be made illegal and not others?
- Why do some people become criminals and not others?

According to labelling theory, the answers to both these questions reflect the distribution of power in society. Not only are the powerful able to designate those acts which are illegal in a society, they are also able to influence who gets labelled as a criminal. Labelling theory argues that although we might like to think that laws are somehow God-given or quite definitely in everyone's best interest, things are not quite as cosy as this. They stress that we have to recognize that the construction of legal rules is a political act. The decision that *this* action should be allowed, whereas another should not, is made by those humans who have the power to decide. Furthermore, 'the powerful' in this regard does not simply mean the actual law-makers, but also individuals or groups who are able to influence the law-makers – those people in a society whom Becker calls its 'moral entrepreneurs'.

Because of the relationship between power and the construction of legal rules, it is not surprising, say labelling theorists, that the acts that are not illegal in a society tend to be the acts in which the powerful engage. So, although it is perfectly possible to imagine a society in which it is illegal to inherit wealth, or profit from rent, or exploit black labour in South African mines, or avoid paying taxes, yet legal to smoke marijuana, make homosexual advances in public, and engage in 'adult' activity at a much younger age than eighteen, this is not how things are. Laws reflect the distribution of power in that the less powerful are more likely to engage in those activities which the laws prohibit.

You might consider this a rather far-fetched view. After all, what about laws prohibiting tax evasion, the placement of contracts by public officials in return for reward, company fraud, or the monopolization of production? Labelling theory grants that of course there are some laws which particularly affect the activities of, say, the wealthy, but it argues that these tend to be the laws that are the least strenuously enforced. And even if they are vigorously enforced they tend to be the laws least likely to furnish a successful prosecution, because of the resources available to the powerful to defend themselves. In effect then, the SI position is that the role of power in the construction of crime is not just restricted to the definition of illegal acts, but influences the investigation of crime too. And nowhere is this latter influence more apparent than in the selection of the individual criminal to prosecute – in the labelling of a particular person's actions as illegal.

## Law-breaking

Why should some people be labelled as criminals and not others? The obvious answer to this is that only some people choose to commit crime. From this point of view, the job of any explanation of criminality – sociological, psychological or biological – is to discover what it is about these kinds of people that led them down the criminal path. For labelling theory, however, things are not as straightforward as this, primarily because such an analysis ignores the huge discrepancy between the number of crimes committed and the number of criminals convicted.

Research demonstrates without doubt that the incidence of criminal activity bears little relation to the number of crimes known to the police (the CKP index), and even less to the number of crimes for which the police get a conviction (the 'clear-up' rate). The degree to which the official statistics underplay the real level of crime depends on the particular category of crime. Almost all cars that are stolen are reported, since it is the only way owners can receive compensation from insurance companies. Probably for the same reason (because more private property is now insured than before), the number of burglaries reported has increased. But other property crimes have much lower reporting rates. For example, very few acts of vandalism are reported, and it is estimated that probably only 1 per cent of all shoplifting offences are reported. Why should this be? Many crimes, such as vandalism, are not reported because of their petty nature. Yet even many violent crimes go unreported – only about 20 per cent of all woundings, sexual attacks and robberies are reported, for example. The main reason for this low rate seems to be the young age of many of the victims and their lack of faith either in the way the police will handle the complaint, or in the capacity of the police to solve the crime. Studies have also shown that even when crimes are reported to the police they are not always recorded. The reasons for this include overwork, doubts about the validity of the allegations, and the temptation to improve the clear-up rates by not including insoluble crimes.

As well as such victim surveys, self-report studies also illustrate the wide gap between the commission of crime and the CKP index and the even wider gap between commission and clear-up. Such studies ask people to volunteer their past illegal actions under a guarantee of absolute confidentiality. They reveal that anything between 50 per cent and 90 per cent of people admit some kind of illegal behaviour that could result in a court appearance if detected. Even more significant, they also indicate that criminal activity is distributed across all sections of society. They show that crimes are just as likely to be committed by the middle class as the working class, and they certainly demonstrate the error of assuming that crime is more likely to be concentrated in the lower strata of the class structure. Yet this is precisely what the official conviction statistics – of crimes cleared up by the police – *do* indicate. The overwhelming impression from these figures is that crime is mainly committed by young, urban working-class males. Why should this be?

If, as self-report studies indicate, crime is committed by no particular kind of person, why do only certain kinds of people get caught?

The labelling theory answer, of course, is that only certain kinds of people are likely to be *labelled* as criminal. Being human, police can only take action against acts and people they *perceive* as breaking the law. That is why certain kinds of people become criminals. It is not because they are the only people who have committed crimes. Indeed it is not even because they necessarily *have* committed any crime at all. It is simply because they have been interpreted as having done so. But why is there such a distinctive pattern to these interpretations? Labelling theorists argue that the perceptions of the police inevitably emanate from the **stereotypes** of criminals with which they and other agents of law enforcement operate. Why stereotypes should prevail in law enforcement is clear enough. If, as self-report studies show, criminal activity is distributed equally throughout any population, then whatever stereotype of the 'typical criminal' you choose to operate, your judgement is going to be vindicated. So, the next important question is: why have some stereotypes come to prevail in the pursuit of crime and not others?

According to labelling theory, we need look no further for our answer than at the distribution of power in society. In the same way that the powerful are able to influence the designation of certain acts as illegal rather than others, they are also able to encourage certain perceptions of the criminal – advantageous to themselves – to prevail. So although the official conviction statistics tell us very little about the actual distribution of crime in society, they do tell us much about the kinds of people police officers and other law enforcers are most likely to label as criminal. In turn, this tells us about the kinds of influences on stereotypes employed in law enforcement that the powerful have been able to bring to bear. The picture painted by the conviction statistics makes this clear. The chances of matching up to the stereotypes typically employed in law enforcement decrease as a person moves up the social hierarchy. According to Bilton et al. criminal labels await the least advantaged members of society because they are powerless:

> We should not be surprised to find blacks and working-class people over-represented in the official statistics of crime, since they and their behaviour are more likely to fit law-enforcement agencies' perceptions of 'criminals' and 'crime', and they are less likely to be able to mobilize the material and social resources necessary to convince others that 'they're not like that'. (Bilton et al. 1981: 595)

Of course, once the powerless receive their labels, the self-fulfilling prophecy just referred to will come into effect. The successful application of the stereotype will mean that its validity is confirmed for its users and it can be employed with even more conviction in the future. The process of criminal labelling thus increases the chances of the least powerful becoming criminals and decreases the chances of the most powerful becoming so. In this way, inequalities of power in society are cemented by the process of law enforcement. Furthermore, once the stereotype is applied and the label attached, the existence of the label promotes the usual self-fulfilling prophecy so far as any particular individual actor is concerned. Others react to the label in such a way that makes future 'normal' activity very difficult. Following a criminal conviction, other people may ostracize the labelled person or treat him or her with suspicion. Occupational opportunities may also become unavailable, and so on. The stigma of being branded a criminal overwhelms all other attributes; something someone is supposed to have *done* becomes what he or she *is*. Because of the reactions of others to the stigma of the label, the labelled person – whether guilty or innocent in fact – is, according to labelling theory, often impelled into pursuing the 'career' of a criminal, simply because all other normal options are closed down. Obviously, this process of being forced into a deviant career by the reactions of others – known as *deviance amplification* – is not as immediately problematic for the self as, say, the misinterpretation of mental illness. After all, one usually knows whether one was guilty of an offence or not. Nevertheless, it can still mean that the labelled person's self-image is in danger of alteration, especially if the opportunities for a 'normal' existence are sufficiently restricted. Lacking any choice, labelled persons come to see themselves as the people they have been forced to become.

## Structure versus action: the analysis of crime

In an area such as crime, therefore, structural and action theory assumptions meet head on. Pursuing the external determinants of any social activity located in the social structure, the structural theorist looks for the reasons why, as the conviction statistics show, certain kinds of people come to commit criminal acts and some do not. Armed with conviction statistics, which feature the urban working-class male above all other categories of person, those giving structural explanations of crime attempt to identify the reasons why a person in this sort of structural location is impelled to commit crime more often than other kinds of person. One of the most popular explanations of this phenomenon is known as *sub-cultural theory*. Here crime is explained as the product of cultural or normative influences. The young working-class male, more often than any other kind of person, finds himself in a cultural setting where criminal activity is normal, and where conformity to such norms via socialization gives rise to law-breaking. The sociological task is therefore to identify those cultural features that promote crime in this kind of social world and not in others. As in the case of all structural explanations then, the emphasis is on identifying the origins of the *external* social forces whose existence is manifested in the behaviour of individuals.

In contrast, labelling theory's approach to crime features the opposed action theory assumptions about social behaviour. Armed with their evidence – that crime is much more widespread among all social groups than the conviction rates show – labelling theorists are interested not in why young working-class males commit crimes more often than other people, but why they are more likely to be *labelled* as criminals than others. The interesting questions here, therefore, concern the reasons for their behaviour being interpreted as criminal, while that of other people is not. The labelling perspective focuses on the social construction of the reality of crime by the members of a society themselves, rather than on the determining influence on behaviour of a structural reality outside these members.

Yet, as the study of crime also shows, the structural and SI emphases are not as mutually exclusive as they might at first appear. The reason is that SI does not completely embrace an action theory approach to social life. In fact, as Ian Craib points out, the SI emphasis on the actor's interpretative abilities sits quite easily with the structural functionalist account of socialization as the internalization of norms and values (Craib 1992). We can see this in two aspects of its explanation of crime. First, the idea of 'stereotypes' in the application of criminal labels refers to generally held views among those whose job it is to enforce the law. Since such generally held views will, for example, be encountered and embraced and therefore perpetuated by new recruits, this is clearly much closer to the structural view of socialization into pre-existing normative definitions than pure action theory allows.

Second, the idea that powerful groups influence both the construction of laws and the stereotypes of the criminal is quite close to an orthodox structural perspective. For such a process to take place, particular groups must have the power to exercise influence while others must lack the resources to resist. This vision of social life as being crucially influenced by the unequal distribution of advantage between groups is, of course, a conventional structural-conflict standpoint.

SI is a fairly moderate version of action theory which, while emphasizing the primacy of interpretation in the social construction of reality, does not deny the existence of a fund of commonly held definitions – a common culture, if you like – from which people choose their interpretations. Furthermore, the fact that it insists upon a recognition of the existence of some kind of structure of power and advantage within which the labelling of deviants takes place, also shows that it cannot be seen as adopting a fully fledged, anti-structural position.

In contrast to at least some examples of SI analysis, ethnomethodologists explicitly take issue with the structural functionalist explanations of social action. For structural functionalists such as Parsons, the social world is orderly and predictable because social actors have been conditioned by their culture to want to follow prescribed courses of action. Harold Garfinkel, the founder of ethnomethodology, argues that in presenting social actors as blindly following cultural orders, Parsons presents them as 'cultural dopes' (Garfinkel 1984 [1967]: 68). For Garfinkel, the problem with Parsons' theory of action is that it utterly excludes from its analysis any account of actors' knowledge of their circumstances. Garfinkel's work offers a radically different account of social action to that of structural functionalism. For Garfinkel, what professional sociologists call 'society' is in fact created in and through the sense-making abilities of ordinary social members. But the skilfulness and creativity involved in conducting everyday life has gone unnoticed. Garfinkel's work is devoted to revealing the nature and the significance of these sense-making abilities, as we shall see below.

## Ethnomethodology

Ethnomethodology rests upon three assumptions:

- social life is inherently precarious; anything could happen in social interaction; however:
- actors never realize this, because
- they unwittingly possess the practical abilities necessary to make the world appear an ordered place.

The primary ethnomethodological interest is rather different from that of other action theorists. Instead of being concerned mainly with the *outcome* of interpretation – the creation of self-image, or the consequences of labelling, for example – it focuses on the shared 'stocks of meaning', the methods we all use to arrive at our interpretations.

(Ethnomethodology literally means 'people's methods'.) The aim is to reveal the methods used by the participants ('members') in any particular social setting to communicate to each other what they think is going on – what the situation means to them – and the efforts they each make to have this interpretation corroborated by the others. Ethnomethodology is not interested in 'the' social world, but in specific pieces of interaction between its members. The stress is on how order in a social setting is the (unknowing) accomplishment of its participants.

This interest in describing the practical abilities of members derives from a theory of reality called *phenomenology*. Phenomenology emphasizes that things and events have no meaning in themselves. They only mean whatever human beings take them to mean. It stresses that for the members of such a meaningfully created world to live together, meanings must be shared. Members must agree about what things are and social order depends upon shared meanings. Members *do* share meanings. This is because of the way they interpret reality. They do so by using 'common-sense knowledge'. This is embodied in language. Through language we acquire an enormous amount of knowledge about the world, knowledge we can take for granted and which others who speak our language possess too. We have actually experienced only a tiny number of the things that we know about. The rest of the knowledge, shared with other members, is sense that is common to us all. In the words of the founder of phenomenology in sociology, Alfred Schutz (1899–1959):

> I take it for granted that my action (say putting a stamped and duly addressed envelope in a mailbox) will induce anonymous fellow-men (postmen) to perform typical actions (handling the mail) . . . with the result that the state of affairs projected by me (delivery of the letter to the addressee within reasonable time) will be achieved. (Schutz 1962: 25–6)

Because members can take for granted this shared knowledge about reality, they can also take for granted the reality it describes. They can assume that the world is a given, objective place. It must be. After all, we all know what it is, and what happens in it.

This concept of shared, common-sense knowledge may sound rather like the consensus theorist's notion of culture. But culture refers to a body of rules which are *obeyed* by actors, thereby producing social order. For the ethnomethodologist common-sense knowledge is *used* by members to create order in a particular situation that would otherwise lack it. Ethnomethodologists define their task as showing how members do this.

Armed with common-sense knowledge and with a confident belief in the factual, ordered character of the world, members can go ahead and make sense of any situation in which they participate. Ethnomethodology stresses that each social situation is unique. The words people utter, the actions they take, are **indexical** – that is, they only make sense on the particular occasion in which they are used. But they also stress that members, unwittingly engaged in identifying order and an objective reality, see things differently. They identify the similarities of an event with other events. They select from all the things happening around them evidence which supports the view that things which exist or which happen are *typical* of the world. For them, a social situation is 'a lecture', 'a dance' or 'a meeting', and a pattern is imposed on it by the application of common-sense knowledge. By common-sense knowledge too, gaps in the accounts of happenings by others are filled in in similar ways by different listeners to reassure themselves that things are as they seem.

In a famous analysis of a two-year-old child's story, ethnomethodologist Harvey Sacks (see Silverman 1998) gives an example of the way the use of common-sense knowledge can be depended upon to generate the same interpretations. According to Sacks, there is a predictable response upon hearing the following two phrases uttered consecutively by the child:

The baby cried.
The mummy picked it up.

We can be assured that, on first hearing the two-year-old's story, any listener will hear the mummy as the mummy of the baby; will assume a relationship between the two events (that the mummy picked up the baby because it was crying); and that these interpretations will be arrived at without having to know anything about the mummy or the baby or of the two-year-old who told the story.

As R. J. Anderson says about this example: 'The import of this . . . is enormous, for if it is the case that competent users of the English language are able to find the same things from the same fragment of talk, then the methods that are used to do so must be of the highest order of generality. They must be part of the foundations of our common culture' (Anderson 1979: 64). It is these methods that ethnomethodology is interested in. Without realizing it, members use them as they work to create the meaning that they believe occasions or events have. Having done this unwitting work, and having arrived at an interpretation, they then engage in yet more unwitting work to have this confirmed by the corroboration of other participants. The founder of ethnomethodology, Harold Garfinkel (1917–), delighted in showing how members identify sense in occasions, even when corroboration from others is actually lacking. This is how Paul Filmer describes a very well-known Garfinkel experiment designed to demonstrate the lengths members will go to create meaning, to discover sense in an occasion, in spite of deliberate efforts to frustrate them:

Ten undergraduates were asked to participate in research being carried out by a university's department of psychiatry to explore alternative means of psychotherapy. Each was asked to discuss the background to a serious problem on which he wanted advice, and then to address to an experimenter – who had been falsely presented to him as a trainee student counsellor – a number of questions about it which would be amenable to monosyllabic 'Yes' or 'No' answers. The subject and the experimenter/counsellor were physically separated, and communicated by two-way radio. After the answer to each of his questions had been given, the subject was asked to tape-record his comments upon it, out of radio-hearing of the experimenter/counsellor. The subjects were told that it was usual to ask ten questions, and they were, of course, led to believe that they would be given bona fide answers to them. The experimenter/counsellors, however, were given a list of monosyllabic answers, evenly divided between 'yes' and 'no', but whose order had been pre-decided from a table of random numbers. Thus, in this experiment, certain crucial variables of everyday interaction situations had been neutralized: the shared language of subject and experimenter had been reduced to the verbal spoken dimension (intonation, in all probability, would also have been relatively unimportant as an agent of meaning, owing to the distortion of spoken sounds by radio); there was no chance of gestures or physical expressions intervening in the communication process because of the physical separation of subject and experimenter. Also, the possibility of the experimenter/counsellor's answers making sense to the subjects depended entirely on their interpretations of them; indeed, the possibility of answers even being those anticipated by the subjects was reduced to a matter of chance. Garfinkel published two unedited transcripts of the exchanges and of the subjects' comments upon them [see Garfinkel 1984], plus a detailed explication of his interpretive findings from them. The burden of these is where the random answers to the carefully thought out and phrased questions of the subjects appeared nonsensical, irrational or in some other way inappropriate or unexpected, then the subject reinterpreted them by reformulating what he assumed to be the context of meaning he held in common with the experimenter/counsellor (and which he had attempted to communicate to the experimenter/counsellor by the phrasing and content of his questions), in order that the latter's responses made sense after all. Even where a succession of plainly contradictory

answers engendered the suspicion in the subject that he was being tricked,
he appeared reluctant to proceed upon the assumption that this was so.
(Filmer et al. 1972: 223–4)

Ethnomethodology is clearly a very different kind of sociology from
the others we have been looking at so far in this book. For structural
theorists the most significant features of human social life are forces
external to the individual actor. To understand social behaviour we
have to understand the structural determinants of people's lives. We
do this by going beyond our actors' *own* theories of their existence and
instead construct expert, objective *observer* theories that explain social
structures.

In contrast, for interactionists/labelling theorists, the actor comes
to the fore. Whether a person is in control of the interpretations of
others, or is a more passive recipient of their labels, the focus is on
the capacity for meaningful interaction. To understand social action
we must understand the processes of interpretation that give rise to it.
We do this by taking advantage of the fact that, just like our subject
matter, we too are human beings. This means we can put ourselves in
the place of the other humans in which we are interested, and, by using
our ability to empathize – by using *verstehen* – work out how the world
must seem to them.

For ethnomethodologists, however, the interest is different. They
criticize other sociological approaches for taking for granted what
they believe is actually the essence of social life – members' sense-
making methods. They also criticize their assumption that the use of
these methods to produce one human's account of an aspect of reality
– a particular social theory, for example – can ever be considered a
true, or correct, depiction. According to ethnomethodology, calling
an account produced by the use of members' methods a 'sociological
theory' does not privilege it over non-sociological accounts.

We can only measure the rationality of any account of social reality
on the basis of its success in helping us to make sense of and therefore
sustain a specific social encounter. For ethnomethodology, the only
thing we can describe with certainty is the one thing we all *do* have in
common: the sense-making methods all humans, sociologists or not,
have to use to arrive at their respective accounts, and this is what sociology should study. It is thus interested in the practice of making sense
of the world, in how members accomplish social life. Though members
are always the architects of social order in any social occasion, ethnomethodology believes it cannot tell the truth about *what* they have
built by their efforts, only about *how* they built it. The focus on the

importance of language in constituting social life reaches its extreme with ethnomethodology; here the nature of human language itself becomes the topic for sociological investigation. Thus, the technicalities of *how* it is used by humans to construct order in social situations is the concern of the best-known ethnomethodological research device – conversational analysis. In ethnomethodology's account of social action then, instead of *verstehen* being the *instrument* sociology uses to understand and explain actors' meanings, it becomes the collective resource employed by all social members to produce social reality.

## Language and social life

Unsurprisingly, ethnomethodology's rejection of the belief that sociologists know better than other social members about their society proved to be highly controversial. In the 1970s and 1980s, the ethnomethodological insistence that any order or coherence we believe society to have is just that – a belief we all need and proceed to make "true" using ethnomethods – was regarded as a worrying denial of the reality of objective social structures because it seemed to question the very need for a structural sociology. As we might recall, for structural **functionalists**, **social systems** were regarded as entities existing independently of individuals' knowledge and understanding. Individuals fulfil the needs of such systems unwittingly through acting according to commonly instilled values, but these structures could not be reduced to the level of individuals actions. Conflict theorists argued in similar terms that by focusing only on small-scale social settings ethnomethodology and other 'microsociologies' ignore the ways in which such settings are established and scripted by the power structures of society. Once again the fault lines between structural and interpretive approaches that we examined in Chapter 1 re-appear. However, as we will now go on to discuss, the recognition of the importance of language as a principal means by which social members construct social order has been taken up by more recent theorists as a means by which to reconcile the analyses of structure and of action.

In fact, two accounts of the sociological significance of the fact that humans are language users have become increasingly influential to the development of social theory since the 1980s, and, as we shall see, they have significantly shaped the theories to be discussed in the remaining chapters of this book. However, there are important differences between these two accounts which have a bearing on the analysis of the relation between structure and action. The first account is influenced by what are broadly known as **hermeneutic** philosophies. As we shall see when we discuss the work of theorists such as Roy Bhaskar, Anthony Giddens and Jürgen Habermas, the usefulness of hermeneutic philosophies to these social theorists lies in their emphasis on language not only as a means of conveying meaning to and for individual language users, but also as a skilled, practical social activity that underpins the continuous production and reproduction of social structures (Giddens 1976: 20). This account of language allows us to see that actors' interpretations are the basic elements not only of specific social settings and social practices (as interpretive sociologies argued) but also of the more embedded or institutionalized structures of society.

The second account of the sociological significance of language in the construction of social reality derives from French structuralism and post-structuralism. As we shall see in the following chapter, in this view, the emphasis is not at all on the skilfulness of language users as a significant factor in the production of society. Instead, language is treated as a system through which power is exercised. According to this view then, individual language users are little more than the vehicles through which this power is channelled.

## Further reading

### Symbolic interactionism

Goffman, Erving et al. (1997): *The Goffman Reader*, Blackwell.
Manning, Philip (1992): *Erving Goffman and Modern Sociology*, Polity.
Scott, Susie (2009): *Making Sense of Everyday Life*, Polity.
Smith, Greg (2006): *Erving Goffman*, Key Sociologists, Routledge.

### Ethnomethodology

Sharrock, W. W. and Anderson, R. J. (2010): *The Ethnomethodologists*, 2nd edn, Routledge.
Garfinkel, Harold (1984): *Studies in Ethnomethodology*, Polity.

# 6 MICHEL FOUCAULT: LANGUAGE, DISCOURSE THEORY AND THE BODY-CENTREDNESS OF MODERNITY

Michel Foucault: born Poitiers, France, 1926, died Paris, 1984

## Major works

*Madness and Civilisation* (1961)
*The Order of Things: An Archaeology of the Human Sciences* (1966)
*The Archaeology of Knowledge and the Discourse on Language* (1969)
*The Birth of the Clinic: An Archaeology of Medical Perception* (1975)
*Discipline and Punish: The Birth of the Prison* (1979)
*The History of Sexuality*, volumes 1–3 (1980–5)

## Introduction

Foucault was an historian who focused specifically on the transition from traditional to modern forms of social organization. His work has been at least as influential as it has been controversial within the social sciences, as well as within modern philosophy and literature studies. Foucault's analysis of the ways in which the development of modern forms of knowledge, within medicine and the social sciences, gave rise to new forms of power over the populations of modern societies has been taken up by social theorists working in areas including the sociology of medicine, gender and the body. His analysis of the exercise of power via bodies was seen to offer an important alternative to Marxian treatments of power.

The latter's rather heavy-handed conviction that significant forms of authority and control stem only from class conflict appeared incapable of recognizing the ways in which modern societies govern their populations by placing them in sexual, ethnic and gendered categories rather than only in economic ones. Therefore the burgeoning scholarship and political activism of the feminist and gay movements of the late 1970s and 1980s found an important source of theoretical rigour in Foucault's *Discipline and Punish* and *The History of Sexuality*. However, Foucault's analysis of modern forms of power has proven controversial within social theory because it questions the foundations of the modernist project. For Foucault, modern rationality is not a means by which we can analyse and therefore challenge the interests of the powerful, instead it is the very vehicle by which such interests are implemented and sustained. To understand and then assess the significance of Foucault's analysis of **modernity** within contemporary social theory, we will begin with his concept of **discourse** (see Glossary: discourse (2)).

## Foucault, structuralism and discourse theory

Foucault developed his analysis of discourse by drawing on the work of fellow Durkheimian structuralist Claude Lévi-Strauss (1908–2009). According to Lévi-Strauss, language originates in the unconscious human mind. Since all human minds work in the same way, whatever differences languages may appear to exhibit, they are in fact organized on the same principles. Furthermore, culture is also the creation of these same unconscious thought processes; thus, the structural features of social organization inevitably mirror those of language. In effect, according to Lévi-Strauss, human thought structures the world of language and of behaviour (social organization) in the same way.

Lévi-Strauss is thus interested in the form, not the content, of language and culture. Culture, like language, is a system of signs and symbols whose organization reflects the manner of human thought. Roger Trigg's view of Lévi-Strauss is that:

> He interprets myths and symbols in this way, saying that 'the world of symbolism is infinitely varied in content but always limited in its laws' . . . he analyses kinship systems in a similar way, viewing them as languages . . . He is concerned . . . to uncover the systems, whether of kinship or language . . . which are built by the mind, as he puts it, 'at the level of unconscious thought'. (Trigg 1985: 190–1)

There is, then, nothing in social life that is the innovative creation of the conscious or imaginative mind; human beings are not the authors of their life stories, for these are written for them, in language and in culture.

A system of language exists independently of its learners and users, and they are obliged to use the meanings referred to by its constituent symbols both to think for themselves and to exchange thoughts with others. Trigg puts this argument as follows:

> The nature of language and culture, viewed as systems, cannot be discovered at the level of the subject . . . this kind of structuralism offers a threat to any idea that man (*sic*) is the centre of the universe. The very categories of human thought are given to us . . . we can no longer be understood as subjects thinking about an independently existing world and devising language to describe it. We are not the source of language or of culture. Being human involves living in a world which has already been determined. (Trigg 1985: 190–1)

The reason for using the term 'structuralism' to refer to ideas about language and its role in social life is clear; as with functionalism and Althusserian Marxism, the individual actor, agent or subject is irrelevant. The origin of social life lies in structural influences beyond the actor; but here it is a system of *language* – rather than a social system of functioning *institutions* – that we must understand and explain. Thus, not only does social life depend upon language, but language defines social reality for us.

## Foucault and post-structuralism

Though agreeing about the linguistic authorship of human life stories, Foucault's *post*-structuralism (*after*-structuralism) goes beyond the kinds of ideas produced by Lévi-Strauss in two ways. First, he rejects the idea that there are universal features underpinning all languages. Second, in part as a reaction to Marxian ideas that power primarily operates in society only along the route of economic class, and that human history is one of the progressive development of the economy, Foucault injects a strong dose of Friedrich Nietzsche (1844–1900) into his work. As Loïs McNay explains: following Nietzsche, Foucault views history as 'a constant struggle or warfare between different power blocs which attempt to impose their own system of domination' (McNay 1994: 89). These systems of domination do not rely on ownership of the means of economic production but instead take control of systems of knowledge – of the production of meaning. Therefore, if we want to understand how power operates in our society we need to adopt Nietzsche's genealogical method of historical analysis to uncover how our ideas of truth and beauty and goodness, for example, are the results of these power struggles.

This means that what counts as true, as morally right, and as beautiful is *relative* to a particular time, place and power struggle; truth changes according to whoever is powerful enough to define it. To summarize then, Foucault follows the structuralist line in placing language at the centre of the picture. But the 'languages' in which he is interested are not the kind normally referred to by the term – like English, French and Spanish. He is concerned to show how specific ways of thinking and talking about aspects of the world are forms of *knowledge and power* which work like languages and which we learn in the same way as we learn ordinary languages. He calls such 'languages' – systems of connected ideas which give us our knowledge of the world – *discourses*, which is why his version of post-structuralism is sometimes called discourse theory. As we shall see in the following chapter, this approach to analysing the relationship between truth, meaning and power has shaped the theoretical and research agendas of the social sciences.

Foucault used post-structuralist theories to understand the ways in which the body has become the focus of new forms of power in modern societies. These elements of his work are closely linked since he uses post-structuralist theory to explain the ways in which social and cultural influences on the body define its universal, natural features in different ways, depending on time and place. Of course, sociologists of the body do not deny that the bodies of males and females have the same organic constitution irrespective of the societies in which they live. However, they argue that these natural features mean different things in different cultural settings. According to many such sociologists, this is because people in different social worlds are taught to think differently about their bodies.

Foucauldian sociology of the body concentrates on the way in which cultural definitions of normal and abnormal behaviour regulate people's ideas about their bodies and what they should and should not do with them. Foucault believes we can make sense of the presence of these different social rules in different times and places by understanding the wider social and historical contexts in which different kinds of societies are located. He is particularly interested in how and why, in modern societies, the body needs to be managed and regulated in ways not necessary in pre-modernity.

## The body in modernity

Foucault suggests that modern societies have two crucial reasons for the systematic regulation of the body:

* the population pressures produced by urbanization
* the needs of industrial capitalism.

The regulation of the individual body – e.g. rules governing sexuality – he calls **anatomo-politics**. The regulation of bodies en masse – e.g. health and safety rules or rules governing physical movement around cities – he calls **bio-politics**.

As a post-structuralist, Foucault is interested in the way in which different forms of knowledge – different versions of what is true and false, right and wrong – produce different ways of life. According to Foucault, the most significant aspect of a society becoming modern is not so much the fact it has a capitalist economy (Marx), or a new form of solidarity (Durkheim), or that it is the outcome and embodiment of rational action (Weber). It is the way in which new forms of knowledge – unknown in pre-modernity – emerge. For him, it is these new discourses that define modern life.

## Discourse theory

According to Foucault, acquiring a discourse is the only human way of *knowing* about reality there is; the only way we can think/talk at all is by using a discourse of one kind or another. Furthermore, since we are compelled to know by means of discourses, they exercise *power* over us. Who we are – what we think, what we know, and what we talk about – is produced by the various discourses we encounter and use. Thus, the 'subject' – the creative, freely choosing and interpreting agent at the centre of action theory (and at the heart of both **Enlightenment** philosophies and later existentialism) – does not exist. People's subjectivity and identity – what they think, know and talk about – is created by the discourses in which they are implicated. To use the post-structuralist jargon: the individual is *constituted* by discourses. So discourses – ways of thinking, knowing and talking – provide us with the only ways in which we can 'be' anybody at all. They provide us with our thoughts and our knowledge and, therefore, can be said to direct, or be behind, any actions we choose to take. This link between thought, language, knowledge and action Foucault summarizes with the phrase '*discursive* *practices*' – meaning that social life consists of activities promoted by discourses.

For Foucault, the study of history involves working out how and why different discourses came to be established when they did, because this will achieve the historian's goal – to discover why people thought, said and did what they did. According to Foucault, this is also ultimately a question of power. The question here is: 'By what means and for what reasons did *this* form of discourse come to be established and to prevail at *this* time in history?' That is, Foucault sees the historian's task as one of unearthing the foundations of different discourses. The use of the archaeological metaphor is not accidental. Foucault himself describes his aim as the digging out of evidence about past discourses in an archaeological fashion; his project is literally to discover what lies underneath the emergence of various discourses.

To summarize then, people are who they are – they think what they think, know what they know, say what they say and do what they do – because of their implication in a configuration of different, and sometimes competing, discourses. These discourses determine what people think and know, and therefore how they act. So, for Foucault, discursive practices are at the root of social life; and the exercise of power through discourse is everywhere. For Foucauldians, if you want to understand human behaviour in a particular place and time, find out the discourses that dominate there. The underlying reasons for the existence of these discourses can be unearthed by the historian/archaeologist; to discover these is, in essence, to discover the basis of a particular kind of knowledge and a particular kind of power. Foucault's claim is that identity is constituted by discourse. For Foucault then, power is exercised in two ways. First, it is exercised in order that a discourse will come into being. Second, it is exercised *by* a discourse, since it constitutes identity.

We acquire **discursive knowledge** in the same way as we acquire language, and the chances of us resisting this knowledge are as remote as our chances of not learning a particular language as we grow up. This is not, however, the same as *repressive* power (the exercise of power in order to stop us doing things). It is the exercise of power to *enable* us to be human (rather than remaining merely animals), and to possess the knowledge we need to attach meaning to our experiences. Just as the child is only able to become properly human through learning some language or other, so we are only able to know truth and falsehood, right and wrong, as a result of the influence of discourses of some kind or other. However, this does not mean we can therefore claim to know things for certain. We are only able to know the truths provided for us by our discourses; we are clearly hamstrung and restricted by the particular discourses we encounter. Just as a child has no choice about the language(s) it has to learn as it grows up, so we have no choice about the particular knowledge of the world we have to acquire. To put this another way, for Foucault, it is through the discourses that dominate a time in history and a place in the world that people acquire their mindset, or worldview. This way of looking at things through discourse Foucault calls an '**episteme**'.

## Discourses and modernity

A brief look at Foucault's own historical work shows the sorts of factors he regards as significant in providing the foundations for the establishment of particular discourses. He argues that the emergence of particular ways of knowing and talking about any area of social life depends on the prior existence of specific organizational and institutional arrangements.

For example, he claims that it was only the appearance of the clinic that made medical discourse possible. As we saw earlier, because we now live in a world where the presence of medical concepts and their use in various areas of social life is taken for granted, it is a little difficult for us to appreciate just how pervasive such a discourse has become. For us, notions of 'health' and 'ill-health' are not just applied to bodies, but to societies (as in the ideas of Durkheim), desires, sexual orientations, appetites, pastimes, interests, families, marriages, economies, and so forth. This list shows how contagious (another use of medical discourse!) the use of such concepts has become. It therefore draws attention to the constitution of thinking and consciousness that Foucault argues a discourse can achieve. It is evidence of the power of both the discourse and the practitioners who enforce such a way of knowing about the world.

Powerful discourses whose function is bio-political – the management and regulation of bodies en masse – come into being as part of the development of modernity. For example, planning and planners begin to organize the utilization of urban areas, while transport experts emerge to regulate the movement of bodies through space. Penology and penologists provide the knowledge base for the management and punishment of criminal bodies: prisons confine and control such bodies. Demographers devise instruments to gain knowledge of the characteristics and attributes of large populations; if you are reading this book, you probably already know something about that ubiquitous aspect of modern life – the social survey. Theories of education promulgated by educationalists inform the management and discipline of immature bodies in the schools in which they are confined. All of these are modern forms of knowledge deemed necessary to control and police the accumulation, concentration and congregation of bodies in modern environments. The exercise of such knowledge, argues Foucault, is the exercise of a certain kind of power – bio-politics. However, for him, the most important discourses in modernity are those which regulate both the social body and the individual body. According to Foucault, Western medicine provides us with the best example of a modern form of knowledge that exercises both considerable bio-power and anatomo-power.

## Bio-medicine

To understand life in modernity, says Foucault, you need only to realize the huge extent to which we modern humans have become subject to the power of medical definitions of normality and deviance – that is, the extent to which we are so preoccupied with our bodily health. According to Foucault, the power of notions of health and illness in our lives is analogous to the power of notions of good and evil in the lives of pre-modern humans. Foucault characterizes the exercise of a discourse's power as a form of *surveillance* to ensure the conformity of a population to particular notions of truth and falsehood, good and bad. He concocted the idea of the *gaze* of a discourse and its enforcers to represent this. Thus he describes the shift from the dominance of religion in pre-modernity to the dominance of medicine in modernity as the emergence of the *Medical Gaze* or the *Clinical Gaze.*

There are a large number of discursive ways in which health and illness are understood by human beings. Why someone should fall ill when others remain well is the question many of these forms of knowledge address. Being bewitched (attacked by witchcraft); having affronted a deity; being punished for a misdeed in this or another life; being unable or reluctant to behave appropriately in relationships with others; being unable to cope with the stresses and difficulties of everyday living – all these kinds of explanation, and many others, link bodily illness to external causes. The body is the site of an illness of course, but its origins lie elsewhere, and therapies are prescribed accordingly.

In contrast, much Western **bio-medicine** merely treats the physical/bodily symptoms rather than the origins of illness; it concentrates on eradicating the disease present in the body rather than on searching for an external cause. This is what distinguishes it from so-called *holistic* or whole-person therapies which typically understand health and illness in terms of a relationship between the social, the mental, the emotional and the physical – between the mind, the spirit and the body. External causes are recognized by bio-medicine, of course, but they are also usually assumed to be physical, such as viruses, bacteria, tobacco or alcohol. Preventive medicine is therefore also body-centred: eat properly, take exercise, avoid dangerous substances and so on. For most of the time, the kinds of non-physical sources of bodily ill-health presumed to be potential causes by other perspectives – misery, social isolation and loneliness, feelings of helplessness and low self-esteem – are relatively neglected.

## How bio-medicine treats illness

The body-centredness of bio-medicine results in a diagnostic and therapeutic regime with which we are all familiar. It is usually the persistence of physical discomfort of some kind or other that leads us to visit a doctor's surgery. During the course of a (usually very short) consultation, the GP – whom we may or may not know – attempts to diagnose our condition by interpreting what is happening to our body. This is achieved in two main ways: first, we try to describe the physical sensations we are experiencing as best we can and second, if deemed necessary, the doctor will physically examine the relevant area of the body by sight, sound and/or touch. If a diagnosis is still difficult, or supporting evidence for the GP's opinion is needed, further tests on the body take place. This usually involves testing blood, urine, stools, saliva, or other bodily products. These and other kinds of highly technical testing can also take place in a hospital – a building and organization designed for the purpose of examining and treating sick bodies. Hospitalized bodies are either out-patients or in-patients. As out-patients, we attend clinics, where bodies are examined by hospital medics. After examination, we are usually free to leave the building. Confined as an in-patient, the body becomes subject to the hospital regime. We eat, drink, sleep, dress, receive visitors, take medicines, are tested further and undergo surgery as we are told to. The body is under the strict control of the hospital staff; the needs of the organization take precedence over the personal whims and fancies of the person whose body is hospitalized. Indeed, one of the most common criticisms of the management and regulation of hospitalized sick bodies is the **depersonalization** involved. Unless this is specifically addressed, there is always a tendency for large organizations and buildings to demand the rational and efficient control of their populations and this is particularly true of hospitals. For individuals used to a considerable degree of choice in their everyday behaviour, the strict ordering, management, regulation and surveillance involved in hospital life can be difficult to adjust to. To be treated as 'the liver in bed 6'; or as 'a difficult patient' if personal autonomy is insisted upon; or to be given only the minimum information about the treatment one's body is undergoing; or to have to request to do the kinds of things taken for granted in the world outside the hospital; or to be forced to do things one would not normally choose to do, can seriously erode feelings of autonomy and **agency** and create a powerful sense of dependency. To have so much attention focused on you as a body rather than you as a person with ideas, feelings and emotions can also lead to feelings of helplessness, isolation and powerlessness. As we saw in Chapter 5, the symbolic interactionist Erving Goffman has provided a famous and telling account of this process, which he describes as 'the **mortification of the self**' (Glossary, see: depersonalization) (Goffman 1968).

## The medicalization of modern life

According to Foucault and his followers, the policing power of the medical gaze in modernity can also be seen in the widespread **medicalization** of modern life. This term refers to the way in which universally experienced features and functions of human existence are, in modernity, appropriated and commandeered by medicine, defined in terms of its essential categories of health and illness and managed accordingly.

### The medicalization of childbirth

Thus, many writers (e.g. Ann Oakley 1980; 1984; 1993) have pointed to the medicalization of childbirth in modernity – the domineering way that medical discourse demands control over the biological reproduction of children in modern societies. Once conception is confirmed, unless a woman fights hard to resist, medicine routinely and systematically polices and monitors both her body and that of her unborn child throughout the pregnancy. The complaint is that such non-stop technological surveillance and control reduces the mother to being merely a body – a reproductive machine – dehumanizing and depersonalizing her experience. In effect, the argument goes, the appropriation of pregnancy and childbirth by medicine defines this most natural of human events as an illness.

## The medicalization of madness

Other commentators, including Foucault himself (Foucault 1965; 1975), tell a similar tale about the medicalization of madness. Unhappiness, hopelessness, distress, fear, social estrangement and social marginalization are all inevitable aspects of the human condition and all human worlds deal with them in some way or other. But only in modernity is madness medicalized – defined as mental *illness* and therefore subject to medical intervention, regulation and control. As a society modernizes, psychiatry and psychiatrists emerge to define, police and manage this kind of illness with their ultimate power residing in their ability to confine and control mad bodies in mental hospitals and other places of surveillance.

## The medicalization of death

Finally, just as modern humans are brought into the world under the control of medicine, so most of us are also ushered out of it under its supervision, a process known as the medicalization of death. In pre-modern societies, someone's death is seen as much as a community matter – a rent in the social fabric that needs to be repaired – as it is the loss of an individual. A death is therefore handled by the community as a whole, as is shown in the protracted public funeral rites that typically take place. Not so in medicalized modernity. Most of us will either die in hospital or else under medical supervision at home. A death in hospital is in essence a *sequestered* death (Giddens 1991), hidden away from the public world in which the dying person's life has been lived, deliberately organized so that it is left unobserved and unnoticed except by the hospital staff and close loved ones. For in a body-centred society dedicated to the triumph of the physical, death is an affront. The body – our principal source of identity and the object of so much of our attention while alive in modernity (a central part of modern existence that we go on to discuss in more detail below) – must die. No wonder death must be hidden away: how could we maintain our commitment to the body if its inevitable decay and demise were an ever-present part of the life of the living? No, ageing, frail and incontinent bodies are best kept out of sight during the 'death sequence', in 'old people's homes' and suchlike, and death itself best sequestered away, witnessed only by other sick and dying bodies.

## Body-centredness in modernity

Foucault links the rise to power of bio-medicine in modernity to the needs of its characteristic form of production – **capitalism**. In order for industrial and commodity production to be effective bodies need to be reliably placed in the production process. However, this is not just a matter of the rational organization of bodies. They also need to be fit and healthy so that their productivity can be maximized. According to Foucault, it is therefore unsurprising that modern capitalist societies have the discursive promotion of bodily health as a strong and central cultural feature. Medical ideas about maintaining bodily health and avoiding illness by means of diet, exercise, the avoidance of bad/unhealthy habits such as smoking and drinking all emerge to regulate and discipline the population. In pre-modern worlds, religious prescriptions focus on the soul, stressing the importance of living good, virtuous and sin-free lives in order to achieve salvation in an after-life. In modernity, by contrast, medical prescriptions focus on the here and now, stressing the importance of 'looking after' oneself physically in order to gain maximum benefit from life on earth.

## Body fetishism

Rather as an incoming tide gradually soaks and then covers in water more and more of a beach, so, as discourses become entrenched and gain in influence, they begin to direct more and more of a population's concerns. In a medicalized, body-centred society, people become increasingly obsessed with their bodies. Living a good or happy life becomes all about possessing not so much spiritual virtues as physical ones. The moral obligation to be healthy develops beyond the strictly medical – avoiding illness and treating the symptoms of bodily disease when they occur – to advertising the fact as well. How the body appears to others takes on a new importance, with huge implications for **consumption** and, therefore, production. Body-centred products flood the marketplace, advertising for them is everywhere, and shopping for them can verge on the obsessive.

This narcissism does not just result in well-stocked wardrobes and chests of drawers, so that we can clothe our bodies fashionably and to suit every occasion. It also re-defines the function of the bathroom and the bedroom from places in which we clean and rest ourselves to ones in which we adorn and transform ourselves. As well as non-prescribed medicants – which, of course, we have been taught to depend upon for our bodily health – the shelves and cupboards of these rooms groan with all manner of lotions, creams, perfumes, conditioners, powders, gels, waxes, deodorants, oils, mascaras, rouges, lipsticks, varnishes, glosses and depilatories. Body fetishism is rampant, fuelled by the beauty industry, the fashion industry, the youth industry, the diet industry and the fitness industry. Nothing matters more than how we look and the resulting obsession with slimming and dieting, working out, looking young and keeping fit reaches its zenith (or nadir) for those wealthy enough to buy the 'benefits' of cosmetic surgery. These days this can extend to women choosing to give birth by caesarean section, so as to minimize the impact on their bodies of being in labour. Among the very rich, there are even cases of surrogate mothers being hired to carry the child conceived by IVF, so that the biological mother's bodily appearance need not be affected by the ravages of pregnancy. Such a discourse is promoted by a panoply of medical and quasi-medical experts. These repositories of modern knowledge range from GPs, hospital consultants and dentists to dieticians, beauty therapists, fitness trainers, hairdressers, chiropodists and so on.

A Marxist would explain this phenomenon as a result of market manipulation by profit-seeking pharmaceutical companies and their promotional allies. Some feminists would point to the gendered nature of such body-centred consumption, though the rapidly increasing proportion of males now preoccupied with their bodily appearance raises questions about such an analysis. But the Foucauldian approach, while acknowledging the partial relevance of such accounts, prefers to see the phenomenon as fundamentally the inevitable outcome of the penetration of body-centred discursive regulation into the very limits of contemporary human existence. It is traceable back to the rise of body-centred medicine, which itself has its foundation in the needs of modernity.

## A case study in Foucauldian analysis: female sexuality

In principle, physical sexual urges can be satisfied by all manner of bodily activities. But in all cultures, only some of these activities are considered legitimate; for Foucauldians, that is, all cultures derive their rules about sexuality from the power of some discourse or other. For example, members of societies governed by religious knowledge 'know' that certain forms of sexual activity are good (right) and others evil (wrong). Religious experts are on hand to enforce these rules of normality and deviance, and their prescriptions are preached in the pulpit, the confessional or wherever. In secular cultures it is more common for ideas about what is 'natural' and 'unnatural' to provide the knowledge base from which designations of normal and deviant sex are derived. Typically, such discursive regulation is conspicuously gendered; it is usual for male and female bodies to be subject to very different prescriptions regarding sexual activity.

In pre-modern Europe the role of regulating female sexuality in order to facilitate property transference was undertaken by the Church. According to religious teaching, sex outside marriage – fornication – was a sin and the dutiful wife was a woman whose body and reproductive capacities remained the exclusive property of her husband. To thwart this rule would bring eternal damnation. Furthermore, for a woman to be reluctant, or refuse, to live the virtuous life of a wife/mother could bring earthly retribution as well. As Bryan Turner puts it:

> Women were closely associated with witchcraft, because it was argued that they were particularly susceptible to the sexual advances of the devil . . . Women were seen to be irrational, emotional and lacking in self-restraint; they were especially vulnerable to satanic temptation . . . Between 1563 and 1727, somewhere between 70 and 90 per cent of witchcraft suspects throughout Europe were female . . . The attack on women as witches was primarily a critique of their sexuality. (Turner 1995: 88–9)

## The medical regulation of female sexuality in modernity

With the onset of modernity and **secularization**, from the beginning of the nineteenth-century, bio-medicine and bio-medical accounts of bodily illnesses took on the role of regulating the female body, with psychiatry and psychiatrists in the vanguard. Women who resisted medical definitions of a healthy life were in danger of being classed as mentally ill. In some places, having a child out of wedlock could lead to a diagnosis of mental imbalance and disturbance. The desire to explore your sexuality with a number of different male partners – being 'promiscuous' or 'loose' – could well lead you to being diagnosed with nymphomania, an illness like hysteria, from which only women could suffer. Indeed, at the end of the nineteenth century, medicine had been so influential in linking female sexuality with bodily health that the antidote for hysteria – abnormally neurotic behaviour – could well be a hysterectomy. (The Greek word for womb is hystera.) This treatment reveals much about bio-medical assumptions concerning the relationship between a woman's body and her personality at the time. Only by living a normal, healthy family life – as a virgin before marriage, faithful yet productive afterwards – could a woman avoid suspicions of mental or physical illness.

In more recent times, medicine continued to exert its control over women. Although deviant sexuality on the part of men – homosexuality was being treated as an illness in Britain up until the 1960s – could also be seen as evidence of sickness as well as the commission of crime, it was on women's bodies that the medical gaze was more sternly directed. Not to want to be married was unnatural. Once married, so was not wanting to have children. Once a biological bond between a woman and her child had been created, medicine ruled that it must be a sign of psychological disturbance not to be able to subordinate all other interests to being a mother. After all, according to medicine, nature takes over once a child has been born; the mother's maternal instinct will guarantee her commitment, her parenting ability and, thereby, the safety and health of her child. To find motherhood difficult, exhausting or unrelentingly stressful was (and to some extent still is) also to invite medical intervention. Often, it is not until the birth of a child that the enormity of the responsibility of being a mother sinks in for a woman, especially in a world where mothers are often isolated from wider kin or other support networks. Asking for help, even if a sensible and practical move, can, in a medical culture, raise suspicions of 'not being able to cope' (mental instability) or, even more alarmingly, evidence of 'post-natal depression'. As with all powerful discourses, the inability to match up to its definitions of normality can not only bring with it the threat of outside intervention but can also engender feelings of failure and worthlessness.

## Self-surveillance

As Foucault explains, it is this combination of external enforcing and internal self-policing and self-surveillance that gives discourses their irresistible power. As we have seen from our examples, a discourse always has its experts to enforce normality and punish deviance. However, one of Foucault's key points is that it is because, as humans, we constantly assess what we should and should not do in relation to the cultural knowledge we have acquired – because *we police ourselves* – that the delivery of a discursively directed order is ensured. He compares the life of a human being in a discourse-directed world – and there *can be* no other kind – to the life of a prisoner in a panopticon. The panopticon was a prison designed by Jeremy Bentham in 1843. The prison warders were located in a circular tower surrounded by the cells that also formed a circle. The idea was to ensure that the prisoners could never escape surveillance – or, rather, that they could not guarantee that they were *not* being observed by the warders. This knowledge, Bentham believed, would lead the inmates to obey the prison rules at all times – that is, they would police themselves and constantly monitor their behaviour – just in case. Though this prison was never built, Foucault used it as a metaphor for self-surveillance in everyday life – a phenomenon he termed **panopticism**. As Foucault describes self-surveillance: 'Just a gaze. An inspecting gaze which each individual under its weight will end by exteriorizing to the point that he is his own overseer, each individual thus exercising this surveillance over and against himself ' (Foucault 1980: 155).

## Governmentality

Foucault's analysis of the spread of discursive power both throughout society and within individuals has been influential within sociological theory and research, as we suggested above. One particularly clear example of Foucault's influence within sociology is the work of Peter Miller and Nikolas Rose (2008). Their work takes up Foucault's analysis of power by examining how our behaviour is governed by discourses which connect more general forms of power, including political, economic, institutional and technical, to the precise management of people's conduct. Foucault uses the term 'governmentality' to convey this idea that in contemporary society power works on individuals through the concentration of a range of different discourses on specific aspects of our conduct. Miller and Rose describe this as the conduct (as of an orchestra) of conduct (behaviour). This behaviour, including that within the workplace, parenting, shopping, and, more obviously, sex, has increasingly fallen into the hands of 'experts'. The range of these expert discourses which are the focus of Miller and Rose's attention are what they call the 'psy' disciplines – those professions associated with psychology and psychoanalysis such as GPs, health visitors, human relations departments, family therapists and occupational psychologists. These disciplines together have the effect of making certain kinds of behaviour both visible and worthy targets of their intervention (a process Miller and Rose call the 'problematizing' of individuals' conduct). The 'psy' disciplines operate, according to Miller and Rose, by creating a proliferating list of categories within which individuals are placed, including those individuals who have no medical or otherwise 'deviant' condition. And, as Foucault suggests, in being identified under such categories, the individuals concerned learn to understand themselves in the same terms.

For example, Miller and Rose (2008) document the increasing involvement of these 'psy' disciplines in the government of the worker throughout the twentieth century. The authors identify a series of identities created by this range of discourses – identities which the worker is then taught to identify with and police themselves in relation to. In the early part of the twentieth century, the worker was categorized as 'a psycho-physiological machine' whose performance must be measured to ensure maximum efficiency, in the manner of Taylorism, as we discussed in Chapter 4. From the 1930s this category was abandoned and emphasis placed on the worker's mental health as 'an adjusted or mal-adjusted individual'. Within this discourse the worker was seen as someone who sought gratification in work, as in the rest of their life, rather than merely a package of skills. So the worker's character and intellect were now the targets of observation, testing and measurement to ensure they were fitted into the right job (Miller and Rose 2008: 179). This concern with the worker's mental health and aptitude helped to establish an interest in 'human relations' in governing (or as Miller and Rose put it, 'interfering with') the social relationships between people as workers: The worker was now governed under the category of a 'social being seeking solidarity' (Miller and Rose 2008: 197) and the workplace was now understood as 'pervaded by an attitudinal and communicative atmosphere, a social-psychological overlay to the actual organisation and the productive process itself' (Miller and Rose 2008: 180). As Miller and Rose observe, none of these categorizations or the practices associated with them were judged as successful in producing contented, productive and peaceable workers and workplaces, but this lack of success, rather than encouraging anyone to question the whole approach, in fact tended only to encourage the production of new categories.

By the 1960s a new category was constructed within a discourse of 'quality of life'. The worker is now seen as 'a responsible and autonomous subject' (Miller and Rose 2008: 197) who seeks 'control, variety and a sense of worth, and finding this in the carrying out of meaningful tasks within a dynamic system of small-group relations' (Miller and Rose 2008: 186). Finally, post-Fordist technical transformations to the work process were linked to a new set of ideals based on a concept of 'the enterprising self'. 'Enterprise here meant not simply an organisational form – that of separate units of competition – but an image of a certain mode of activity that could be applied equally across a range of organizations from hospitals to universities, to individuals within these organisations whether these be managers or workers, and, more generally, to persons in their everyday existence' (Miller and Rose 2008: 195).

Rose and Miller regard these discursive creations as equally significant to those surrounding sexuality, which we looked at above:

> For it is in work, as much as in 'private life', that human beings have been required to civilise themselves and encouraged to discover themselves. It is around work, as much as around sexuality, that truths about the nature of humans as persons have been elaborated, and that norms and judgements about the conduct of individuals have crystallized. It is in relation to work, as much as in relation to intimacy, that authorities have gained a legitimated competence to pronounce truth about persons and about the ways in which our lives should be conducted. (Miller and Rose 2008: 196).

## Foucauldian theory and the project of modernity

While Miller and Rose add little to Foucault's own theoretical work, they do offer extended examples of its application. How can we assess the significance for social theory of the Foucauldian approach to the relationship of power to knowledge? So far in this book, we have seen that for the structural theorists who engage in the **project of modernity** the task is to generate knowledge which can then be used to enable societal progress and make possible individual freedom and liberation. For Foucauldians, however, forms of knowledge are used to regulate, control and discipline. Thus they turn the **modernist** definition of knowledge on its head, claiming that since we can only know reality through discourse, this knowledge must control who we are. We do not use knowledge to create better worlds; social change simply means the emergence of new discourses, which in turn define and control subjects in new ways. These 'new' ways of knowing are not 'better' or 'worse' than what has gone before – they are simply different, reflecting different forms of power. Defining madness as the possession of sacred knowledge, or as representing lack of reason, or as evidence of a diseased mind, is not a matter of 'falsehoods' being replaced by 'truth'. It is simply a shift in power relations – the replacement of one way of defining reality by another. The same applies in the case of the 'psy' disciplines extending their influence into workplace psychology and culture; each new category comes with a range of assumptions and practices which together contribute to creating a series of different work cultures and identities over time. The impact of each category does not lie in the overt exercise of power over workers but instead in the neutral and gradual re-definition of what counts as efficient, or well-adjusted or otherwise. To refuse human relations-led mediation in a dispute with a colleague may lead to 'gardening leave', or other sanctioned absence, and, without a recognized form of resolution, perhaps to 're-deployment' or 'voluntary severance'. This represents the exercise of a 'different' but not necessarily better form of authority than the strict and obvious 'hiring and firing' leadership from the top.

This Foucauldian portrayal of the power of discourses to create reality thus offers a radically different view of the Enlightenment belief in progress through reason. Here, through the post-structuralist and Foucauldian lens, the very belief in a free subject is seen as the basis for discursive domination. None of the above processes of surveillance and self-surveillance would be possible without the belief, enshrined in Western philosophy, theology, politics and art, that to be human means to have an inner life, whether referred to as a soul, psyche, libido or self. Once this inner chamber has been assembled by such discursive materials, it offers the perfect location for what appear to be the most intense forms of policing and control – the kind of control which we welcome as the means for our individual emancipation. From this Foucauldian perspective, notions of agency are treated as yet more means for such control rather than as evidence of its limits.

This brings into question one powerful justification for the whole enterprise of social theory, at least in so far as the latter proceeds on the basis that understanding the social world increases the possibility of being able to change it. Minimally, such a project would have to believe that knowledge produced by the social sciences could reach an audience capable of receiving and acting on it. Miller and Rose explicitly distance their work from such social critique, as we shall see below.

## Foucault and feminism

However, Foucault's work has also been pivotal in the development of analyses which do seek to criticize discursive power, particularly from the perspective of feminism. A very good example of such work is that of Sandra Bartky (1990). She argues very forcibly that discourses of femininity operate as highly repressive forms of power that maintain women's subordination to men by instilling a deep sense of bodily shame in women. Skin-care regimes, dieting, wearing make-up, attention to bodily deportment – all such disciplinary practices are regarded by Bartky not merely as attempts to sustain differences between masculine and feminine bodies, as we outlined above, but to produce a feminine body as a body on which an inferior status has been inscribed. Bartky regards such shaming discourses as the answer to why all women are not feminists:

> The woman who checks her make-up half a dozen times a day to see if her foundation has caked or her mascara run, who worries that the wind or the rain may spoil her hair do, who looks frequently to see if her stockings have bagged at the ankle, or who, feeling fat, monitors everything she eats, has become, just as surely as an inmate of the panopticon, a self-policing subject, a self committed to a relentless self-surveillance. This self-surveillance is a form of obedience to **patriarchy**. (Bartky 1990: 80).

Foucauldian and **postmodernist** discourse theory have provided powerful tools for feminists who have sought to identify how women learn to regard themselves as different and inferior to men. However, their work has been criticized by other, non-Foucauldian feminist theorists on precisely the grounds that it appears to rule out the possibility of human agency and the capacity to challenge discursive control. If humans, of any gender, are viewed as being no more than effects of discourse – and, in the case of women, as effects of a discourse which renders them as passive 'objects' – it becomes hard to see how resistance to male control is possible.

Many critics have pointed to the basic dilemma facing a Foucauldian who wants to use discourse analysis in the manner of Bartky – i.e. as a way to criticize the effects of power on its subjects. Perhaps Peter Dews' identification of the dilemma Foucault faced applies more generally. According to Dews, Foucault assumes that every mode of experience, system of meaning or form of knowledge is entirely determined by operations of power. 'Yet, in order to function as a political critique of these operations, Foucault's work must appeal to some form of meaning, experience or knowledge which is not so determined' (Dews 1987: 185). Dews suggests that Foucault does not manage to resolve this dilemma in his own work. We will look at this issue in greater detail in relation to postmodernism more generally in Chapters 8 and 9.

## Governmentality and agency

At this point we can ask what the implications of a Foucauldian perspective are for those who do not seek to ally their work with 'modernist' political critique and change, but who do see their work as contributing to the analysis of social practices. Miller and Rose make it clear that social and political critique is not their objective. They explicitly distinguish their work from those forms of sociology that seek to ground their criticisms 'on values of personal identity, agency, self affirmation which are seen as essential to the human subject' (Miller and Rose 2008: 173). Miller and Rose, then, seem content to chart rather than criticize the shifting nature of discourses of governmentality. In this respect their work returns us to the question we referred to at the end of the previous chapter, that of the relationship between actors' knowledge and the kind of knowledge produced by social scientists. As we suggested there, **hermeneutic** and post-structuralist accounts of the social significance of language differ radically in terms of the importance they give to 'ordinary' human communication in understanding and thereby contributing to changing society.

Let us briefly consider whether the Foucauldian approach discussed in this chapter recognizes any distinction or potentially critical space between the discursive networks sustained by the 'psy' disciplines and the meanings, intentions and knowledge of those who are the subjects of such disciplines. Are those subjected to these disciplines left with any possibility of challenging them? Despite attempts by Foucault and by his followers to distance their project from the grand modernist ambitions of conventional structural sociology, we might point to what appear to be some striking similarities between them.

Like **functionalist** and conflict theorists, these Foucauldian authors appear to direct their work only at other specialist producers of social science. It is not quite clear whether Miller and Rose are content to assume that the 'psy' disciplines will have their intended effect on those who are subject to them, in other words that their truth is simply and passively accepted by its intended targets. As in the case of structuralist sociologies, the knowingness of the authors is assumed, but what the actors know is left unexamined. It is, therefore, an open question as to whether the circuit between collective values, institutional stability and individual motivations is as securely in place for Miller and Rose now as it was in Parsons' time.

Perhaps Rose and Miller believe that questions relating to social actors' knowledge are not worth asking, or perhaps they consider such questions to be adequately addressed by the definition of discourse as creating the very notion of the agent or subject on whom their critique would rely. In this context, if the subject or agent is created by discourse then such agents' views become inherently predictable and unworthy of detailed exploration. For the theorists we will now look at, however, the question of what actors know is absolutely central not just to the nature of social practice and meaning but to the nature of social theory.

## Further reading

McHoul, Alec and Grace, Wendy (2002): *A Foucault Primer: discourse, power and the subject*, Routledge.
McNay, Loïs (1994): *Foucault: a critical introduction*, Polity.
Shilling, Chris (2003): *The Body and Social Theory*, 2nd edn, Sage.
Turner, Bryan (2008): *The Body and Society: explorations in social theory*, 3rd edn, Sage.

# 7 SOCIAL STRUCTURES AND SOCIAL ACTION

## Introduction

It is now time to examine a series of important contributions to the re-formulating of conceptions of **social structure** and social **action** or **agency** which were developed in parallel with, and in contrast to, the post-structuralist themes of Foucault's work. As we shall see, the theorists whose work we will be discussing look beyond the boundaries of social theory to find ways to re-think the structure–agency relationship. In this they were influenced by challenges to **positivism** within the natural sciences which became important sources for attempts to dislodge positivism from within the social sciences.

As we saw in the early chapters of this book, Marx, Durkheim and Weber offered conflicting accounts of what a scientific analysis of society would entail, with Durkheim most explicitly doing so within a positivist framework and Weber at the furthest distance from positivism. As we also suggested, the intention of each of these writers to at least in part address their specific historical and political contexts was laid to one side by later theorists who attempted to develop more generalized sociological frameworks within which to analyse the relationship between 'the individual and society'. However, the belief of both Weber and Durkheim that the study of the causal structures of society requires an explanatory framework which allows us to see more than the subjective meaning of actions persisted long into the twentieth century.

In the context of the mid twentieth century, once the structures of industrial capitalism had become established within Western societies, structural sociological analysis focused largely on issues relating to how individuals were socialized into conforming to the values of those societies. Within this framework, interpretivist sociologies 'drilled down' further to reveal some of the processes of meaning-creation and interpretation by which individuals conducted their lives in relation to each other. As we have seen, Foucault and later Foucauldians, while offering a clear framework for analysing the effects of discursive power, may be criticized for neglecting the agency of discursive subjects. In one way or another then, the question of how we might try to analyse both the ways in which social structures shape our lives *and* how we as individuals might relate to such structures as social agents rather than as mere effects remained unclear.

In fact, many theorists argue that the concepts of structure and action or agency actually represent mutually exclusive explanatory frameworks: If we try to explain social practices from one of these perspectives we thereby rule out the possibility of explaining them from the other. On one hand, symbolic interactionists and ethnomethodologists emphasize the importance of the methods that actors adopt in the interaction process, and the ways in which they account for their social actions or the meanings they place upon things and events. On the other hand, structuralist social theorists explain individuals' actions not in terms of their performances and interpretations of social encounters but by studying what lies beyond the awareness of these actors – namely, the unacknowledged conditions and unintended consequences of their actions.

In this chapter we will discuss social theories which have in their different ways sought to radically re-write the conceptual framework of social theory and tried to bring the analyses of structures and of action together. As we shall see in more detail below, the 'genetic structuralism' of Pierre Bourdieu, the **critical realism** of Roy Bhaskar, and the **structuration theory** of Anthony Giddens each offer different attempts to challenge the 'structuralist versus interpretivist' orthodoxy of social theory.

A common theme in the work of all three theorists concerns the importance of social science recognizing that social structures are not created independently of what actors do and know but are in important respects the collective creations of actors' **practical knowledge** and interpretations of the social world, and of their social relationships with each other. Likewise, actors are able to act, to pursue their projects and goals, only because they employ this practical knowledge. Seen in this light then, social structures and social agents are parts of the same overall process of action, meaning and interpretation. This does not mean that following this circuit of action and structure is the beginning and end of sociological analysis, but it does remove the strict division between *either* looking at the actors *or* looking at the structures.

Let us now turn to Bourdieu's theory of genetic structuralism to see how he understands the significance of this more dynamic or fluid co-mingling of actors and structures, or the subjective and the objective, within social practices.

## Pierre Bourdieu's genetic structuralism

Pierre Bourdieu (1930–2002) wanted to construct a theoretical framework that would be of direct practical use to social researchers – a toolkit for understanding what actually happens in the social world. This drove his attempts to produce a sociology that would avoid the dangers both of the structuralist account of social actors as mere side effects of social structures and of the restricted interpretivist viewpoint in which social structures are reduced to those aspects of social situations of which actors are directly and intentionally aware. His work is intended to allow for what he describes as an 'escape from the ritual either/or choice between objectivism and subjectivism in which the social sciences have so far allowed themselves to be trapped' (Bourdieu 1977: 4).

Bourdieu, like Giddens, referred to his research as **reflexive sociology**. For Bourdieu this reflexivity referred to two issues – firstly, the need for the sociologist to be aware of his or her social background as a source of possible bias, and secondly, the need to give more importance within sociological explanation to the ways in which an actor's practical knowledge is not just knowledge *about* their society but part of the material that *creates and sustains* that society.

### Overcoming the subjectivism and objectivism divide

Bourdieu was schooled at the prestigious École Normale Supérieure in Paris where he studied philosophy and came under the influence of three forms of knowledge: French Marxism, the existentialism of Jean-Paul Sartre, and the structural anthropology of Claude Lévi-Strauss. The Marxist and existentialist philosophies he encountered were treated as examples of, respectively, the structuralist and the excessively interpretivist positions we identified above. However, as John Thompson points out, Lévi-Strauss' anthropology seemed to offer a more sophisticated model of society, and Bourdieu labelled his own work 'genetic structuralism' or 'structuralist constructivism' (Thompson 1991: 29). As we saw in the previous chapter, Foucault too was influenced by structuralism, and it was this which led him to emphasize the all-pervasive impact of **discourse**. Bourdieu, in contrast, wanted to give more space within this structuralist framework to people's practical knowledge of their everyday worlds. This led him to the work of Goffman and Garfinkel. For Bourdieu it was important to recognize that people knew much more about their world than they would be able to express in theoretical terms.

Bourdieu borrowed the term '**doxa**' from the Ancient Greek philosopher Plato to describe this practical knowledge. Plato used the term *doxa* in a rather derogatory manner, to refer to the common knowledge or understanding of things or ways of doing things. For Plato, perhaps like Durkheim, *doxa* was the muddle of ordinary citizens' views and served as a threat to political order. Bourdieu's account of *doxa*, however, is not intended to be disparaging: 'doxic experience' here refers to that which is taken for granted by the actor in their daily activities, but which is not part of their conscious knowledge. Bourdieu argued that the more rigid and ordered the objective structures of society are, the more social actors will be reliant on doxic experience. Routines can be carried on more or less without conscious attention (Bourdieu 1977: 165–6). This notion of *doxa* is closely related to the most well known of Bourdieu's concepts, that of **habitus**, and it is to this that we now turn.

## Habitus

Habitus is where doxic experience is stored as a series of memories of how to behave. Habitus is thus the agent's practical or common-sense knowledge about ways of doing things, responding to situations, and understanding what is going on. It is the kind of knowledge we do not consciously refer to but which we routinely employ. This form of understanding covers a diverse range of situations from the trivial and the mundane – 'ways of walking or blowing one's nose, ways of eating or talking' – to, for example, the politically significant divisions 'between the classes, the age groups and the sexes' (Bourdieu 1977: 466). For Bourdieu, habitus is an acquired way of seeing the social world and is dependent on one's position and upbringing in that world. While habitus is a shared vision of the social world, differences of class, age and gender, etc., will colour this vision accordingly. In summary, habitus is something that belongs to the individual or resides in the self, but which also reflects shared and common understandings about the social world. This might remind us of Durkheim's collective moral beliefs, and it is the case that habitus refers to that which belongs to a social collective. However, Bourdieu also departs from Durkheim most clearly in his emphasis on how our habitus contributes to the objectivity of the social world. One's habitus is a product of socialization and of social position in a field of social activity, while the external world (in this case the world of positions, fields, and **capital** – see below) is produced and reproduced through the activities and actions of individuals. It is important to see, then, that despite Bourdieu describing habitus as a social structure which is internalized by individuals he is not adopting the structuralist **functionalist** position that habitus is a mechanism which simply reproduces social conformity. It is seen to shape our orientation but not in the manner of an objective law. Likewise, Bourdieu avoids arguing along interpretivist lines that an actor's stock of knowledge is either always correct or ultimately responsible for the outcomes of any given social encounter.

Bourdieu's model of the interchange between subjective and objective processes moves away from both positivism and structuralism, but this is not to say that he abandons hope of developing a science of society. Indeed, the opposite is true. As Wacquant and others have observed, he leans very much in the direction of an objectivist view of the social world but one in which the potential of an agent to alter that world is always maintained (Bourdieu and Wacquant 1992: 11).

## Field, position and capital

Bourdieu next turns his attention towards the objective or external aspects of the social world. Here a number of concepts are of fundamental importance, in particular: field, position and capital. All of these exist within what he calls a social space. This is an arena in which various interconnected fields, and positions within fields, exist in a semi-autonomous manner. Fields criss-cross all societies. Bourdieu studied a range of fields in his own sociological research on taste and judgement, academia or higher education, language, and the bureaucratic state. Other areas we might think of as fields include business and commerce, art, juridical politics, religion and science.

According to Bourdieu, the common characteristic of all fields is that they are 'arenas of struggle'. These struggles for power may be undertaken by individuals, groups or institutions, each of which attempts to appropriate the products that are at stake in the field. Entities exist within a field in what Bourdieu calls positions, which relate to each other in terms of opposites or differences. For example, in a general sense, the position of a man is opposed to that of a woman, good taste is opposed to bad taste, well educated to poorly educated, and so on. In a more concrete way, to consider an area that Bourdieu himself researched, the field of higher education is partly constituted by faculties or disciplines. In this arena academics positioned in the faculty of law will be endowed with different resources to those positioned in the sciences, who in turn bring to the field different assets to those academics belonging to the arts and humanities faculties. Hence, positions carry with them different resources which individuals and groups utilize in confrontation with other individuals and groups in their attempts to secure different means and ends. As López and Scott observe: 'In a field, agents and institutions constantly struggle according to the regularities and the rules constitutive of this space of play . . . with various degrees of strength and therefore diverse probabilities of success, to appropriate the specific products at stake in the game' (López and Scott 2000: 102).

Strength in this context is dependent upon the resources that individuals or groups can bring to bear – that is, on what Bourdieu calls 'capital'. This term seems at first to be misleading since it implies, especially within sociology, a reference to economic resources. In fact, Bourdieu discusses four types of capital: economic, cultural, social and symbolic. Some of these are self-explanatory. Economic capital, for example, refers generally to resources such as income, land and financial assets, while **cultural capital** is defined in terms of manners, taste, language, knowledge and skills. Social capital relates primarily to valued social relations – who one knows and who might be used in order to achieve a given end. Symbolic capital, finally, relates to honour, prestige and reputation. Capital is only capital when it can be used in a given field, and those who are in possession of the right sort and the right amount of capital will be able to dominate a field – they are its well-positioned agents, groups or institutions. Equally important, it should be noted that capital often begets capital. For instance, an individual who possesses a great deal of cultural or social capital may be able to use these resources to obtain more economic capital.

To return to an example used earlier, one of Bourdieu's best-known texts is *Homo Academicus*, a study of French academia during and leading up to the student riots of 1968. In this work he shows how the various faculties of a university can be differentiated in terms of the types and levels of capital they possess in the field of higher education. In France in the 1960s the dominant faculties in this field (those with most power and authority) were the faculties of law and medicine. Their prestige and power largely rested upon the amount of social and economic capital they could use to dictate how French universities should operate. The subordinate faculties belonged to the natural sciences, which were rich in cultural capital but poor in relation to social and economic capital. The struggles that took place in the French higher education sector at this time raged around cultural capital versus social and economic capital. The faculties of the arts and the social sciences, Bourdieu observed, straddled these two extremes, occupying academic positions that could easily fit into either camp, the social and economic or the cultural.

In his study Bourdieu also observed the way in which capital was passed down from one generation of academics to the next in a reproduction of the system and its distribution of positions and power. This, he claimed, resulted in and encouraged intellectual stagnation in many faculties. For an agent to succeed in, for example, the faculty of philosophy, he (and occasionally she) must conform to a system that placed at least as much emphasis on social capital as it did on cultural capital. The reproduction of French academia was thus not freely chosen by academics but was a result of the objective positions and interactions between positions characteristic of French university life.

The concepts Bourdieu developed, from *doxa* and habitus to fields and forms of capital, provide the social theorist and researcher with a repertoire of instruments with which to study the social world and try to show how objective structures and subjective actions relate to and affect each other rather than stand opposed. However, some critics have argued that Bourdieu is still offering a model of social structure and action which follows earlier structuralist lines too closely. Too little attention is given, it is claimed, to the ways in which actors can transform social structures as well as reproduce them. In failing to give full scope to the degree of exchange between actors and structures, Bourdieu leaves us with too sparse a framework to understand the full range of processes involved in either social reproduction or change.

These criticisms will be easier to evaluate when we come to discuss Giddens' structuration theory, to which Bourdieu's work is often compared. However, before doing so, we will examine Roy Bhaskar's attempts to develop, like Bourdieu and Giddens, an analysis of how structures are produced and reproduced in social life. Both Bhaskar and Giddens argue for the removal of positivist methodologies from the social sciences, and both argue that such methodologies prevent any adequate explanation of the relationship *between* social structures and social action. There is, however, a major distinction between their respective positions on this point.

Like Bourdieu, and echoing Durkheim, Bhaskar wants to produce a science of society. In fact, his claim is that such a science should be seen as producing knowledge of causal laws in the same way as do the natural sciences. However, he argues that such a causal analysis is only possible once we see that positivists such as Durkheim were misdescribing the procedures of scientists. Once we re-think what natural scientists do we will see that social scientists can share the same methodology – a realist one. As we suggested briefly at the end of Chapter 5, in developing his argument in this respect, Bhaskar makes use of more specialized philosophies of natural science as well as **hermeneutic** philosophies (those focused on how humans interpret and communicate). Giddens also incorporates important insights from hermeneutic philosophy into his own work. However, while Bhaskar uses such insights to move social science closer to natural science, Giddens uses them to establish a radical distinction between the two types of science. For Bhaskar – and even more so for Margaret Archer, who takes up his arguments for a causal science of society – the aim appears to be that of producing a series of generalized statements about the structural properties of society, statements that can then be shown to stand as laws which are independent of human agency. Giddens, for his part, does not believe that we can make any such claims for generalizing statements within the social sciences. We will examine his arguments in relation to this point below. But first we will briefly introduce the relevant aspects of hermeneutic philosophy common to both Bhaskar and Giddens.

## Science, language and interpretation

Bhaskar and Giddens develop their own arguments by drawing on debates within philosophy, and particularly the philosophy of the natural sciences, around the positivist insistence that theory and empirical experiment should remain clearly demarcated aspects of the scientific process. As we can recall, positivism gives priority to the measurement of cause and effect relationships through empirical means – by observation of what is detectable we can hypothesize the presence of non-detectable laws which explain the patterns and regularities in what we are observing. This kind of scientific activity thus relies on the use of two distinct languages – the one *theoretical*, used to explain what we think is going on beyond what we can observe, and the other *empirical*, used to describe what we are observing. These two languages should be kept separate from each other to ensure that we 'see' the facts as they are, rather than contaminate them with our own assumptions and biases. This allows science to arrive at generalizations that are true in so far as they correspond to the facts. As long as we can be sure that we have accurately observed what is there, we can with confidence proceed from observations of regularities in what has been observed to general explanatory statements of causality. Within the social sciences, the languages of theory and observation should also be kept separate from the understandings of the social world held by social actors themselves. The positivist insistence on these boundaries between different kinds of scientific procedures and languages was intended to support the process of **induction** – the movement from observation to generalization.

The problem with these rules of demarcation between languages is that they limit the social scientist to observing behaviour – to observing *what* people do rather than *why* they are doing it. By extension, people's own interpretations or theories of social practices have no place in the causal explanation of the persistence of these practices. Despite influential attempts to argue against positivist methodologies within the social sciences, it was the impact of ideas developed in disciplines other than sociology that most decisively broke the stranglehold of positivism within social theory. Again in general terms, the early twentieth-century hermeneutic philosophies of Martin Heidegger, Hans Georg Gadamer and Wittgenstein, combined with post-empiricist philosophies of natural science such as that of Mary Hesse (1924–) (1974), contributed to two crucial shifts in perspective:

- to treat language as the means by which humans *create* their world rather than as a set of symbols to be applied to a pre-given reality
- to move scientific thought and action closer to non-scientific practices.

The overall effect of these two moves was a blurring of the boundaries between all of the different languages within which humans encounter their world and communicate. This new approach to what it means to be a language user rejected the approach to knowledge-gathering enshrined in positivism. Rather than assuming that we come to know the world by attaching our concepts onto it like sticking labels on parcels, hermeneutic philosophers argued that we encounter and come to know both ourselves and the world only in and through language. Put simply, there is no 'world' without language. This account was most clearly set out by Gadamer, using a term that will be familiar to us from Weberian sociology – '*verstehen*', or, as it is normally translated, 'interpretive understanding'. Gadamer argued that *verstehen* should not be seen merely as a specialist procedure used by social scientists as a way into individuals' private inner worlds. Rather, *verstehen* now refers to the ontological condition necessary for us to carry on in the world. We know what we know – scientists, sociologists and every other language user – through language 'disclosing' or opening up the world to us.

Hesse argued, with a more specific reference to the practices of natural science, that positivism is mistaken in its belief that the only way to secure objective validity is to maintain a strict demarcation between theoretical and observation languages. She claimed that such a rule is futile because we cannot in fact separate out the two languages, since in practice they always overlap. In other words, it is a mistake to believe that we can notice anything without at the same time interpreting or theorizing about what it is.

On this basis, then, Hesse argues that we should see scientific languages as *extending* in different ways the means by which ordinary languages disclose the world to us. Scientific and natural languages are all part of the same network of human communication. Distinctions between scientific and ordinary languages, along with distinctions between scientific and artistic or moral meanings, are applied according to what we are doing at any given time. In fact, in practice such languages and meanings are often used together. Imagine the inner conversation we might have when, in attempting to send an email to a friend we discover our computer will not work. On fairly swiftly coming to the end of our technical expertise (perhaps no more than pressing the on/off button), we consider whether we can justify phoning the suppliers and trying to get the machine repaired under the guarantee we are pretty sure ran out a week ago. Even in this short, if rather vexed, moment we will have moved between private, technical, moral and legal frames of meaning quite easily in order to solve a routine problem. The problem is thereby disclosed to us in each of its dimensions through social and linguistic meanings. Even 'the computer' is not something out there and independent of our frames of meaning. When it works we barely notice it and just get on with using it. It becomes 'the computer' perhaps only when it stops doing what we want it to do, and so we foreground it as a recalcitrant object. In this sense then, our languages and practical projects carve into and throw into relief what 'the world' is to us at any particular time.

This attention to the world- and human-making powers of language is sometimes rather generally referred to as the 'linguistic turn' in philosophy. More specifically, this refers to the deeper and

more important recognition that we do not live in splendid isolation as 'subjects' but first come to know ourselves and our world(s)
through the inter-subjective medium of language. The mastery of different frames of meaning is common to natural, social and ordinary
language.

This point is particularly significant when it comes to thinking about
the human and social sciences. Bhaskar and Giddens each try to think
through the implications of this 'linguistic turn' in their respective
attempts to move beyond the structuralist versus interpretivist opposition within social theory. Arguably, Giddens travels further along the
hermeneutic road than does Bhaskar. The latter does, however, argue
that the insights of hermeneutic philosophers such as Wittgenstein
and Winch open up a much richer and more fluid way of analysing
the individual–society relation. For Bhaskar, these philosophers effectively allow us to see how social scientists always encounter a world
that has already been interpreted by lay actors; this then means that
those actors' own interpretations have an important role to play in
explanations of the persistence of social practices. Bhaskar's work is
distinctive in that it uses a critique of both positivism and of interpre-
tivism to argue *for* the scientific study of the causal laws of society. To
this end, Bhaskar uses Hesse and other contemporary philosophers of
science in an attempt to place both sociology and natural science under
a common methodology.

## Roy Bhaskar's critical realism

As its title suggests, Roy Bhaskar's (1944–) *The Possibility of Naturalism*
offers an argument for the social and natural sciences sharing a methodology (realism), but on the basis of an abandonment of positivism's
rigid separation of the languages of observation and of theory. In
simple terms, he argues that positivist methodologies rely on a theory
of causality which says that unless you can *observe* that something has
caused something else you can't say you have established a real causal
law. Bhaskar argues that causality should not be taken to rely on
observability – instead, causal powers are evident in what they *do*, and
not on whether we can observe them doing it:

> The positivist tradition is correct to stress that there are causal laws, gen-
> eralities, at work in social life. It is also correct to insist (where it does)
> that these laws *may* be opaque to the agent's' spontaneous understanding.
> Where it errs is in the reduction of these laws to empirical regularities, and

in the account that it is thereby committed to giving of the process of their identification. (Bhaskar 1979: 27)

The second key argument Bhaskar makes concerns the extent to which interpretivist theories have accepted the accuracy of positivism when applied to the natural world (in other words, they too have accepted the idea that causes need to be observed to be real) and then merely attempted to argue that the social world is not subject to the same rules and therefore cannot be explained in causal terms. According to Bhaskar then, interpretivist sociologies are wrong on both counts. Once we reject positivist ideas as mis-descriptions of causality we can see that yes, interpretivist sociologists are right, and social science *does* need to take into account that actors' meanings help to constitute social structures. But they are nevertheless wrong in insisting that such a social science cannot therefore offer a causal explanation of the laws of society (Bhaskar 1979: 27).

New philosophies of science allow us to see that nature and society operate as 'open systems' – this means that we cannot predict that the laws we know to exist will actually take effect at a particular time. Natural science can perform experiments, but even in this case natural scientists recognize that what might happen under carefully controlled conditions may not happen outside of the laboratory. Countervailing conditions and other unexpected factors can suddenly come into play. Social scientists also operate in open systems where we cannot predict that a causal power we know conceptually to exist will actually exert its influence at any particular time. Bhaskar develops his argument for natural and social science sharing a realist methodology while recognizing that the material of social life is different to that of nature because it is made up of 'a pre-interpreted reality, a reality already brought under concepts by social actors' via shared frameworks of meaning (Bhaskar 1979: 27). Let's see how he does this.

Bhaskar's description of social structure bears some similarity to Bourdieu's. In both cases social structures consist of relations between individuals in positions within a structural sphere, and structure meets action at the point of intersection between positions and activities. However, Bhaskar begins to explain his concept of structure and action by comparing it to a 'sculptress at work, fashioning a product out of the material and tools available to her' (Bhaskar 1998: 34). Here, then, the implication appears to be that social structures are akin to objects in nature – they are things that pre-exist us, and have to be worked on and adapted or else they remain obstacles to our will. It is hard to see any room for interpretivist ideas here. Similarly, Bhaskar's conception of agency is detached from his notion of social structure. For him, agency is directly related to the psychological characteristics of reason and intention. Again this appears to resemble closely the oppositional account of the relationship between structures and action which Bhaskar criticized above, rather than offering a more fluid or dialectical account of various kinds of capital as the common currency of agency and structure as does Bourdieu.

Bhaskar's argument is that while agents' frames of meaning do contribute to some extent to the structural properties of society – and therefore those agents do, in principle, have the power to change their society – most of the time what agents know about their social structures is more superficial than that relating to the deep causal structures. In other words, even though these deeper causal powers are continually affecting what we do, we will most likely never know it. Realist social scientists, however, can help out here. Remember that for realists, just because we can't observe that something is happening, this doesn't mean we can't conceptually understand that it is happening. This opens the way for social science to elucidate the process: to move from 'the manifest phenomena of social life, as conceptualised in the experience of the social agents concerned, to the essential relations that necessitate them' (Bhaskar 1979: 32).

Bhaskar's position can be summarized in the following ways: On the one hand, in order to resist the interpretivist danger of reducing social structures to what lay actors might think they are, he claims that people and societies are fundamentally different kinds of things. But on the other hand, he does not want to fully embrace **naturalism** by treating social structures as if they exerted the same degree of causal power over human agents as does gravity, for example. He argues that social structures are not entirely like natural structures for the following reasons:

1  Social structures, unlike natural structures, do not exist independently of the activities they govern.
2  Social structures, unlike natural structures, do not exist independently of the agents' conceptions of what they are doing in their activity.
3  Social structures, unlike natural structures, may not always exist or remain in the same state. (Bhaskar 1998: 38)

But, Bhaskar still wants to insist that whatever the differences between the causal or structural properties of natural and social worlds, social scientists can still produce a scientific account of the causes or 'structural conditions for various forms of conscious human action' (Bhaskar 1979: 45).

Bourdieu's genetic structuralism attempts to overcome the divisions between subjectivism and objectivism by showing how social structures function in the minds of agents and arguing that social subjects and social structures shape each other in a continuous process. This emphasis on the common features of structures and agents is often referred to as a **duality** of structure, to signal not only that both parts of the duo interact but also that, in so doing, each makes the other. As we have just seen, Bhaskar seems to envisage some interchange between structure and action but also to hold onto the idea that social structures have causal powers that are in some ways independent of actors. This 'qualified naturalism' is dismissed by Margaret Archer. She reads Bhaskar as offering a stronger justification for a scientific study of society than he recognizes, and one which gives a much clearer role to the independently causal properties of social structures. Archer refers to this as the **dualism** of structure and agency, signalling a separation or clear distinction between these two elements of social theory. This represents a return to a more conventional notion of social structure and one in which structures directly constrain agents from acting in a purposeful manner. This version of critical realism thus returns to Durkheim's insistence that society and social structures exist as *sui generis* entities – that is, they exist in their own right.

## Margaret Archer's revised realism

The main influence upon Margaret Archer's (1943–) version of critical realism comes from Bhaskar's seminal works in the 1970s. Throughout her texts, Archer (1982, 1995, 1996, 2000) is primarily interested in demonstrating how social structures are of an historical nature and how actors encounter them as a pre-given force to be reckoned with or to be lived with. This is not to say that the reflective or monitoring role of actors is suddenly neglected in favour of social determinism. For Archer, actors, like structures, are also autonomous entities with causal powers to intervene in the social world. The influence of Bhaskar is clear here. But, importantly, she insists that actors encounter social structures as pre-given entities, and that therefore Bhaskar was being too timid in trying to retain any kind of relationship between actors and social structures in which the former actually help to create the latter.

In *Realist Social Theory: the morphogenetic approach* (1995), Archer argues against all three of Bhaskar's limitations to naturalism, listed above, as we will briefly outline below. Archer is particularly concerned with the specific features of historical structures, or in her terms, of social structures that are more dependent on past-tense human actions than on present-tense purposes and intentions. An example of such past-tense actions which constrain the actions of current agents is the demographic structure. Its shape, the proportion of people in particular age ranges, is partly a consequence of the actions of the long-dead, and its causal powers are capable of resisting any attempt to change it in a fundamental way. This is something we are all aware of in terms of concerns about providing adequate pensions for the retired. The present workforce have no control over the numbers of those who are retired and who are entitled to pensions, but they nevertheless have to adjust their actions accordingly to meet the financial costs, whether in terms of accepting higher taxes or longer working lives, for example. For Archer, then, if the demographic structure has governing powers and also resists change it must be seen as existing independently of the activities of agents. She is also critical of Bhaskar's second point, above, that social structures do not exist independently of the conceptions that agents have of them. As evidence for Bhaskar's error here, Archer points to the structural relations that are maintained by law, coercion, censorship or ideological manipulation. These social structures are kept in place by *overriding* actors' concepts of what they are doing.

Archer thus presents what she refers to as a 'stratified model of society' made up of both structures and actors. People, as actors, have the power to make changes to the structures of a society. But social science needs to specify carefully when such interventions into structures are possible. Structures, Archer claims, exist in two forms, as social structures (material resources) and as cultural structures (or knowledge). Following Bhaskar's lead, she argues that each of these is made up of **'emergent properties'** – those which are irreducible to people, generate causal powers, and are relatively long-lasting. As such, structures exist as autonomous or independent things. There is therefore, she claims, an 'inescapable need for a two-part account' of society (Archer 1995: 154): one part that looks at the pre-given structural features of the social world, and another that considers how actors intervene or change these structural conditions. Archer maintains that, using this two-part account, it is possible to distinguish when societies are being re-shaped (morphogenesis) and when they are being reproduced (morphostasis). Archer calls her revised critical realism 'analytical dualism', and observes that it requires a methodology that separates structure from action but equally allows causation to be two-way: coming from structure(s) to agent(s), and agent(s) to structure(s).

Critical realism has gained many adherents in recent years. Its popularity perhaps derives from its no-nonsense approach to the problem of structural constraint. It is clear to sociologists that all societies are shaped by unequal distributions of power and resources. It is also true that one of the main tasks sociology faces is to explain the presence and persistence of such inequalities. The main attraction of the critical realist approach is that it allows for a conceptualization of structural constraints in a way that makes it clear that inequalities persist despite attempts by actors to change things for the better. In other words, critical realism allows social critics to highlight not just the deficiencies of society but the limits that we face when we try to change society. And it does this within the context of attempting to solve the subjectivism-objectivism divide in social theory.

Critics of realism have claimed that it does not really achieve its goal of providing a coherent structure–action account of society, and that analytical dualism is ultimately flawed in its insistence on treating social structures as real entities (see Harré 2002). Analytical dualism, the critics say, makes the fundamental error of treating what is only a *concept*, namely social structure, as an actual entity, when it is clear that social structure is wholly dependent on people and the meanings that individuals place upon things. In what way, therefore, can we talk about social structures as real entities? Archer's response is to argue that structures are real in the sense that they possess causal powers to either make something happen or to prevent other things from taking place. And any phenomenon which has the ability to change or to prevent change must, she argues, be considered to be real by definition.

Let's try to summarize where we are: Bhaskar and Giddens both reject positivist methodologies as inappropriate for social science. We will look at Giddens' views on this point below. But for Bhaskar this rejection is based on his argument that positivists are wrong to claim that we can only detect causality through observation. Laws are not discoverable through neutral observation techniques – they are not 'out there' waiting to be noticed. Instead, scientists establish the existence of laws through their own conceptual processes. The conceptual connections and arguments developed within scientific communities enable them to go beneath the surface appearance to get at the deeper causal processes generally hidden from non-scientific actors. The structural properties of society are not created by us, and always pre-exist us, but we can nevertheless produce and reproduce them. In this process, the structural properties take on an independent status, but because social causes are open-ended, human intervention can make a difference and can transform social structures, once we know enough about how they work. Bhaskar, then, seems to want to preserve the independent causal powers of social structures without claiming that those structures would exist without actors' meanings and activities. Archer, too, emphasizes that structures pre-exist us, and pushes the argument back into Durkheim's territory – structures are causal and entirely independent of actions and meanings.

In the work of Bhaskar and then Archer we find examples of two sustained attempts to develop theoretical support for the kind of sociological knowledge committed to maintaining the revelatory role of classic **Enlightenment** thought as a science of social causation. Such a science would provide the means by which to correct the errors or fill the gaps in lay actors' knowledge about their world. We will now examine Giddens' different interpretation of the relation between lay and social scientific knowledge.

## Anthony Giddens' structuration theory

Giddens' (1938–) development of structuration theory took place from the mid 1970s through to the mid 1980s (Giddens 1976, 1977, 1979, 1984). His work since then has covered a striking range of subjects, focusing on the specific character of modern and late modern social practices, from politics to intimacy, and including, as we shall see in the following chapter, issues to do with '**modernity**' and the 'risk society'.

Like Bhaskar, Giddens argues that positivist methodologies do not accurately describe what natural or social scientists actually do, but, unlike Bhaskar, he wants to maintain a clear boundary between natural and social science. His argument on this point becomes clear when he discusses the relationship between two different kinds of generalizations about the social world – those produced by social theorists and those produced by lay actors.

As we suggested above, Giddens draws heavily on hermeneutic and post-empiricist philosophers of science to argue, along parallel lines to Bourdieu and Bhaskar, that social theory must re-think the conceptual map it uses to understand how social structures are produced and reproduced. Again like Bourdieu and Bhaskar, Giddens insists that social theorists must approach the social world as one that is made and re-made by actors' practical and theoretical knowledge. This world, or more accurately, these worlds, are disclosed to actors via the multiple frames of meaning they employ. Giddens thus reminds us, as do Bhaskar and Bourdieu, that the social world is always encountered by social scientists as one which is pre-interpreted by actors. However, unlike Bhaskar and Archer, Giddens argues that this unique feature of social worlds means that we can never, in principle, say that the explanatory frameworks or generalizations produced by professional social scientists should be treated as invariant laws. For Giddens, the idea that this kind of generalization is what sociological knowledge should be looking to establish betrays a residual trace of positivism. In some ways, both the novelty and the simplicity of Giddens' position can be seen to develop from this point. We will therefore examine it in more detail.

There are a range of generalizations in use within social life; some of these hold because actors more or less consciously use them, and they are therefore not so much 'discovered' by social scientists as expressed by them in a more formal way. Another kind of generalization is understood by structural sociologists to 'refer to circumstances, or aspects of circumstances of which agents are ignorant and which effectively "act" on them, independent of whatever the agents may believe they are up to' (Giddens 1984: xix).

Structural sociologists are usually only interested in this latter kind of generalization – in explaining what actors didn't know about their situation but which nevertheless, or, more strongly, *because* of their ignorance, affected them. The effects of an actor's positioning in a class or gender hierarchy would be examples of this kind of circumstance. For his part, Giddens does not rule out the presence or value of generalizations deriving from what actors are unaware of, but his distinctive claim is that the status of these generalizations is only ever *provisional*. These generalizations cannot be given causal status of 'laws'. The uniqueness of social structures consists in the fact that they only ever have what he calls a 'virtual' existence. This means that such structures continue to exist only in so far as social actors continue to use them in their everyday lives. We will look in more detail at what Giddens might mean by this virtual existence below. For now we can draw out the clear implication of this provisional status: if structures are dependent on actors' knowledge and use of them, then the generalizations structural sociologists make about the conditions under which actors act, and of which they are unaware, will only hold for as long as the actors involved remain unaware of them. 'The circumstances in which generalizations about what "happens" to agents hold are mutable in respect of what those agents can learn knowledgeably to "make happen"' (Giddens 1984: xix).

Giddens makes a further distinctive claim: that the first kind of generalization, the kind made by people in their daily dealings with each other, is *as* important to social science as the second kind so valued by structural sociologists. Archer's work, for example, is devoted to establishing that this second kind of generalization can be made and can be granted the status of a causal law. Likewise, structural functionalists such as Parsons and Robert Merton, despite rejecting positivist methodologies, sought to produce generalizations of this second kind. For Giddens, the key point is that 'each form of generalization is unstable in respect of the other' (Giddens 1984: xix). In other words, social scientists cannot with any certainty predict the impact of their generalizations about social structures because once lay actors become aware of those generalizations they will incorporate them into their own frames of meaning and shape their future actions accordingly. For Giddens this means that it becomes absolutely essential to social science that those who engage in it have a detailed, highly reflexive understanding of actors' generalizations. Too often, he suggests, structural sociologists claim to have identified a causal power within social structures when all they have really identified is a gap in their own knowledge:

> the designation of just what is unintentional in regard of the consequences of action can be adequately grasped empirically only if the intentional aspects of action are identified, and this again, means operating with an interpretation of agency more sophisticated than is normally held by those inclined towards functionalist premises. (Giddens 1984: xxxi)

Until social scientists have thoroughly established what actors know about their situations the specification of actors' ignorance, and therefore of their being constrained by structures and 'caused' to do something, will be premature. This would appear to challenge Archer's point, above, when she argues that examples of the independent power of social structures include structural relations involving coercion, in which actors' meanings about what they are doing are over-ridden by ideological or more explicitly forceful measures. For Giddens, even this situation is in principle provisional, and cannot be used as an example of an invariant law.

As we might expect, Giddens' challenge to structural sociological approaches has not been taken lightly. Many of the criticisms levelled at his work concern what is often referred to as its excessive '**voluntarism**'. In this context, this term usually means that too much freedom to change social structures has been attributed to social agents and too much emphasis has been placed on their knowledge as the principle ingredient of such structures. The overall charge is that Giddens gives too little attention to all those situations where actors really do lack the power to alter their circumstances for the better. In a world so riven by inequality and exploitation, are Giddens' ideas not rather complacent, and perhaps really only applicable to the rich, western middle class?

Before this criticism can be evaluated we need to examine more closely what Giddens actually claims about the relationship between structure and agency. At this point it will be useful to look in more detail at what he believes is involved in actors' generalizations. What kinds of knowledge do actors have about their social world? Giddens breaks down such knowledge into two main kinds: **discursive** and **practical**. The former refers to an actor's ability to give an account of their conduct, an account which will rely on the actor's routine monitoring of their actions and their motivations for acting. However, alongside this, Giddens (like Bourdieu) also wants to draw out the significance of the actor's practical knowledge about their world. Both kinds of knowledge provide a home for social structures, as we shall see. Practical knowledge is tacit in nature; it is present in all actions of an habitual or taken-for-granted nature. Actors do not as a rule monitor such activities and would perhaps struggle to give an account of them.

## The duality of structure

Giddens' notion of social structures moves sharply away from the traditional conception a structure as a framework or girder which constrains social action. For Giddens, social structures are both enabling and constraining: they help us to make sense of the world, to achieve our purposes or goals, but they can also limit our room for manoeuvre in the social world. This leads him to define social structures in terms of the 'rules' and 'resources' that actors employ in their social relations, and which form part of their discursive and practical knowledge about the social world. However, the concepts of 'rules' and 'resources' have a specific meaning here. Giddens observes that a 'rule' tells an actor how to act in a particular social situation. Rules may provide either a tacit understanding of what one should do right now, or discursive knowledge of what is called for next. They are understood by all participants involved in a social interaction process and only make sense in the context of such interaction. It is important to note that these are not merely formulas. To take a well-known example, the rules of chess tell us how the knight can move or when the king is in checkmate, and they tell us what we, as players, can or cannot do next. It is obviously true that the rule of 'checkmate' only makes sense within the context of playing chess; applying it elsewhere would make no sense at all. The rules of social action are similar in that they are action-guiding, telling us, in the words of Wittgenstein, 'how to go on from here' in this or that social setting.

Resources, Giddens claims, relate to power relations, and are what actors bring to the interaction encounter. They come in two forms. As 'allocative resources' they refer to our command over material objects, and as 'authoritative resources' they stipulate command over other actors. Social structures are enabling in so far as actors have some degree of control over both kinds of resources. Those actors with the most useful resources possess what Giddens refers to as a 'transformative capacity' to change social structures.

Giddens' idea that social structures are both enabling and constraining is not the only sense in which his theory of structure is novel, for he also binds structure and social action together through the actors' memory. Social structures are, he says, mere memory traces, or the knowledge (both tacit and discursive) that actors in any given society possess. It is because action is here tied to structure and structure to action that Giddens' framework is described as a 'duality of structure'. This is the defining point of his account of social structure: actor and society are inseparable, each is dependent for its existence on the other. Duality here contrasts with the dualism of action and structure which we find in Archer's work, for example. In the latter case, as we may recall, action and structure are treated as separate aspects of a society or culture.

As Giddens makes clear, this dualism of action and structure is exemplified in our use of language. He observes that while speech and dialogue are complex accomplishments of their individual producers, we can only use and understand speech acts because each individual act employs the rules of language. These rules structure the speech act, and we draw on them even though many of us may not be able to state them formally. In our everyday language usage we also unintentionally reproduce the rules of the language being spoken. As a system of grammatical or syntactical rules, a language only continues to exist in so far as it is spoken by people in their everyday life. Hence, social structures are not things which exist separately from everyday interaction. They are produced and reproduced only within such interaction, and, furthermore, they exist in a virtual form. The rules of language, for example, only have existence in so far as they are held in the minds of actors who actually employ them or instantiate them in speech.

For Giddens, 'agency refers not to the intentions people have in doing things but to their capability of doing those things in the first place' (Giddens 1984: 9). Agency is thus best thought of in terms of an individual or group's access to the resources we outlined above. This idea of access to resources links to Giddens' specific use of the concept of power. He claims that power should not be tied to the idea of domination over someone else but instead is a more diffuse concept relating to the capacity to 'intervene in the world' (Giddens 1984: 14) or to refrain from intervening. If one has enough of the appropriate resources one can influence others' access to resources, but all social agents, by definition, have a degree of power, including the power to subvert or challenge the power of others.

## Social systems, agents and power

Critics of Giddens' structuration theory argue that it strays too far towards an **interpretive theory** of social action, or that it fails adequately to explain the ways in which social structures may prevent actors from doing what they want to do. These criticisms turn on Giddens' definitions of social structure and agency, as we have outlined above.

The criticisms levelled at Giddens' definition of social structures have varied considerably, but roughly they fall into the following categories. First, some have argued that the notion of 'rule' is either ambiguous or cannot do the job required of it (Held and Thompson 1989; Archer 1995; Mouzelis 1995, 2000). Second, but not unrelated, other more friendly critics have wondered whether it makes any sense to treat 'resources' in the same way as 'rules' as belonging to a 'virtual' order of reality. As Sewell observes, some resources, such as land or factories, have a material existence in the world, unlike rules (Sewell 1992: 10).

It has been pointed out that Giddens' definition of 'social structures' as rules and resources is quite unlike the traditional model of this concept (see Held and Thompson 1989). As we have seen in previous chapters, social structures are usually represented in social theory as if they are material objects that act like walls within **social systems**. But for Giddens a social structure only exists in the moment in which it is produced or reproduced by actors. This leads many to wonder how a study of virtual structures could explain the existence of systematic inequalities, for example. Giddens' response to this has been to refer his critics to a third dimension of society: that of social systems. The social system can be understood as the clustering of social structures into 'regularised relations of interdependence between individuals and groups' (Giddens 1979: 66). Social systems are standardized practices that exist in actual time and space as opposed to social structures that exist in the virtual world of individuals' memories. Whereas social structures are outcomes of social action, the analysis of social systems allows us to identify the unacknowledged conditions of action and the unintended consequences of such structures. Some of these activities may also be discursive or deliberately monitored attempts to maintain a systemic order or inequality.

Giddens offers an example of the way in which structuration theory may explain system inequalities and unequal power relations in his discussion of the 'poverty cycle' (Giddens 1979: 79). The poverty cycle, he claims, takes the following form: Material Deprivation → Poor Schooling → Low-level Employment → Material Deprivation. This cycle is maintained by many factors. Some might be described as controlling factors, such as the use of entry exams at secondary schools or the location of 'good' schools in middle-class neighbourhoods and 'bad' schools in working-class districts. Such factors may follow from deliberate policies aimed at maintaining a class hierarchy or based upon misguided assumptions concerning class and intelligence or class and vocational attributes. Other factors, Giddens observes, are unacknowledged conditions of action, such as the presence of a negative attitude towards education that can be found amongst working-class children, or the embedded nature of speech codes that either aid or hinder an individual's progress in an educational system that promotes those with elaborated speech structures. In this cycle we can observe all kinds of interrelated reasons (concerning intentional, unintentional and unacknowledged factors) as to why a working-class individual born into material deprivation is likely to stay in this condition throughout his or her life.

The second Giddensian concept that has caused concern is his notion of agency. His critics (see, especially, Archer 1982; Carlstein 1981; Held and Thompson 1989) have complained that Giddens' concept is overly voluntaristic, or that his definition appears to make it impossible for an individual not to be an agent. Giddens says that agency 'concerns events of which an individual is the perpetrator, in the sense that the individual could, at any phase in a given sequence of conduct, have acted differently' (Giddens 1984: 9). But he has repeatedly defended himself from charges of excessive voluntarism and has argued that his notion of agency is tied to a particular definition of power which, he says, is historically and empirically variable. As such, any understanding of both freedom and inequality must be based upon research, rather than assumed in advance.

To return briefly to the implications of these re-formulations of agency and structure for the production of sociological knowledge: Giddens is clear that in principle there is nothing that social scientists can discover about the social world which non-sociologists could not also know. From the point of view of action, Figure 7.1 shows that those parts of their social situation which the actor is not reflexively monitoring appear as unintended or unacknowledged aspects of the reproduction of social systems.

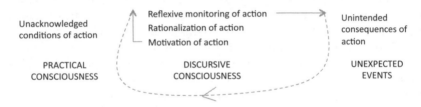

**Figure 7.1:** The Stratification Model of Action
Adapted from Giddens (1979: 56)

On the right-hand side of the diagram is what Giddens calls the unintended consequences of action. They and the unacknowledged conditions of action on the left-hand side of the diagram take place in a taken-for-granted realm. These are important because they indicate the way in which social structures are interdependently related and how systemic features of a society may be maintained even though they escape the purposes of the actors engaged in their reproduction. Giddens argues that social scientists can usefully contribute to our knowledge of such aspects of social experience, as well as of their longer term consequences. And, as he points out, social scientists belong to the same community of language users as those they study. In this context, the knowledge and theories that sociologists produce are always going to feed back into the knowledge used by lay actors. Giddens refers to this process as a 'double hermeneutic'.

## Conclusion

The three approaches that we have looked at in this chapter share the goal of overcoming the subject–object divide within social theory. They each recognize the importance of incorporating into social theory a toolkit for understanding action and the power that regularized or institutionalized structures of behaviour have upon social life. At the same time there is an attempt, in each account, to incorporate essential elements of the interpretivist emphasis upon the meaning that actors place upon events and social activities and the ability of actors to purposefully change society. Each theory might be said to start with Karl Marx's famous dictum from 1852 that people 'make their own history, but they do not make it just as they please; they do not make it under circumstances chosen by themselves, but under circumstances directly encountered, given, and transmitted from the past'.

The issues raised by Bourdieu, Bhaskar, Archer and Giddens pick up the threads from an earlier period of social theory and also offer somewhat contrasting visions of its future direction. The overview of social theory's past, present and possible futures offered by these authors closely overlaps with the subject of the final chapters in this book, which more explicitly focus on debates between **modernists** and **postmodernists** about what the ideals of the Enlightenment might mean for us now. As we shall see in the following chapter, much of the debate between modernists and postmodernists concerns whether a belief in the possibility of furthering freedom through reason is actually an attempt to justify controlling the natural and social world, or whether the critique of such Enlightenment hopes is itself an excuse for a dangerous from of irrationalism within which how deeply one feels about something becomes more important than being able to give good reasons for believing it.

## Further reading

Baert, Patrick and Carreira da Silva, Filipe (2009): *Social Theory in the Twentieth Century and Beyond*, 2nd edn, Polity.

Bryant, Christopher and Jary, David (eds) (2010): *Giddens' Theory of Structuration: a critical appreciation*, Routledge.

Collier, Andrew (1994): *Critical Realism*, Verso.
Parker, John (2000): *Structuration*, Open University Press.
Robbins, Derek (2000): *Bourdieu and Culture*, Sage.
Stones, Rob (2005): *Structuration Theory*, Palgrave Macmillan.

# 8 POSTMODERNITY, POSTMODERNISM AND ITS CRITICS

## Introduction

In the last chapter we looked at how contemporary social theorists have attempted to overcome problems which arise in the study of agents and social structures. Each of the approaches we discussed necessarily begins from the premise that it is possible to study and make judgements about social relationships and practices. Such a view is by its very nature a **modernist** one. However, there is an alternative view to this, and it is one that rose to prominence in the 1990s. 'Post-modern' social theory does not exactly ignore debates about the relationship between social agents and structures, but it casts all modernist claims as poorly disguised longings for a kind of control and certainty that, if it ever existed, is certainly long dead now. For the thinkers of the **Enlightenment** – the modernists – an important goal of the sciences was to establish distinctions between aspects of social life. By contrast, the authors we will be discussing in this chapter claim that in a postmodern society any such boundaries that did exist are now largely erased. For example, in **modernity** we could easily distinguish between high and low culture, reality and representation (TV, film, literature), politics and advertising, economic life and culture, or production and exchange. Today, however, such differences are not straightforwardly obvious, as each of these categories tends to blur into the others. For postmodernist thinkers, this fragmentation of social life represents an exhaustion of the social scientific **project of modernity**. Of this project, they claim, there now exists nothing but shrapnel, and any attempt to build a system of knowledge around this debris is doomed to fail.

Before we unpack this claim, and look at the response of its critics, we must first introduce a distinction between **postmodernity** and **postmodernism**.

'Postmodernity' refers to the view that the institutions and ways of living characteristic of modernity have been replaced by new institutional features to such a profound extent that it is no longer plausible to see the twenty-first century as a continuation of modernity. Modernity has ended and we now live in a new era, that of postmodernity. We thus need new ways of making sense of this transformed world; as Bauman puts it: 'a theory of postmodernity . . . cannot be a modified theory of modernity . . . it needs its own vocabulary' (Bauman 1992: 188). In contrast, the term 'postmodernism', though obviously intimately connected to postmodernity, refers to new ways of thinking about *thought* – to new ways of understanding *ideas*, *beliefs* and *knowledge* – rather than to new ways of living and organizing social affairs.

## From modernity to postmodernity?

It is clear that, in recent times, the preoccupations of the classic theorists of modernity have been found wanting when it comes to making sociological sense of significant aspects of how we live. For obvious reasons, Durkheim, Marx and Weber have little to say directly about issues that are of crucial importance for us living now, such as threats to the environment, the dangers posed by the proliferation of nuclear weapons, and the risks and uncertainties associated with scientific and technological advances. It is perhaps less obvious why they should have neglected to look in a sustained way at gender and race issues, or issues surrounding war and nationalism, but these, too, are major concerns for our times which require us to go beyond traditional theorizing to properly address.

The task of producing new conceptual frameworks that will help us to understand the world as it is today has driven the work of some of sociology's major living theorists, such as Anthony Giddens, Jürgen Habermas (1929–), Ulrich Beck (1944–) and Manuel Castells (1942–). We will look at some of Habermas' ideas towards the end of this chapter, and at the current views of Giddens and Beck in the next chapter.

These writers, however, though sensitive to the new concerns that need to be addressed by sociology today, are most certainly not postmodernists. They believe that the contemporary world is still best interrogated by building on the intellectual and theoretical tools that have helped us to understand modernity and modernism. It is this continuation of the modernist approach that postmodernists disagree with, arguing instead that radical new ways of thinking sociologically are needed to make sense of what is, for them, a new Great Transformation.

In Chapter 1 we briefly summarized the transformations ushered in by the emergence of modernity. These included the rise of **capitalism**, of mass production techniques, of large urban conglomerations, of the nation-state, of Western global dominance and of the **secularization** of knowledge. The question now is: in what ways have these characteristic elements of modern life been so dramatically altered that some have been led to describe the contemporary era as a time of postmodernity? For many commentators, one of the key features of life today is **globalization**. There is much debate about the meaning and precise significance of this concept, and we do not have the space here to even begin to do justice to the different viewpoints involved. It is therefore important to remember that what follows is merely an outline sketch of some of the features of our lives today to which the term 'globalization' generally refers.

## Dimensions of globalization

### Global capitalism

Capitalism has dramatically altered since its establishment as the economic dynamic behind modernity. It has long since left its moorings in the harbours of individual countries and is today rampant on the high seas and throughout the globe. No longer confined to the West, the relentless pursuit of profit has penetrated into the furthest reaches of the world. It has become a global phenomenon, far beyond the reach of national regulation. The significant players in contemporary capitalism are the multinational – or, more accurately, *transnational* – corporations. Owing no allegiance to particular nations, transnationals operate *in* countries, but not *for* countries. Profitability determines the location of manufacturing. If wage costs can be kept down by locating production in countries without trade unions – and therefore without established wage-bargaining procedures – then this is considered good business, even if it involves using so-called 'sweatshop' labour. Research and development may still have to be located in the educated West, but the manufacturing of the developed product usually takes place where returns can be maximized. This profit-driven tendency to relocate production away from the West has been accompanied by a corresponding expansion of the service industries in Europe and the USA, and by the rise of fears about long-term mass unemployment in these countries.

## The nation-state in the twenty-first century

The emergence of these features of global capitalism has in turn threatened the power of the nation-state. Even when corporate decisions go against their national interests, there seems little that governments can do to restrict the rampaging dominance of transnational capitalism. Indeed, it could be argued that the only time transnational corporations consult national governments is when it makes good business sense – when there is something in it for them. For example, governments often have to offer considerable financial incentives to the corporations to get them to locate their production in the West.

## Population growth and urbanization in the twenty-first century

Along with the decline in power of the nation-state, two other original features of modernity have been reversed. Today, rapid population growth and urbanization is taking place in the Third World, whereas cities are in decline in the First World. Furthermore, there has been a real shift in global power relations; recent years have seen a considerable expansion of wealth and power in Asia at the expense of Europe.

## The globalization of markets and marketing

Markets have become global too. Go into any supermarket and look at the place of origin of the products on sale there, or go into a clothes store such as Gap, or French Connection, and look at the labels which say where the garments were made. The global nature of manufacturing production and distribution will become all too apparent. The marketing of these products is another global activity. Advertising and promotion knows no national boundaries and exactly the same techniques of image-construction and branding designed to entice and seduce can be found in all parts of the world, West, East, North and South. However, unlike in the production process of early modernity, the mass production of a standardized good is a thing of the past. Mass production has been replaced by a much more flexible system enabling both a wider range and faster turnover of goods, and mass marketing has been replaced by promotion tailored to local circumstances, a process known as 'niche marketing'.

## The network society

The Information Revolution – the way in which instant electronic communication has obliterated traditional notions of time and space – has been another principal impetus behind globalization. It has transformed the management of capitalism, particularly finance capitalism: dealing in investments of various kinds is now a global activity and mainly conducted electronically. Mass media communication is another clearly global phenomenon. Thanks to TV, video and film, few parts of the world are unaffected by the images and narratives pumped out on a 24/7 basis by the media. This means our knowledge of the world is no longer limited by time and space. We now routinely peer into the worlds of others whose existence we would never have known about unless we had physically visited them. For the Spanish social theorist Manuel Castells, this communication revolution has been *the* defining transformation of our existence; indeed, he labels our contemporary global world the 'network society' (Castells 1996).

The changes involved in globalization are recognized by all kinds of contemporary theorists. What is distinctive about postmodernist analyses are the conclusions and inferences they draw from these changes and the emphases they place in their accounts.

## Identity in postmodernity

> Our world is being remade. Mass production, the mass consumer, the big city, big-brother state, the sprawling housing estate, and the nation-state are in decline: flexibility, diversity, differentiation, and mobility, communication, decentralization and internationalization are in the ascendant. In the process, our own identities, our sense of self, our own subjectivities are being transformed. We are in transition to a new era. (Hall et al. 1988: 24–9)

As the penultimate sentence in this quote indicates, it is the relationship between institutional changes and *identity* that has been the focus of much sociological attention in recent years. This is particularly true of postmodernist analyses. One of the principal elements in a typical postmodernist account concerns the way postmodern humans live their lives and see themselves. In modernity the centrality of work in people's lives found expression both in their sense of themselves –

'I am what I do' – and in the work-based social groupings to which they belonged. For example, as we noted in Chapter 1, two of the distinctive features of modernity are class membership based on occupational rewards and the existence of workplace organizations, such as trade unions, set up to engage in collective bargaining with employers/managers.

For many postmodernists, one of the central features of postmodernity is the way work and production have given way to **consumption**, both as the lynchpin of social cohesion and as the source of individual identity. One of the leading supporters of the idea of postmodernity is Zygmunt Bauman. Here is how David Lyon describes Bauman's view of this profound shift in our lives:

> Bauman rightly argues that for the first part of its history, modern capitalism placed work (or at least paid employment) in a central position. Work held a pivotal role, linking the individual motivation of the worker, the means whereby a network of social relationships and friendships was developed, and the way that the whole system was kept running efficiently. But work as paid employment has undergone some radical changes over the past quarter-century, and the idea of a secure lifelong job, trade or profession has increasingly become history. Employment has become casualised, part-time, uncertain and insecure (and this affects both women and men), and the multiple career, retraining and early retirement (or layoff) seems more like the norm. This is hardly a basis for personal motivation, let alone the fostering of stable communities and liveable localities. (Lyon 2000: 227)

For Bauman, since we can no longer slot into pre-existing identities based on occupation and class, we have to be more creative in the way we construct ourselves. For him, this is where the purchase of consumer goods comes in. According to Bauman, what is postmodern about these circumstances is the way consumption has become the central feature of our existence as we have turned to focusing on possessions as the main means of expressing who we are. Lyon summarizes this view as follows:

> The consumer system needs credit-card-happy shoppers, and there is also a sense in which consumers feel themselves bound to shop. They are pressurised both by the constant need to keep up with others and to demonstrate their style, up-to-dateness and social fit; and also by merchandising companies who both define the good life – above all through relentless advertising – and go to great lengths to channel the choices of consumers ... Both symbolic rivalry and social management together

form, not a mode of pressure felt by oppression, but a system of (what Pierre Bourdieu . . . calls) seduction. (Lyon 2000: 227)

According to Bauman, this preoccupation with consumption produces a new form of stratification. For those with the means to join in, consumption fetishism offers a choice of lifestyle unimaginable in modernity. But for those whose lack of means disenfranchises them from living in consumer society – those whom Bauman calls 'flawed consumers' – their inability to acquire possessions makes their outsider status only too visible. However, even for those happily on holiday, inside the shopping mall, or tuned in to the shopping channels, postmodern life brings new uncertainties and insecurities. This is how Lyon characterizes Bauman's take on this aspect of postmodern existence:

> Any apparent 'order' is local, transient and emergent, rather like a river whirlpool that maintains its pattern but is constantly renewed. Rather than use 'society', the term 'sociality' should be adopted to express the processual, the play of randomness and pattern, and the notion of structure as an emergent accomplishment. Human agency . . . is foregrounded, such that choices made in the agent's life add up to self-constitution or self-assembly. The corresponding item to be dropped is any notion of 'progress'. Mobility and change there may well be, but not in any clear direction. Time is thus unbound, in that ties with the past are weakened, leaving less space for the future to be colonised. (Lyon 2000: 228)

This leads us neatly to the other main element of postmodernist thinking – the rejection of modernist notions of progress through truth. Here we turn our attention away from the nature of postmodern*ity* to the ideas of postmodern*ism*.

## From modernism to postmodernism?

Postmodern thinking applies not only to social organizations, but also to all other realms of human activity and production, like art, architecture and literature, for example. The focus is on pluralism and on competing accounts of the nature of virtue, style, truth and falsehood. It is also on the impermanence and instability of such definitions – the transience of certainties and the chronically brief life of truths. Postmodernism thus represents a reaction to the modern Enlightenment-sponsored search for *the* truth, for ultimate meaning, and the true nature of reality. Instead, the superficial and ephemeral nature of contemporary human life is emphasized. Here, because of the persistently impermanent character of claims to truth, it is fashion, trend and image that have come to matter more than substance and meaning. In particular, the cultural dominance of the mass media is highlighted, where reality and identity are constructed for us by advertising, popular music and television soap operas. So although the mass media shrinks our world, with its ability to transcend time and space, this gives us no more meaningful a purchase on 'reality' – it simply multiplies the number, frequency and impermanence of the accounts of reality we consume. What we 'see' via the media inevitably constitutes a major source of our knowledge in a postmodern world – but what we see and know, and therefore are, operates merely in the here and now, and then only until another story comes along.

Postmodern forms of representation are, according to Fredric Jameson (1934–), superficial and lack real understanding of the world. Jameson claims that we no longer delve into the underlying meaning of things or objects but are satisfied with surface meanings and images. This is a world emptied of emotional and ethical meaning. Jameson offers the example of Andy Warhol's paintings of Campbell soup cans, which are nothing more than perfect representations – they are simulacra, copies of a copy, allegedly painted from a photographic image. Contrast this with Edvard Munch's modernist series of paintings entitled *The Scream*. Munch's art offers a depth of emotion which seems to seek out an observer, whereas Warhol's paintings are emotionless or without sentiment. Stephan Meštrović argues that this loss of depth in understanding affects our sense of empathy towards other people. He calls this the post-emotional condition, and describes it in the following way:

> It is a society in which people do not react to what, in an earlier era, would have been stirring occurrences and crises. Rather, individuals have become blasé, allergic to involvement, yet intelligent enough to know that the events are significant, and perhaps even to know that in an earlier era individuals would have responded with deep emotional empathy, or equally deep emotional antipathy, to particular individuals, and to the events surrounding them. (Meštrović 1997: ix)

Ralph Fevre, in *The Demoralization of Western Cultures*, provides an example of post-emotional confusion following the revelations in November 1998 that the American President Bill Clinton had been involved in an affair with a White House intern named Monica Lewinsky. When the affair first came to light Clinton denied any involvement and lied in court and in public about his having had sexual relations with Lewinsky. Eventually the truth came out and

Clinton was impeached by the House of Representatives for perjury on 19 December 1998. What shocked Fevre in this news story was not the affair itself but the reaction of the American people to Clinton's behaviour – and to the subsequent lies he told. In such circumstances, Fevre argues, one would expect a President's standing amongst voters to take a substantial dip. Instead, American opinion polls at this time recorded an increase in Clinton's popularity as voters again and again defended him on the grounds that 'he is only human', or asserted that they too 'would have lied in his situation'. Thus, according to Fevre, Americans did not so much excuse their President as refuse to judge him.

With similar concerns to those of Jameson, the French social philosopher Jean Baudrillard (1929–2007) characterized postmodern society as a form of what he called 'hyperreality'. That is, a world in which there is a breakdown between reality and the media representation of reality. In this world, Baudrillard claimed, the image is more 'real' than the real itself. Television is one example of this. TV allows no space for a relationship between the real and the imaginary as real life dissolves into television similes and it is these images that we take as the real. Thus, hyperreality is characterized by simulacra – copies of the real that are taken by audiences to be the real. Baudrillard, for example, claimed that the first Gulf War was fought not as a real war but as a 'simulacra of a war' where the allied military targeted and attacked their foe through the use of computer simulations rather than real objects. Disneyland and Las Vegas are other examples of simulated reality. In Vegas, Baudrillard observed, one can visit Paris, London and other great cities within the space of a mile. Such simulacra make the real redundant. Baudrillard saw no way out of hyperreality. Looking below its surface, he explained, would be pointless, for it is nothing but surface representation.

We can draw an analogy between this postmodernist account of the acquisition of knowledge and the social construction of consumption in general. It does not take much thought to realize the pivotal role of media manipulation in the establishment of (deliberately transitory) notions of what is fashionable and what is not in the minds of consumers. Take clothing for example. The exercise of power in advertising is designed to produce in the consumer a belief in the attractiveness of, and (sometimes) therefore the desire to possess, an item of clothing. According to postmodernism, this is how the social construction of knowledge works too. Just as consumers of clothes are subject to the power of advertising and promotion, so the consumers of, for example, moral positions are subject to the power of *their* promotion. There is no objective or inherent beauty in one item of clothing that elevates it over another. The one *appears* more beautiful than the other as a result of the power exercised on its behalf to define it as being so. For postmodernism, the same is true of moral positions. There is no moral judgement that is objectively right or objectively wrong. One appears right and the other appears wrong because more power is being exercised to promote the former rather than the latter.

## Modernism versus postmodernism

The debate between modernists and postmodernists about the nature of knowledge is reflected in their respective views on the nature of freedom. According to one view held by modernist thinkers, we can only become free if we live according to what it is reasonable to expect in relation to a series of goals and calculated risks, whereas for postmodernists we will only be free when nobody feels able to tell us how to live.

We might see extreme proponents of the modernist position as, in effect, Truth merchants – purveyors of the one and only answer. The missionaries we normally encounter in our everyday lives are religious ones – for example, Mormon elders (though in my experience they are always very young men) who stop us in the street to talk to us about their faith. What they are doing is trying to sell us what they know to be true.

But perhaps all promoters of modernist theories are in effect secular missionaries. For example, Marx used the word *praxis* to describe the importance of not just knowing the truth – understanding the human world – but of taking political action to re-organize the world according to these insights. Thus, in good modernist Truth-merchant fashion, he demanded that the 'Workers of the world unite! You have nothing to lose but your chains!' Feminists have been among the twentieth-century heirs to this unification of theory and practice: from the suffragette movement onwards, feminist theorists have advocated the importance of women taking action on behalf of feminist politics. This is the meaning of the term 'consciousness-raising' after all. Whether their goal is anti-racism, anti-sexism, anti-homophobia or whatever, activists invariably represent the political wing of a modernist theoretical analysis.

Such political action in support of the Truth takes place on a grander scale too. For example, the US-led war against the Taliban in Afghanistan was self-consciously portrayed by the protagonists – in the rhetoric of President George W. Bush, Prime Minister Tony Blair and their successors – as a 'crusade' on behalf of freedom, liberty and democracy. Years later it is still seen as justified in moral terms as well as retaliatory and strategic ones. But the Taliban see their fight in exactly the same terms: a *jihad* is a holy war, fought against infidel unbelievers, and also on behalf of freedom and liberty. How can this be? How can two sides in a bloody war be fighting for the same thing?

For postmodernism, of course, it is because notions of freedom and liberty are *relative* – someone considered a terrorist from one standpoint will almost certainly be considered a freedom fighter from another. It is this fact – that human concepts such as right and wrong, truth and falsehood or good and bad are inevitably relative to the way the world is looked at – that has led postmodernists to reject modernist thinking. This is precisely the position of Jean-François Lyotard (1924–98), author of *The Postmodern Condition*. Lyotard argued that modernist authors who claim to have found a formula for reaching a consensus or rational agreement about moral and political issues are misguided cultural imperialists. He asserts that the modernist's ideal of seeking universal agreement through dialogue is impossible, and is bound to result in ethnocentric outcomes. The principles that are adopted belong to Western thought and it is the West that has the force to impose them. Lyotard's alternative to what he describes as the grand narratives of Western philosophy is a celebration of difference that is designed, so he claimed, to take account of cultural pluralism. For Lyotard, knowledge can only be advanced by seeking out and accepting uncertainty and paradox, instead of searching for a higher truth.

Lyotard's work borrowed heavily from Ludwig Wittgenstein's later philosophy, and in particular the latter's notion of 'language games'. Wittgenstein likened social rules to the rules of games. Social rules, like those of, say, chess, only make sense within the context of a specific culture, just as the rules concerning checkmate or the way in which the knight piece moves only make sense within the context of chess. Social rules, then, understood as language games, cannot be naturalized or made real outside of the milieu in which they are found. Lyotard, in basing the core of his social theory around this concept, argued that each culture has its own set of language games or social rules that only really make sense within the context of that culture or society. Dialogue between cultures, he claimed, must begin with a paradox: the fact that language games are not translatable from one culture to another and do not follow fixed universal principles. In this sense the idea of universal reasoning or agreement makes no sense. Instead, Lyotard argued, we must accept what he called 'differends'. That is, we must learn to live with cultural differences and not attempt to settle disparities through forceful manipulation. Forceful settlements by the powerful abound in Western history, not just in terms of imperialism but also within Western societies themselves, as for example when workers must negotiate the objectification of their own labour in the language of employers, or feminists must challenge men in a **patriarchal** idiom, or, perhaps some might suggest, when members of an Islamic faith must address their protagonists in the language of Western principles of democracy.

From this point of view, missionary work by Truth merchants is actually no more than cultural imperialism – the imposition of one cultural version of truth onto others. Like most imperialism, it is of course carried out in the name of liberation, but, again like most imperialism, it is in fact no more than an (often vulgar) exercise of power. It involves the use of power to degrade and, ultimately, to destroy, other equally legitimate ways of thinking and living simply because those who subscribe to them are powerless to protect themselves and resist. According to postmodernism, only when we come to accept that there can be no objectively 'True' human knowledge, just as there can be no 'True' human language, will we be free. This will be a freedom from the dogmatism, bigotry and intolerance that always characterizes the behaviour of those who believe they have a monopoly over Truth. For postmodernism, humankind does need liberating – not *by* 'the Truth' but *from* the whole idea of 'the Truth'. Real liberty means being given the freedom to be different – to be tolerated even though we are 'the Other'. This kind of liberty means being free to be who we have to be, as our knowledge permits, without being distrusted or despised, or hated or punished for it, just as those different from us can also do the same. Postmodernism insists that the only real freedom possible for culturally constructed human beings is that which comes from abandoning the modernist fallacy that humans can use reason to know things as they really are. Such a view implies that using reason somehow gives us the means to step outside of our culture and its influence and to know right and wrong, truth and falsehood for certain. For postmodernism, however, since we can never escape culture, we can never know anything for certain. Humans can only ever know via language and **discourse**, and languages and discourses can never be true or false or right or wrong.

Many different kinds of objections have been made to the postmodernist account of human existence. In the following chapter we will look at the criticisms raised by Ulrich Beck and Anthony Giddens. First though, we will examine the highly critical response of the German social and political theorist, Jürgen Habermas.

## Habermas and communicative rationality

Habermas is very much the modern heir to the ideals of the Enlightenment. His 1987 work, *The Philosophical Discourse of Modernity*, shows him to be a fierce advocate of the virtues and continued relevance of modernist thinking for our times, rejecting the postmodernist assault on the possibility of humans achieving progress through Truth. For Habermas, we can – and must – keep faith with the Enlightenment belief in the power of human rationality to enable us to know things for certain, because this power resides in our basic human ability to communicate with each other.

For Habermas, we are not hamstrung by culture, as the postmodernists argue. No matter how divergent our cultural backgrounds, and no matter how radically different our life-experiences, humans always have one thing in common – our unique ability to use language to communicate. Habermas insists that so long as we are earnest in our desire to do so, it is this ability to communicate through language that will always enable us to reach out to each other across cultural divides, and so to forge a cross-cultural moral community.

Habermas has been influenced by a wide range of theories and his approach represents an imaginative fusion of previously disparate ideas. In particular, he makes strategic use of important Marxian, Weberian and action theory concepts as major constituents of his perspective.

Habermas is critical of Marx for over-emphasizing the political significance of the economy and of labour in human societies and relationships, and for underplaying the significance of interaction (Habermas 1986). This critique is an important part of Habermas' overall project to re-think the significance of interaction and communication in line with the key insights of **hermeneutic** philosophers such as Gadamer, who we discussed in the previous chapter. Our capacity to use language to disclose the world to ourselves and to others is, Habermas claims, the route by which we can strive to realize the positive and humane potential of modernity. He does not suggest that social practices associated with labour are unimportant, but he does insist that all such practices must be brought under the control of the wider community via moral-ethical communication.

Habermas describes activities within the economy, and the instrumental values and forms of communication associated with such activities, as belonging to 'the system' (Habermas 1984). Those practices and communication strategies belonging to the rest of our dealings with each other as social agents he describes with a term taken from Schutz: 'the life-world'. For Habermas, the most deep-rooted and serious problems modern societies face, from human exploitation to environmental destruction, are caused by the needs and values of 'the system' encroaching upon the 'life-world'. In Weberian terms then, Habermas is arguing that the problems facing modernity are not our 'fate', but have arisen from a specific imbalance.

Like Weber, Habermas distinguishes between two types of rational action – **instrumental rationality**, action oriented to the achievement of efficiency in human life, and *value-oriented rationality* – the use of reason to distinguish between right and wrong. As we saw in Chapter 4, Weber saw instrumental rationality gaining a tighter and tighter grip on human behaviour in modernity and was profoundly pessimistic about the chances of this stranglehold ever being broken. For Weber, the modern preoccupation with efficiency, calculation and predictability means the increasing neglect of spiritual matters, a process he termed **disenchantment**. He saw the future for modern life in extremely bleak terms. He predicted a future characterized by an overwhelming obsession with how to get things done in the most efficient ways possible with little or no thought given to values – to notions of good and bad, right and wrong. That is, he foresaw a world in which concerns about the essence of being a human – concerns about how we *should* live, how we *should* behave, what kinds of people we *should* be – would become increasingly irrelevant. For Weber, then, modernity is the triumph not just of rationality, but of instrumental rationality. In other words, it is not the fault of rationality as such. We can use reason to think about how we should live as well as using it to calculate how to be efficient, but we hardly ever do, and we will do so less and less. This is why, for Weber, the prospect for humankind is such a depressing, soulless and disenchanted one.

Habermas does not agree. He accepts that the use of reason since the Enlightenment has been as Weber describes – that human rationality has principally been harnessed to the search for instruments of effectiveness. But unlike Weber he sees the potential for using reason for more noble ends – to enable us to do good and be good – as enormous. All that is required is a new belief in the power of value-oriented rationality. The problem, says Habermas, is that we have allowed instrumental rationality to become our yardstick in areas of life where it is inappropriate. He is certainly perfectly happy for the pursuit of efficiency to dominate in those realms of human activity where it is appropriate – that is, in the social system. Where we have gone wrong, he says, is that we have allowed instrumental rationality to become our yardstick in matters of value as well; as he puts it, we have made the mistake of allowing the life-world to be *colonized* by instrumental rationality.

This point returns us to Marx's insight that since all aspects of society are created by human relationships, any problems we experience can in principle be solved by human means, if we try hard enough and exert our uniquely human faculty of accountable communication in doing so. For Habermas, what we therefore have to do in order to establish a moral community including members of our own and other cultures is to do what we, as humans, do all the time, in every social occasion in which we are implicated. We must talk to each other in order to find common ground and establish a consensus with others over contested meanings. It is because we are capable of being rational and reasonable in these matters – and have to be so in order to co-exist at all with others in our everyday social encounters – that we can employ exactly the same techniques to reach across cultural divides too. Habermas' point is that nobody enters into a conversation with another without assuming that an agreement can be reached about meaning. For example, a customer does not communicate with a shopkeeper except in the belief that the shopkeeper wishes to serve him. Likewise, the shopkeeper speaks to the customer in the belief that he or she wishes to make a purchase. That is, they share a view of their encounter that informs the way they communicate with each other. Each of them reasons that the other will behave reasonably in order to achieve a reasonable outcome.

According to Habermas, much less mundane encounters can operate in the same way. Take political arguments, for example. So long as the parties to a communicative exchange have an equal opportunity to state their views, and so long as they treat each other as equals and honestly seek agreement, such agreement is always possible. It is only impossible if the exchange is one-sided or the desire to reach agreement is fraudulent. Obviously, humans can talk at each other until they are blue in the face and will never agree if reaching agreement is not what they want. If a powerful person wants to use a communicative encounter to humiliate and subjugate a weaker one then of course this is what will happen. If one person is determined not to listen to other points of view and is not prepared to shift their position then of course communication will get nowhere. We are all familiar with communicative encounters where this is precisely the case. But if the parties to an exchange genuinely do want to agree, and everyone has the same chance to state their views, then an agreed outcome is always achievable.

In short, so long as a communicative encounter is approached rationally – with reason – differences can be overcome. Of course we can be pig-headed and unreasonable if we want to be. But, by the same token, we can also be reasonable and rational, if we so choose. Rational communication is unique to human beings, and Habermas argues that it is precisely this ability that gives us the chance of living in a world that is not just physically shared but morally shared too.

It is important to recognize that Habermas is referring here to the ethical significance of those daily acts of communication we all engage in and not only or especially to those belonging to professionals, academics or politicians. Habermas is thus offering another way of reassessing the importance of what Giddens refers to as the inherent knowledgeability of social agents. For both theorists, any attempt to make a difference to how the world works would have to involve ordinary human knowledge and communication. And a common target of both theorists' critiques of other social theorists and philosophers, from positivists to postmodernists, is their tendency to underplay or ignore the moral, ethical and, in broad terms, political significance of ordinary language, knowledge and relationships. This is all some way removed from the postmodernist argument that all knowledge is a form of control, and language a means of domination and exclusion of the other.

## Conclusion

We can identify two ways of regarding postmodernism: as a version of relativism that usefully reminds us that we don't know all the answers, or as a form of nihilism arguing for the destruction or futility of all values. Undoubtedly, postmodernism is relativistic. The modernists' dependency on unity, grand narratives, intellectualism and notions of progress are rejected and in their place is a celebration of pluralism, the non-rational and the local (all of which contradict the supposed realities of globalization identified by Jameson and Baudrillard).

There is some defence for the postmodern position. First, in relation to the claim that it subverts objective standards of truth and thus the distinction between knowledge and belief, it does not necessarily follow that holding a relativist position is the same as rejecting the view that some forms of argument or knowledge are better than others. And, of course, many recent versions of social theory or research are essentially relativist – ethnomethodology and conversation analysis are prime examples – but they do not hold that, for example, all scientific knowledge is worthless. Stephen Crook sums up this point, as offering a more moderate version of relativism, when he observes that 'to consider scientific (or any other) knowledge as a "construct" is not to debunk it, but to focus attention on the way it is produced' (Ritzer and Smart 2001: 313).

Equally, the influence of postmodern social theory in more substantial areas of sociology – studies of gender, deviance and multiculturalism are good examples – has had the salutary effect of emphasizing the existence of difference rather than debunking any notion of rational order in general. Furthermore, theorists such as Bauman might argue that one of the aims of postmodern social theory is to re-enchant the world – to rescue social research from linear rational models. As he remarks:

> The postmodern world is one in which mystery is no more a barely tolerated alien awaiting a deportation order . . . We learn to live with events and acts that are not only not-yet-explained, but (for all we know about what we will ever know) inexplicable. We learn again to respect ambiguity, to feel regard for human emotions, to appreciate actions without purpose and calculable rewards. (Bauman 1993: 33)

On the other hand, the relativism of some postmodernist social theorists has verged on the nihilistic view that any one form of knowledge is as good as any other. The critique of postmodern normative concerns is in some respects more important. The playfulness of postmodernism does appear to lead to the conclusion that it is marked by a failure to set limits to the scope of moral and political values. And, as Crook again notes, 'postmodern approaches are at their least compelling when they seem to be in the grip of attenuated, residual ghosts of modern dreams or purity – whether in epistemology and method or values and politics' (Ritzer and Smart 2001: 315).

Habermas himself has been very critical of postmodern social theory. He rightly points to the notoriously vague answers that have been supplied by postmodernists in relation to questions of political action. For modernists, answers to contemporary problems are usually clear cut – consider the response of Marxists or contemporary animal rights activists, or environmentalists, or feminists. For postmodernists, the answer always seems to be the same: 'resistance'. For Foucault we should resist relations of 'power'; for Lyotard the weak should resist the strong. But in both cases the concepts used are vague, and, as Habermas has noted, can be as equally aligned to 'conservative' as to 'progressive' thinking (Habermas 1981). As we shall see in the following chapter, Habermas is not alone in his insistence that rather than abandon any hope of constructively applying rational thought to the dilemmas of contemporary society, as postmodernists suggest, we must instead update and renew our efforts to understand the specific problems we late moderns now face.

## Further reading

Cahoone, L. (ed.) (2003): *From Modernism to Postmodernism: an anthology expanded*, 2nd edn, Blackwell.
Delanty, Gerard (2000): *Modernity and Postmodernity*, Sage.
Dodd, Nigel (1999): *Social Theory and Modernity*, Polity.
Harvey, David (1989): *The Condition of Postmodernity*, Blackwell.
Lash, Scott (1990): *Sociology of Postmodernism*, Routledge.
Smart, Barry (1992): *Postmodernity*, Routledge.

# 9 RETHINKING MODERNITY

## Introduction

### Anthony Giddens: analysing late modernity

Giddens attacks strong versions of **postmodernism** on several grounds. First, as we saw earlier, he rejects the term **postmodernity** since it implies that we no longer live in **modernity** – that human existence has left modernity behind. He thinks this is a serious misrepresentation of the situation. For Giddens, the point about contemporary life is that modernity has altered and is characterized by new circumstances, new forces and new turbulence and uncertainty, but not that it no longer exists. As a result, for him, the sociology of modernity still provides us with the right conceptual tools with which to make sense of social existence today.

Second, Giddens rejects the postmodernist portrayal of the human actor as wholly in the thrall of discursive influences and incapable of independent, creative action. For him, the social actor or agent is most certainly not dead. But neither is he or she in any sense an isolated individual, building social order in the total absence of any structural features or constraints. Giddens gives us an account of contemporary existence – *late modernity*, as he calls it – at both the level of structure and at the level of action. Furthermore, these realms, are inextricably linked. As he argues in his purely theoretical work on *structuration* (Giddens 1984), no actor makes choices except in specific structural circumstances and no structural features can come into being except as a result of the consequences of intentional action. In fact, it can be reasonably argued that Giddens' account of life in late modernity is **structuration theory** in practice.

His account of late modernity not only shows how structuration analysis works, but also highlights the centrality in our lives of what for Giddens is one of the defining features of modernity today: *risk*. According to him, the notion of risk 'unlocks some of the most basic characteristics of the world in which we now live' (Giddens 1999: 21). Giddens distinguishes between two types of risk – *external* risk and *manufactured* risk. External risk 'is risk experienced as coming from the outside, from the fixities of tradition or nature', whereas manufactured risk is 'risk created by the very impact of our developing knowledge upon the world' (Giddens 1999: 26). In essence, as Giddens explains, it is the difference between worrying about what nature can do to us – in the form of floods and famine, for example – and worrying about what we have done to nature, for example, the emergence of threats to the environment such as global warming. He argues that the emergence of manufactured risk is one of the hallmarks of late modernity. However, Giddens does not see risk in contemporary life as being solely a matter of the potential for global catastrophes such as nuclear accidents or wars, important though this is to his analysis. He also characterizes our personal lives as suffused with risk too.

In traditional worlds, whether they were based on agricultural or industrial production, to a large extent people did not have to work out how to live or who to be in the way we have to now. This is what living 'traditionally' means – having the assurance that things in the future will be substantially the same as they were in the past. Living in late modernity, says Giddens, means that we cannot depend on continuity and stability in this way and, as a result, we have to accommodate change and uncertainty by creating and recreating our lives on a routine basis – an activity he calls **reflexivity**. We will look at this characterization of late modern personal existence in more detail shortly.

## Ulrich Beck: a risk society

The centrality of the notion of risk in Giddens' account of contemporary existence echoes many of the ideas of the German sociologist Ulrich Beck (1944–). Like Giddens, Beck rejects postmodernism. He acknowledges the new circumstances in which our lives are lived today, but prefers to call this emerging world a 'new modernity', rather than describe it as postmodern. Again like Giddens, Beck analyses contemporary life at the levels of both structure and action, and lays much of the blame for the increase in manufactured risk at both levels on natural science. As he puts it: 'Science has become the protector of a global contamination of people and nature. In that respect, it is no exaggeration to say that in the way they deal with risks in many areas, the sciences have squandered until further notice their historic reputation for rationality' (Beck 1992: 70).

One of Beck's key points concerns the way our relationship to science and scientists has changed in recent years. In the past, we took it for granted not only that science could be relied on to tell us the truth, but also that scientists were experts we could depend upon to guide us in circumstances of uncertainty. It was a case of 'Trust us, we're scientists', as much as 'Trust me, I'm a doctor.' As Giddens puts it:

> In Western society, for some two centuries, science functioned as a sort of tradition. Scientific knowledge was supposed to overcome tradition, but actually in a way became one in its own right. It was something that most people respected, but was external to their activities. Lay people 'took' opinions from the experts. (Giddens 1999: 31)

Of course, there were failures and mini-disasters during this time, but these could always be explained away as the result of individual inefficiency or negligence, thus allowing us to retain our faith in science and scientists generally. For it is one thing to blame an individual practitioner, but quite another to blame the profession itself. That is, we could retain our trust in science, and derive a sense of security from its benevolent presence in advancing our lives, just so long as there were enough malpracticing or inept individuals around to blame for any mistakes.

Beck argues that this no longer describes our relationship with science and scientists. According to him, the consensus so characteristic of modernity – that the development of science and technology will lead inexorably to a golden future in which we humans can harness the power of nature for our own purposes – began to break down in the 1970s. It is no coincidence that this happened at a time when new social movements and protest groups such as Greenpeace and Friends of the Earth began to employ their own scientists to critique those establishment scientists working in government or business. As Beck puts it, science began to turn in on itself, undermining the very foundation on which the reliance on science rests – that the expert knows best (Beck 1992). Now the 'experts' not only fought among themselves, but were seen to be doing so by the wider public. And the more it became apparent that these hugely important sources of our sense of security were divided over matters of fact and of truth, the more risk management had to become a matter of personal responsibility. As a result, in everyday life, our uncertainties began to multiply and our sense of risk began to increase. As Giddens portrays this new world:

> We cannot simply 'accept' the findings which scientists produce, if only because scientists so frequently disagree with one another, particularly in situations of manufactured risk. And everyone now recognizes the essentially mobile character of science. Whenever someone decides what to eat, what to have for breakfast, whether to drink decaffeinated or ordinary coffee, that person takes a decision in the context of conflicting and changing scientific and technological information. (Giddens 1999: 31)

Beck characterizes this process as *reflexive modernization* and stresses that it operates at both a structural and a personal level. To quote Giddens again:

> Whichever way you look at it, we are caught up in risk management. With the spread of manufactured risk, governments can't pretend such management isn't their business. And they need to collaborate, since very few new-style risks have anything to do with the borders of nations . . . But neither, as ordinary individuals, can we ignore these new risks – or wait for definitive scientific evidence to arrive. As consumers, each of us has to decide whether to try to avoid genetically modified products or not. These risks, and the dilemmas surrounding them, have entered deeply into our everyday lives. (Giddens 1999: 34)

Risk management thus involves both institutional and individual reflexivity. Beck and Giddens see the presence of risk in our personal lives as so pervasive that it is not just a matter of second-guessing scientific knowledge. It becomes a question of managing uncertainty in *all* areas of our everyday existence. Thus, as Beck puts it: 'newly formed social relationships and social networks now have to be individually chosen; social ties, too, are becoming *reflexive*, so that they have to be established, maintained, and constantly renewed by individuals' (Beck 1992: 97).

For Beck and Giddens, then, twenty-first-century life is not only much more uncertain and risky in terms of the management of inexorable change and the unknowability of the future at the macro level. It is also much more uncertain and suffused with risk for us as individuals in our personal lives as well. This places social theories of late modernity under the obligation to examine how the macro and micro experience of risk entwine in specific contexts. It is not just a matter of understanding risk and uncertainty as both an objective fact and a matter of perception – as both *objective* and *subjective* risk – important though this distinction is. It is that our identities – who we are – are no longer established and sustained for us by institutional certainties. This is how a culture of risk and uncertainty born of, and reproduced by, constant and rapid change impacts on individual lives. We saw earlier that Giddens developed his structuration approach in order to deal with the dialectical relationship between structure and agency in social life. We will now examine how the same theoretical framework can been used to analyse risk and uncertainty in late modernity.

## Giddens: reflexivity in late modernity

At the level of structure, Giddens insists that any satisfactory commentary on the way things are in modern society has to highlight the incredible changes we are undergoing. As we have just seen, they include the emergence of new dangers and risks – for example, those posed by nuclear weapons and threats to the environment. The threats also include those arising from rapid **globalization**, which impacts not only at a global level but equally also at the local – the level of everyday experience. The technological transformation in methods of human communication, with its obliteration of traditional categories of time and space, is also hugely significant here.

Because of this structural focus, Giddens is contemptuous of the postmodernist preoccupation with representation, and in particular of its central claim that reality is discursively created and exclusively a function of the powerful forms of cultural knowledge that define it. For Giddens, it is absurd to conceive of human existence as being solely a matter of discursive definition, or as being only about meanings. For him, there is nothing more real than, for example, the threat of nuclear war, or the dangers posed to the world by barely manageable environmental change, or by global relations of wealth and inequality.

However, Giddens acknowledges that structural analysis is insufficient by itself, since structure and action must be analysed in relation to each other. His account of the nature of individual experience in late modernity thus forms the other, equally important half of his narrative. His point is that the enormous structural changes in the world he identifies have had huge consequences for the way we live our lives and think of ourselves. Because we exist in circumstances so different from those of any other humans who have ever lived, we have had to find new ways of living and coping. In effect, not only do contemporary humans need to be interpreting, creative agents as never before, but the exercise of this agency will have inevitable consequences for the structure of our world.

## Identity in late modernity: the emergence of the reflexive self

As was mentioned above, in both pre-modern and modern traditional settings people acquired both a sense of social order, and of their having a settled, defined place within it, from the presence of established institutional pegs on which to hang their sense of themselves – their identities. Giddens calls this existential condition **ontological security**. Marriage, family life, working life and community life all had a sense of permanence and stability. There were established – traditional – ways of living there to be used as a life-script, and as a result it was a relatively easy matter for people to be sure of themselves and of their futures. Not so now. According to Giddens, one of the crucial consequences of rapid structural and institutional change is its impact on the everyday business of living – the business of knowing yourself and knowing what to do. Giddens gives the following example:

> Two or three generations ago, when people got married, they knew what it was they were doing. Marriage, largely fixed by tradition and custom, was akin to a state of nature – as of course remains true in many countries. Where traditional ways of doing things are dissolving, however, when people marry or form relationships, there is an important sense in which they don't know what they are doing, because the institutions of marriage and the family have changed so much. Here individuals are striking out afresh, like pioneers. It is inevitable in such situations, whether they know it or not, that they start thinking more and more in terms of risk. They have to confront personal futures that are much more open than in the past, with all the opportunities and hazards this brings. (Giddens 1999: 27–8)

For Giddens, living in modern societies today means we have to make and re-make our selves in order to cope with the changes buffeting us from all directions. Since new circumstances constantly arise and have to be made sense of, we have to manage and attach meaning to a world that is inherently *un*stable. We cannot turn to old ways of living since they have become redundant in this new 'runaway world' (Giddens 1999). Our only course of action is to constantly monitor our circumstances and re-shape our selves accordingly. This means routinely adapting to our sense of what is going on; sculpting a self, an identity, to suit today but not necessarily tomorrow. This is the process Giddens describes as *reflexivity*. Thus, living in late modernity becomes a (life-long) *reflexive project*: making sense of how things are and how we should live has to be undertaken over and over again as the conditions under which we live continually alter. We can expect nothing else so long as we live in a world famously described by Giddens as:

> A runaway engine of enormous power which, collectively as human beings, we can drive to some extent but which also threatens to rush out of our control and which could rend itself asunder. The juggernaut crushes those who resist it, and while it sometimes seems to have a steady path, there are times when it veers erratically in directions we cannot foresee. The ride is by no means unpleasant or unrewarding; it can often be exhilarating and charged with hopeful anticipation. But, so long as the institutions of modernity endure, we shall never be able to control completely either the path or the pace of the journey. In turn, we shall never be able to feel entirely secure, because the terrain across which it runs is fraught with risks of high consequence. (Giddens 1990: 139)

At the level of the agent or actor then, the emergence of late modern life has meant the dissolution of the institutional forms of identity characteristic of more traditional settings, with the result that a sense of self can only come from within. Late modern life is about writing and re-writing an emotional and mental script for oneself: reflexivity is the name Giddens gives to this search for ontological security in the absence of external, culturally defined signposts.

## Managing personal uncertainty: the rise of therapy

According to Giddens, it is this aspect of the reflexive project that explains the dramatic rise in the number of professionals offering to help you do it. If living life has become a matter of making your own decisions about who you are, the explosion in recent years of various forms of counselling and therapy as aids in this task comes as no surprise. Giddens has been criticized for assuming that recourse to therapy is a general feature of late modern life, when in reality it is only a late modern phenomenon among those (like him) in possession of the cultural and economic resources to make use of it. But there seems no doubt that, at least for some, living in late modernity has involved an increasing use of professional guides claiming to map out directions for individuals to take on their personal odyssey.

## The reflexive body

This emphasis on self-reflexivity in late modernity also leads Giddens to offer a very different account of contemporary body-centredness from Foucault. Because, theoretically, Giddens insists that we recognize agency as a principal constituent of human existence, he rejects the Foucauldian view that the kinds of body obsession and body fetishism characteristic of contemporary life that we reviewed in Chapter 6 are discursively constructed phenomena. Giddens argues that in fact they are symptomatic of reflexive agency.

Interactionists like Goffman have traditionally pointed to the creative use of the body in social interaction. For him, as we saw in Chapter 5, effective impression management relies heavily on the self-conscious use of the body. Our ability to manipulate our appearance, demeanour, expression and so on is routinely pressed into service in social encounters so that they can proceed in ways with which we feel comfortable. We use our body in a theatrical way, as part of a public performance. In some of these little dramas we are being 'true to ourselves' whereas in others we are not.

Giddens, however, is saying something rather different. For him, life in late modernity means we can no longer let our job, or where we come from, or where we live, or who our family is, speak for our selves. We have to find other ways of both being our selves and representing these selves to others. For this reason (and here he provides a similar analysis to Bauman), the rampant consumerism that is such a major feature of contemporary life becomes understandable. If possessing things is now the way we reveal the self, it is the material elements of consumer culture that become our expressions of identity. As Bauman puts it: 'The roads to self-identity, to a place in society, to a life in a form recognizable as that of meaningful living, all require daily visits to the market place' (Bauman 1992: 26).

This is why the body becomes so important. It becomes one of the plates on which a reflexively chosen identity is etched: our physical appearance becomes emblematic of who we are. This is how Elizabeth Jagger summarizes this element in Giddens' account:

> By providing a series of 'expert knowledges', for instance in relation to lifestyle, health, fashion and beauty, consumer culture is understood . . . to have contributed to an increasingly reflexive understanding of the self, an awareness that identity is chosen and constructed . . . As Giddens (1991) has pointed out, the self in 'late modernity' has become a reflexive project; it is created (and re-created) through a plurality of consumer

choices and lifestyle decisions. In his view, individuals can now draw on a wide repertoire of symbolic goods with which to fashion and display their own identities. (Jagger 2000: 51–2)

In effect, as Giddens himself puts it, in late modernity the body becomes 'a visible carrier of self-identity and is increasingly integrated into the lifestyle decisions which an individual makes' (Giddens 1991: 31). We may argue that perhaps Giddens is over-estimating the degree to which we can actually express creativity in constructing our identity – in the face of the enormous commercial and media-generated pressure this reflexive project can feel more like an anxiety-inducing obligation with clear sanctions such as social ridicule or marginalization if we 'get it wrong'. Foucault's analysis of discursive power perhaps offers a stronger account of the sense in which we have very little alternative but to choose and construct ourselves from a limited range of options. This may be, however, an issue to be examined through research, rather than by theoretical generalization. In such a context, social science is perhaps under its own obligation to develop highly sensitive devices for mapping and articulating the range of experiences involved in identity construction; including the degrees of enablement and constraint and their complex inter-mingling. Arguably, the Foucauldian lens of 'discursive regulation' would be very hard pressed to capture this complexity.

## Zygmunt Bauman: 'liquid modernity'

As we observed in the last chapter, throughout the early 1990s Bauman's work was closely linked with postmodern social theory. However, when the latter became too strongly associated with an extreme relativism in which it seemed that 'anything goes', Bauman reverted back to the term modernity. It might be said, therefore, that Bauman does not so much reject the postmodern movement as make a gradual withdrawal from its more extreme characteristics. Whatever the case, at the turn of the millennium he introduced a new term to describe contemporary life (in the West at least): 'liquid modernity'. The term is meant to convey, in the most powerful sense, a feeling of up-rootedness and instability, in contrast with the solidity and firmness of an earlier form of modernity. In comparing the two forms of modernity, Bauman explains his metaphor as follows:

While solids have clear spatial dimensions but neutralize the impact, and thus downgrade the significance, of time (effectively resist its flow or render it irrelevant), fluids do not keep to any shape for long and are constantly ready (and prone) to change it; and so for them it is the flow of time that counts, more than the space they happen to occupy: that space, after all, they fill but for 'a moment'. (Bauman 2000a: 2)

For some readers this passage may suggest a similarity with Giddens' notion of a 'runaway world' or the concept of reflexive modernization. Indeed, Bauman references the works of Giddens and Beck frequently. Likewise, his description of the early form of modernity as 'solid' or 'heavy', as well as his account of contemporary modernity as 'liquid' or 'light', are very similar to the social worlds depicted in the accounts of Giddens and Beck.

For Bauman, 'heavy modernity' is characterized by what he sees as its principal institution, the Fordist factory. Vast in size, Fordist production, he says, 'reduced human activities to simple, routine and by and large predesigned moves meant to be followed obediently and mechanically without engaging mental faculties' (Bauman 2000a: 25). Fordism, as the above quotation implies, controlled both space and time. It was solid and predictable. And just as the world of production in 'heavy modernity' was underwritten by this principal of certainty, so too were social relations in general and, in turn, individual identity. Early modernity, he says, disembedded individuals (from earlier feudalism) only to re-embed them into a social world that positioned its members just as firmly in terms of class and gender relations. The challenge to the individual was, Bauman claims, to conform to a social order that seemed as natural as nature itself. Hence, the institutions of this era – of marriage, family life, work and community – held the individual in check. In Giddens' terms, they provided the self with ontological security. But in fluid modernity these features are liquidized, casting the individual into an unstable world without any permanence in which he or she must take responsibility for his or her own being. In liquid modernity, Bauman says, there are no 'beds' available to the individual. 'There are rather', he argues, 'musical chairs of various sizes and styles as well as of changing numbers and positions, which prompt men and women to be constantly on the move' (Bauman 2000a: 33). Everything is liquidized: work, family, love, intimacy and morality.

The cause of this rupture in social relations is a familiar one and follows, at least approximately, the contours of globalization discussed in the last chapter under the heading of 'postmodernity'. Thus, the ideals of heavy modernity were undermined by the technological explosion of new information systems. Multinational or transnational companies chipped away at the economic authority of the nation-state and encouraged the outsourcing of manufacturing to developing nations. At the same time there was a shift in investment in the West, away from manufacture and towards finance, communication and the service sectors. Suddenly, according to Bauman, capitalism shifted from solidity and heaviness to weightlessness and fluidity, affecting all other aspects of social and political life in the process.

Thus far, there is little in this description that had not been said before by Giddens, Beck, or even (partially) by Bauman himself in his earlier incarnation as a postmodernist. However, as we will see, there is a fundamental difference between Bauman's depiction of 'liquid modernity' and the implications of 'reflexive modernity'. Giddens' and Beck's accounts of reflexive modernization offer a cautious optimism that the individual may benefit from the breakdown of the certainties of early modernity. They point to the new forms of freedom available to the reflexive individual arising from the relaxation of the constraints of traditional notions of class and gender. Late modernity offers indi-viduals a far richer palette with which to create their own identity than did any previous epoch. But there is none of this optimism in Bauman's description of 'liquid life'; here identity is put through the same liquidizer as the rest of heavy modernity.

## Individualization and identity

Like Giddens and Beck, the main thrust of Bauman's argument is prem-ised on the individualization thesis. This is the view, outlined above, that traditionally stable aspects or institutions of social life – work, family, community, etc. – have been rendered inoperative by the proc-esses of globalization to such an extent that the individual must now organize and take responsibility for his or her own fate. For Bauman, this has a profound effect upon identity. With no solid or stable place to reside, for the individual liquid life becomes highly precarious. It is a life in which we are compelled to move constantly from one project to the next without any time to stop and relax, or to reflect long enough to say 'this is who I am and this is what I have achieved'. 'These days', Bauman says, 'patterns and configurations are no longer "given", let alone "self-evident"; there are just too many of them, clashing with one another and contradicting one another's commandments' (Bauman 2000a: 7). There can be no fixed patterns in a world in which work is fragile and friable, where personal relationships frequently fail, where authorities in all kinds of fields are too numerous to count, and where the inhabitants of communities are never in one place long enough to become familiar faces. In such a world nothing endures long enough to be taken in and add weight to or anchor our precarious identities. As Bauman observes: 'In the world we inhabit . . . walls are far from solid and most certainly not once and for all; eminently mobile, they remind the traveller-through-life of cardboard partitions or screens meant to be repositioned over and over again following successive changes in needs or whims' (Bauman and May 2001: 45).

In this new chronically insecure world, the freedom of self-creation which Giddens and Beck point to is regarded as an illusion by Bauman. It is, he claims, a negative freedom that promises the individual the right to take responsibility for being ill or unemployed without giving her 'the capacity to control the social settings which render such self-assertion feasible' (Bauman 2000a: 38). Nowadays there are no longer authorities to tell us what to do and release us from responsibility for the consequences of our actions. Instead we have only other equally lost individuals to look to for models of how to go about life's business. Bauman sums matters up in the following way: 'To put it in a nutshell, "individualization" consists of transforming human "identity" from a "given" into a "task" and charging the actors with the responsibility for performing that task and for the consequences (also the side-effects) of their performance' (Bauman 2000a: 31–2).

It might be concluded from this account that Bauman's depiction of identity and the place of the individual in liquid modernity is not so fundamentally different from his own (earlier) postmodernist depiction, or from the outwardly pessimistic views of Fredric Jameson. However, in his more recent writings Bauman at least suggests that, even amongst what he sees as the rubble of contemporary society, 'we need collectively to learn to tackle [these problems] collectively' (Bauman 2000a: 38).

## The consumer society: tourists and vagabonds

In his 1998 text, *Globalization*, Bauman asks what it means to say that we are living in a consumer society. His answer is that it means to live in such a way as to actively seek to be seduced through **consumption**. It is, Bauman observes, to 'live from attraction to attraction, from temptation to temptation, from sniffing out one tidbit to searching for another, from swallowing one bait to fishing around for another' (Bauman 1998: 83–4). According to Bauman, we are all caught up in this compulsion or addiction, although some may be better placed to indulge their habit. The better placed he labels the 'tourists'; the very worse off are the 'vagabonds'. Although both tourists and vagabonds are without home or direction, we all aspire to be tourists. The tourists are the new jet-setting business men or women who work one week in Singapore, the next in New York, and the week after that find themselves in London, Prague or Paris. Each of these places is neither foreign nor unknown to the tourist. When she arrives she will know in advance the menu she will eat from later; she will know where the light switches are in her hotel room; and she will be aware of the conversations and gestures she will encounter at the hotel reception and the meeting rooms she will work in. Tourists are not home-sick, because the comforts they require are met in their life-strategy: the seduction of collecting sensations. Tourists are at the top of the tree of consumers. At the very top are entrepreneurs such as Bill Gates, the chairman of Microsoft. Gates is seen as an iconic consumer, a man who never looks back but roves constantly from one project to the next and is willing to tear up the past in order to pursue a new goal. Tourism, these days, is what we all desire, as it has become the only acceptable (or respectable) way to live.

Other consumers, Bauman says, wander for a different reason. The vagabonds are on the move because they are pushed from behind. They have no choice but to travel because all the places in which they want to stay are inhospitable; they must move on because they are unwelcome. The vagabonds, Bauman claims, are 'the mutants of postmodern evolution [they] are the waste of the world which has dedicated itself to tourist services' (Bauman 1998: 92). These 'mutants' of consumer society are resented, viewed as non-contributors who have no role in society but are costly to the public. But it should be noted, says Bauman, that the vagabond is actually the alter ego of the tourist: 'tourism and vagrancy are two sides of the same coin' (Bauman 1998: 96). The tourist has much to fear when he sees the vagabond. The majority of tourists cannot be sure that their current 'success' will last; that it will, as Bauman observes, see the light of the next day. There 'are so many banana skins on the road, and so many sharp kerbs on which one can stumble' (Bauman 1998: 97). Becoming a vagabond is, for the tourist, always a possibility.

Bauman's depiction of the 'tourist' and the 'vagabond' displays his typically pessimistic view of contemporary society. Of course, most of us live our lives somewhere on a spectrum between tourist and vagabond. But there are two key messages here. First, it seems that we are all caught up in a consumer society aimlessly seeking new sensations; the vagabond dreams of being a tourist just as the tourist fears becoming a vagabond. Second, in this text and elsewhere (see Bauman 1993),

Bauman is keen to point out to his readers the injustices of contemporary society and the presence of marginalized groups. In a world in which identity has become privatized and we are obliged to take responsibility for our individual fate it becomes too easy to scapegoat the poor and the homeless because they unwittingly remind us of the precariousness of our own lives.

## Conclusion: late modernity versus postmodernity

This chapter has set out three different accounts of the key features of contemporary experience. In conclusion, we will outline a general critique of all three approaches. Giddens, Beck and Bauman all share an adherence to the view that twenty-first-century society is inherently individualizing. We have discussed this in relation to Bauman's work, but Giddens and Beck are also of this opinion. Thus, for Giddens, late modernity sets the agent free to explore the normative contours of the social world and to reflexively design their own life. However, perhaps all three authors, despite their differences, share a tendency to exaggerate the degree to which our society has become individualized and the extent to which traditional values have been left behind. Anthony Elliot sums up the opinion of many critics of individualization when he observes, in relation to Bauman's thesis, that 'by focusing attention on the liquidization of the self, social relations and everyday life in a globalized world, Bauman tends to neglect the ongoing significance more structured, solid forms of sociality' (Elliot 2009: 302).

As we have suggested above, both Giddens and Bauman refute the claim that we are now living in an epoch that has broken, wholesale, with the principles of modernity. Bauman does not place us as firmly in late modernity but he is equally concerned to steer away from the **moral relativism** of some postmodernist positions. Beyond this, as noted above, he retains a postmodernist stance in his claim that modern institutions and ways of living have been replaced by others that are so profoundly different that we can no longer see a continuity between the past and the present. In this sense, Bauman's use of the term 'modernity' in the title 'liquid modernity' may appear misleading, unless, of course, what he seeks to retain of modernity is its aspiration to build a sense of collective meaning in the social world. Giddens and Beck offer a less ambiguous account of the gulf between modernity and postmodernity.

For Beck, the postmodern analysis of society tends to overlook the guiding principle of modernity: its commitment to the principles of

equality and freedom. It is this commitment, Beck claims, which justi-
fies the continued use of the term 'modern'. Had postmodern theory
retained this ethical commitment it would have seen that the path that
**modernism** has taken in the past half-century represents not a break
with the past but a continuity and renewal of these principles. Early
(or first) modernity continued the feudal tradition of ascribing social
relations according to characteristics of birth (in the form of gender
and class relations). Second modernity (or the risk society) has, in
contrast, witnessed an enhancement of equality and freedom. For Beck
it is as if early modernity could not quite free itself from the shackles
of feudalism. Finally, in the twenty-first century, the individual is free
to construct an identity based around the personal rather than the
structural or normative dictates of first modernity (upon meeting a
stranger the first question we ask will no longer be 'what do you do
for a living?'). Of course, this has not been achieved without a price.
Our trust in science and in authority in general has been undermined
by modernity's failure to live up to its goal of realizing a golden future,
and by the extraordinary destruction that the relationship between
technology and business has wrought upon the natural world.

Giddens also emphasizes, albeit in a different way to Beck, the
failure of postmodern social theory to observe that which is shared by
early and late modernity. For him, the concept of reflexivity is key to
understanding modernity in all of its forms; it is modernity's defining
feature. In its early version reflexivity was present in two of the fundamental institutions of modernity: in business (or capitalism) and in
science. Late modernity represents, in a sense, a flowering of what lies
at the heart of modernity as this tendency towards self-scrutinization
devolves from the structural level to the individual or agent. For
Giddens, postmodernism, with its caricature of the individual as lost
in a sea of meaninglessness and gripped by the superficiality of the
moment, fails to grasp what it is that makes us social beings – our
ability and desire to be creative and free agents. The social and structural constraints of contemporary life may prevent many of us from
fully developing our creative potential, but postmodernists are, at the
very least, guilty of exaggerating our plight. Furthermore, in its more
radical form, as a version of relativism that proposes a laissez-faire
attitude towards truth, postmodernism also neglects the pragmatic
benefits of reason and analysis. For Giddens, then, postmodernism as
a social theory is mistaken on three counts:

- it neglects the institutional realities of living in the twenty-first
  century

- it wrongly sees the individual as powerless in the face of discursive influences, and
- it cannot make any useful contribution to the business of making our world a safer and better place because it denies that we can ever have the capacity to know how things really are.

As such, according to Giddens, postmodernism is wholly inadequate as a sociological theory. For him, just as for the classic social theorists, sociology and its theories are ultimately worthless if they cannot contribute towards elucidating and thereby helping to keep open the possibility of improving the human condition by human action.

In the light of this penultimate chapter then, we can begin to recognize more clearly the implications for social theorizing of incorporating insights from two contrasting accounts of language and the communication of meaning – the **hermeneutic** and the post-structuralist. As we suggested in Chapter 5, both of these accounts of how the structures of language relate to the production of meaning place communicative practices at the heart of social life. Both involve moving away from the individual as the source of meaning and towards seeing language as a shared social practice, but they each give very different accounts of how meaning is sustained within language. According to post-structuralists, language imposes meaning – language speaks us. We are the vehicles that carry predetermined meaning into social life. According to the critics of post-structuralist views, this account entirely ignores how the rules and conventions of language are continuously negotiated, produced and reproduced within even the most everyday linguistic usage.

For those theorists who emphasize the ways in which human communication creates our shared social world, language becomes a means by which to argue about what meaning and truth – and by extension, what social progress, freedom and rationality – might mean; such ideas are not inherently subverted by language. This appears to open up a way of maintaining some sense of the **Enlightenment** commitment to social progress through human action. For such theorists, processes of communication, debate and discussion in and between all social actors, both specialists and lay members of society, can at their best offer the possibility of agreement about what is important and how it can be achieved.

In this context we are not obliged to be inherently suspicious that human communication is 'really' a vehicle of power-play, manipulation or deceit. On some occasions it may well be, but it is an overreaction to take the fact that our means of communication is rich enough to *include* strategies of manipulation and deceit to mean that this is *all* that we are doing when we communicate.

In our final chapter, we will examine some of the most fertile examples of social theories which have sought to contribute to social change – namely, feminist and gender theories. As we shall suggest, the issues that have led to the development of and debate between feminist and gender theories exemplify many of the themes so far discussed in this book.

## Further reading

Bauman, Zygmunt (2000): *Liquid Modernity*, Polity.

Beck, Ulrich (1992): *The Risk Society: towards a new modernity*, Sage.

Beck, Ulrich, Giddens, Anthony and Lash, Scott (1994): *Reflexive Modernization*, Polity.

Bryant, Christopher and Jary, David (2001): *The Contemporary Giddens: social theory in a globalising age*, Palgrave.

Dodd, Nigel (1999): *Social Theory and Modernity*, Polity.

Mythen, Gabe (2004): *Ulrich Beck: a critical introduction to the risk society*, Pluto.

# 10 FEMINIST AND GENDER THEORIES

---

## Introduction

> *Ever spent a night in hospital?* Yes, I had a concussion. At college I did that thing of holding on to the bike rather than putting a hand out. Apparently women do that: if you push a woman down the stairs holding a cup of tea, in theory she holds on to the cup because she thinks it's a baby. (Sally Philips to the *Observer*, 2 August 2009)

> The prevailing law threatened one with trouble, even put one in trouble, all to keep one out of trouble. Hence, I concluded that trouble was inevitable and the task, how best to make it, what best way to be in it. (Butler 1990: vii)

The concept of gender is perhaps deceptively easy to define. As Raewyn Connell (1944–) succinctly puts it: 'Gender is the structure of social relations that centres on the reproductive arena, and the set of practices that bring reproductive distinctions between bodies into social processes' (Connell 2009: 11). This definition indicates the span of gender's reach. As a structure of social relations gender will be part of the organization of society – and indeed, if we reflect on our own experience we can see that gender provides some of the most significant rules and resources by which social systems are sustained. Globally it regulates the distribution of resources such as wealth (women do two-thirds of the world's work for one tenth of the world's income and own less than 1 per cent of the world's property), education (women make up two thirds of the world's illiterate), or power (only 16 per cent of the world's parliamentarians are women).

As this statistical snapshot shows, at least on a global level, gender regulates the life-chances of men and women in ways that sustain massive inequalities between them. At this global level, inequality is unambiguously evident, and yet there is a great deal of ambiguity surrounding the practices and processes through which gender structures our lives.

The depressing figures just given do not tell us all there is to know about how gender structures or regulates our lives. For one thing, they do not convey the pleasure that any of us who have fallen in love and found it reciprocated, or have delivered a planned pregnancy, will have felt. Likewise, although we can see that the majority of the world's resources still go to men, the experience of masculinity, of 'living up to it', is often treacherous and laced with fear and insecurity. Men are both the overwhelming perpetuators of violence and the overwhelming majority of its victims, and much of the research into men and masculinities strongly suggests that often this violence can be understood to reflect the *struggle* – the competition and conflict – men engage in over the power and status associated with masculinity. Masculinity, perhaps because of the privileged access to social resources it offers, does not come easy. It would seem safe to conclude, then, that both the pleasures and the harms of gender are confusingly and powerfully combined in the structures and the more tangible relationships we each enter into as gendered beings. Perhaps this mixing of pleasure and harm makes some sense of the fact that questions of gender – what it is, what it measures, and how it regulates our collective and individual lives – remain a source of intense political, cultural and academic disagreement and contestation.

If we consider the second part of Connell's definition of gender, much of the disagreement arises from the question of *how* 'practices bring the reproductive distinctions between bodies into social processes'. Over the last 150 or so years in Western societies, this 'how' has involved a massive body of scholarly research, political activism and government policy. At the same time, the structure and organization of households, parenting, work and sexuality have changed markedly from generation to generation. Think for a moment of the differences between your own family experiences or aspirations and those of your grandparents, or even of your parents. The range of choices available about whether, and if so how, when and with whom, to establish sexual and parenting relationships has never been greater. Given what Giddens would refer to as our heightened 'reflexivity' about gendered practices, it is perhaps to be welcomed that so much research is available to inform our decisions. But yet again, all is not as it appears. We might think that the research generated would provide a stable basis for our beliefs and practices, but many of us believe what we believe about gender *despite* and in contradiction to the evidence. The contrariness of many of our gender **belief systems** has been well-documented by gender theorists such as Lynne Segal (1999), Michael Kimmel (2004) and Raewyn Connell (2009). As they each demonstrate, the overwhelming weight of psychological and physiological research shows that women and men are overwhelmingly *similar* in their strengths, vulnerabilities, personality traits, abilities and needs, and yet an enormous amount of funded research is still devoted to identifying those differences that everyday conversations suggest many of us insist must be there. It seems then, that some of the ways in which social practices deal with reproductive distinctions are characterized by confusion, anxiety and irrationality. Our generalizations – 'that's so typical of men'; 'women always do that' – suggest that we see (and perhaps want to see) gender as some kind of law governing our actions.

But what kind of a law is this? Is it a law of nature which social practices and structures merely reflect? Is gender simply the tracing paper and pencil we use to follow our biological fate as sexed beings? Does the female potential to bear children govern the rest of women's lives to the extent that their nurturing instincts will unwittingly extend to inanimate objects, as our first quote from Philips suggests? Do the biological laws of sexual reproduction really bode the kind of trouble for women that leads them to risk serious physical injury by confusing a cup with a baby? Or would it be more accurate to regard the trouble that comes with gender as being of human design, as Judith Butler's (1956–) words imply? In the latter case, if humans have made up the rules of gender, and if these rules appear to cause significant strife, then perhaps they need to be changed.

It is not easy to come up with a single definition of feminism, but for the purposes of this chapter we will take it that those for whom feminist and gender theory is important would agree that the regulation of gendered practices does not come from biology or nature, and that, given the harm the regulation causes, it's better to make trouble for the prevailing law rather than accept its legitimacy.

Since at least the last quarter of the nineteenth century, feminist activists, mostly women, have identified man-made laws as both the cause and the intended target of personal and political trouble. We tend to associate the mainly European and North American feminist writers and political activists of the late nineteenth and early twentieth centuries (often referred to, if rather inaccurately, as the 'first wave' of feminism in distinction to the 'second wave' associated with the 'Women's Liberation Movement' at its peak in the 1970s) with campaigns to change the laws of the land. In Britain, these laws denied women the right to work, to own property, to vote, to divorce, to receive higher education and professional training and to make their own decisions about sexual and reproductive practices (see Rowbotham 1992; Walby 1990).

For most of this period, the varied political forces which resisted such calls for change would use the argument that because women's biology is so radically different to men's they were too ill-equipped to take up the rights and obligations of citizenship. The activists fighting for women's legal freedom and autonomy were successful in winning women the right to move outside the private sphere of the home and the authority of the male head of the household. However, they were well-aware that the laws they were challenging were only one part of the problem, and that these laws themselves were supportive of and supported by a wide range of more informal customs, conventions and values positioning men and women at opposite ends of the possible range of human behaviours and personality traits. According to the dominant view then, men display instrumental values (valuing people in terms of what they can do or how they might be useful) while women hold particularistic values (valuing people for what they uniquely are); men represent culture and women nature; men embody reason and women emotion; men are active whereas women are passive. Men make the stairs and women fall down them. It doesn't take a genius to see that the traits associated with men are also those seen as essential for assuming political and economic power and leadership. In contrast, the so-called feminine traits and values are not only regarded as less important but, as feminists have pointed out, often serve to legitimize or justify the inferior social status of women. As we shall see, the later women's liberation movements of the 1970s are perhaps better known for attempting to make visible and to challenge the structures, practices and values of male authority that defined and regulated both the public and the private spheres.

'How best to make trouble' and 'what best way to be in it': these phrases of Butler's offer us a neat way of summarizing the sources of the debates and disagreements within and between feminist and gender theorists. The question of how best to analyse and then challenge the prevailing law has remained a source of not always productive tension between different theorists and activists. For many, the title of 'feminist' should be reserved for those who believe that reducing the harm of gender relations is best effected by focusing *only* on the ways in which women are damaged by men. In contrast, gender scholars who are critical of aspects of feminist thinking argue that harm-reduction is best attempted by focusing on both men *and* women, and on the relationships between them. This strategy was taken to allow for a more detailed analysis of the impact of circuits of power and inequality both *within* and between the genders. It also enables fuller consideration of the links between gender, class and ethnic inequalities in relation to the lives of individuals belonging to different social groups. In this chapter we will look at theorists who can be loosely grouped as either feminist or gender analysts, but to illustrate some of the complexity of gender politics and theory, we should also mention those whose commitment to harm-reduction leads them to disavow the usefulness of either feminism or the concept of gender. Some **postmodern** and queer theorists adopt this position, for example.

## Feminist theories and women's liberation

As Connell points out, functionalist sociologies of the family were used by feminists in the late 1960s to probe how far gender identities and gender relations might be transformed (Connell 1987). In fact, the social sciences in general were particularly important to this generation of activists. Social, psychological and political theories and research were deployed by feminist researchers and activists in their attempts categorically to distinguish legal statutes, customs and practices which could be changed, from the universal and unchangeable laws of nature. It was this generation of feminists who emphasized the importance of the sociological distinction between sex and gender. This distinction was intended to shore up the boundary between what can and cannot be changed by social and political reforms. Sexual differences were thus defined by second-wave feminists as referring to chromosomal and other physiological differences relating to male and female reproductive functions; whereas gender referred to the socially constructed categories of masculinity and femininity. This distinction was intended to make it strikingly visible that social relations between men and women created gender inequality. Treating the prevailing law as if it originated in biology was now revealed as a cover story used to justify the cultural, economic and political practices sustaining men's power, authority, domination and privilege over women.

Here, then, we can see how useful structural-conflict theory was to the feminist theories of women's liberation that flourished in the 1970s and 1980s. This sociological approach was common to a range of different feminist challenges to the **naturalistic** and **individualistic** approaches that dominated sociological discussion of gender relations prior to the 1970s. Structural-conflict theory, as we may remember from earlier chapters, allows relationships between different social groups, in this case, men and women, to be analysed on the basis of their objectively opposed interests. Structural forces create these interests and cultural norms and values carry them into our daily lives. Aspects of these relationships that were previously treated as only as the private troubles of a woman, or as the lone actions of a psychological disordered man, such as rape, domestic violence, sexual harassment and discrimination at work, were now treated as public and political issues and as evidence of the systematically unequal social relationships between men and women. As we shall see, liberal, Marxist, radical and dual-systems theorists provide different accounts of the structures and values which were responsible for women's subordinate position and the structures of inequality between men and women. Each of these theories differ in terms of how systemically they see women's interests as conflicting with those of men.

## Liberal feminism

> The problem lay buried, unspoken, for many years in the minds of American women. It was a strange stirring, a sense of dissatisfaction, a yearning that women suffered in the middle of the twentieth century in the United States. Each suburban wife struggled with it alone. As she made the beds, shopped for groceries, matched slipcover material, ate peanut butter sandwiches with her children, chauffeured Cub Scouts and Brownies, lay beside her husband at night – she was afraid to ask even of herself the silent question – 'Is this all?' (Freidan 1965: 13)

No doubt too many of us have had similar late-night thoughts to those Betty Friedan (1921–2006) describes above. But for Friedan – a leading North American women's rights campaigner who founded the influential National Organization for Women (NOW), the campaigning arm of liberal feminism – the sense of dissatisfaction was directly caused by the stultifying demands of middle-class American femininity. Friedan's generation, whose birthright was the political successes of first-wave feminism, and who therefore had gained the right to attend university and earn their own living, still felt the weight of continuing legal discrimination and restricting cultural expectations. The term liberal feminism is usually reserved for those writers and campaigners who argued that further reform of prevailing laws was the fundamental task for the feminists of the mid twentieth century. They therefore developed campaigns for educational and legal reforms to enforce anti-discrimination laws and to promote non-sexist attitudes towards both women and men. Such reforms were designed to ensure that gender would no longer be used to ascribe particular social roles or positions to individuals. Men should be able to stay at home and look after their children; women should be able to work full-time. An individual's choices, talents, efforts and ambitions should decide their life course rather than social and legal prejudice.

The powerful campaigning voice of liberal feminism has undoubtedly been effective, but it has also been criticized for lacking a more searching analysis of the systematic oppression of women. Liberal feminism tends to operate at the level of the individual woman rather than looking at the historical and systemic features of women's collective experience (see Walby 1990). Those feminist theorists who sought to apply a more structural analysis of power differences between men and women as social groups rather than as individuals criticized liberal feminism for really only speaking for and to those women who were in a position to compete for middle-class rewards.

Such a perspective seemed to suggest that all that was needed was for feminists to campaign for some women to be able to compete more favourably for a bigger slice of the capitalist cake, rather than offering a more radical critique of its recipe. More radical conflict theories pointed to the extent to which the structural properties of modern, capitalist societies actually *relied* on the subordination of women. This subordination was no accident or mere historical residue. Theorists such as Friedan do not employ a radical analysis of the systematic conflict of interests between women and men such as we find in the radical and Marxist feminist theories to be discussed below. However, we can perhaps see that the audacity of saying 'thanks, but no thanks' to everything women are supposed to want, and the struggle to find the words to express what Friedan calls 'the problem that has no name' – women's experience of subordination – are features common to all the strands of feminist thought and activism of this time. The feminist theories we will look at below return to the traditions of Marxist and other variants of structural-conflict theory to find the words to make women's oppression and exploitation visible.

## Marxist feminism

It was to the nature of the capitalist economy that Marxist feminists turned in their analysis of the origins of and remedies for women's subordination. For Marxist feminists, far from the public sphere offering liberation from the clock-ticking claustrophobia of wifehood and motherhood, the hidden hand of the capitalist economy was responsible for the isolated and lowly status of women's domestic and working lives. According to Marxist feminists, women's subordination serves the needs of capitalism. It is in the economic relationships and ideas characteristic of the capitalist mode of production that we should look for the structures of disadvantage that unequally constrain women's lives in contrast to men's. The solution to the problem of women's oppression thus lies in the destruction of capitalism. This perspective then, offers a more focused analysis of the conflict of interests between men and women than may be found in liberal feminism. For Marxist feminists, the cause of women's exploitation lies in capitalism's reliance on women's labour, both paid and unpaid.

Under capitalism, women live in families, as wives and mothers. In these families, women constitute a source of unpaid domestic labour, which is as vital for capitalism as the paid labour of the commodity producer in industry. By providing the domestic services necessary to sustain the male worker who is her husband, and by reproducing a new generation of workers through childcare, the woman as wife and mother is providing a crucial service for capitalism – for free. It is therefore obviously far more profitable for capitalism to have women as unpaid domestic labourers than to have to pay male labourers the much higher wage they would need to purchase the same domestic services in the marketplace.

Also as a result of the normalcy of the nuclear family under capitalism, when women do enter the labour market, because they are seen as economically dependent on their husbands, they can be given low-paid, low-status and part-time work. Their work is seen as secondary and supplementary to that of their husbands, and so the rewards can be supplementary, too – married women's wages also need not be as high as those of single persons. Writers like Michèle Barrett (1949–) use the kind of approach advanced by Gramsci, arguing that the role of ideologies in extolling the virtues of family life, and of wifeliness and motherhood in domesticating women, are crucial in reproducing the features of the world by which they are disadvantaged. Thus Barratt emphasizes that the destruction of capitalist economic relations is a necessary, but not a sufficient, condition for the liberation of women. Also necessary is the transformation of ideas about sexuality, gender and parenthood, so that men and women are not ideologically coerced into living in only one kind of marriage and in one kind of family.

Obvious problems present themselves with Marxist feminist

accounts. If capitalism promotes women's subordination, why are women also subordinated in non-capitalist societies? Though it is easy to see how the performance of unpaid domestic tasks clearly benefits capital, Marxist feminism does not explain why it should be women who inevitably perform this labour. Why not men? Why not the old?

Radical feminism attempts to address this issue of why and how women specifically are oppressed by men. The radical feminist account uses the concept of **patriarchy** – the systematic exercise of power over women by men. This analysis of patriarchal power offers an account of the far-reaching and deep-rooted extent of the conflict between women's and men's interests. Thus, for radical feminists, it is not an economic system that oppresses women – it is men who oppress women.

## Radical feminism

Radical feminists utterly reject the liberal feminist argument that all women really need to achieve equality is fair access to the public sphere and to the resources required to compete on equal terms with men. For radical feminists women experience patriarchal oppression within both spheres of society, public and private; it shapes and colours every detail of their lives. For radical feminists, patriarchy is the key to understanding all **social structures** and patriarchal relations are universal and elemental parts of the human condition. Why should this be? One of the first radical feminists, Kate Millett (1934–), argued that patriarchy is brought about by male control of ideas and culture (Millett 1977). While this drew proper attention to institutionalized forms of belief oppressing women at work, in education and in the family, Millet's explanation of these processes is rather tautological. In effect she tends to explain patriarchy by the exercise of patriarchy, which is hardly satisfactory. In another early radical feminist theory, that of Shulamith Firestone (1945–), the argument is that patriarchy is based on the biological fact that only females bear children. This approach claims that only when it becomes technologically possible to conceive and nurture children outside the womb will women be capable of being liberated. Then, gender differences will become irrelevant and the biological justification for trapping women in the role of mother in the family will disappear (Firestone 1971).

Other radical feminists argue that the universal phenomenon at the root of patriarchy is not biological motherhood, but the social institution of the family based on marriage of one kind or another. For this version of radical feminism, marriage is what capitalism is for Marxist feminists – according to Bouchier, the 'real institutional source of exploitation' (Bouchier 1983). Here we see a characteristic of radical feminist theorizing that became established quite early on in its development – the notion that the 'personal is the political'. The exercise of power by men over women is found not just in the public structural and ideological features of work, education, the media, and so on. Just as important is patriarchy on the personal level, in the private world of intimate relations between men and women. As Mary Maynard puts it: 'Politics occur in families and between individuals when one person attempts to control or dominate another. It is in the personal and private sphere that women are particularly vulnerable to the power of men' (Maynard 1989: 66). Thus, as Sylvia Walby says, from this point of view, 'The question of who does the housework, or who interrupts whom in conversation, is seen as part of the system of male domination' (Walby 1990: 3).

For radical feminists then, every aspect of life has to be questioned and revolutionized by women in order to defeat patriarchy. So the insistence that the personal is political does not simply mean that the personal dimension of life should be added to the list of what counts as political, but rather that the oppression of women by men is the most intense political subjugation of all. At this point we can see clear similarities between radical feminism and the political rhetoric of Marxists. Just as the *Communist Manifesto* was written to stir the proletariat of Europe into revolutionary action, so radical feminism can also be appreciated as a provocation to women to wake up and take action to transform their lives. And just as Marxism in campaigning mode treats the working class as just that, one class united in a shared experience of economic exploitation, so radical feminism emphasizes an equally polarized picture of men as oppressors and women as the oppressed. For many radical feminists, rather than economic exploitation, the practices and meanings associated with heterosexual sex are seen as being the source of women's oppression.

As Adrienne Rich (1929–) argues, women are living under a regime of **compulsory heterosexuality**. 'I am suggesting that heterosexuality, like motherhood, needs to be recognised and treated as a political institution' (in Kemp and Squires 1997: 321–2). Heterosexuality, in other words, should be regarded as something that has been 'imposed, managed, organised, propagandised, and maintained by force'. Rich implies that without the compulsion towards heterosexuality and the systematic discrediting of lesbian existence, women would seek out other women, not just for sexual experience but also for 'the sharing of a rich inner life, the bonding against male tyranny, the giving and receiving of practical and political support'. Rich's argument neatly reverses the dominant cultural assumption that a lesbian existence needs to be explained or justified. She suggests that women who identify as heterosexual are deceiving themselves and/or under coercion.

This emphasis on heterosexuality as the basis of patriarchy has led radical feminist theorists to explore the links between sexual hegemony and violence against women. The work of Andrea Dworkin (1946–2005), among others, is notable here. In societies like Great Britain, a significant element in the social construction of heterosexuality is the public presentation of women as sexually available and accommodating to men, in pornography and other cultural forms. The radical feminist point here is that if women are presented in this sexually available way, with the explicit invitation to be used by men, then sexual harassment, assault or rape should not be seen as surprising. In fact, Dworkin's analysis is even more pointed than this: 'We will know that we are free when the pornography no longer exists. As long as it does exist, we must understand that we are the women in it: used by the same power, subject to the same valuation, as the vile whores who beg for more' (Dworkin 1981: 224; see also Mackinnon 1989).

For many radical feminists then, the woman's world is suffused with the prospect of real or potential violence by men. If some men structure some aspects of their lives because of the threat of physical assault – avoiding certain places at night, or refusing to drink in 'rough' pubs – then radical feminism points at the much more routine problems faced by women. According to Elizabeth Stanko:

> Women know about the unpredictability of men's physical and sexual intimidation. We plan our lives around it: finding the right street to walk down when coming home, cooking the eggs the way the husband likes them, and avoiding office parties are examples of strategies designed to avoid male sexual and physical intimidation and violence. (Stanko 1985: 70)

## Dual-systems theories

Dual-systems theories fuse Marxist feminist and radical feminist ideas. They want to take into account both the ways in which men oppress women and the ways in which such oppression has become an integral part of capitalism. Zillah Eisenstein (1948–) sees capitalism and patriarchy as being so intimately connected that they actually form one system, which she calls capitalist patriarchy (Eisenstein 1979). Their interconnection is so profound that changes in one part of the system cause changes in the other. Thus, for example, an increase in women working in the labour market because of the needs of capital will necessarily cause pressure for political change, because of the impact of this on women's role as domestic labourers.

In her essay 'The Unhappy Marriage of Marxism and Feminism' (1981), Heidi Hartmann (1945–) also insists on the need to see women as oppressed by both men and capitalism, but she sees these features as constituting separate, though connected, systems of oppression. Thus, women are exploited by men both in the labour market, where men have the better rewarded jobs, *and* in the household – women do more domestic labour than men, even if they are also wage-earners.

Patriarchy came into being prior to capitalism through marriage and family relations, and with the development of capitalist relations of production men have, as it were, 'done a deal' with capitalism to secure the kind of advantages over women in this new sphere of waged work which they had previously enjoyed in the domestic sphere. Thus the Labour movement in Great Britain has mainly promoted the interests of men, not women. Capitalism benefits from women's economic dependence on men because this ensures their availability for insecure, low-paid employment, and men benefit because they get the better jobs and have domestic services provided for them at home.

## Feminist theories: an evaluation

Radical, Marxist, dual-system and, to a lesser extent, liberal feminist theories successfully challenged some of the deep-rooted assumptions of traditional social theory and made visible to sociological analysis the impact of gender in all areas of social life. We can see the affinity that this collection of feminist theories has with social theory in that the sociological framework provided by conflict theory allows them to make the case that gender is a matter of social and political regulation rather than a law of nature. But however politically committed, these feminist theories also illustrate the theoretical limitations of conflict theory. As we shall discuss in the remainder of this chapter, one of the unfortunate ironies of using structural-conflict theory to criticize biological determinism (the assertion that differences between men and women are rooted in biology) is that one form of determinism tends to be replaced by another, namely, structural determinism. Connell argues that radical, Marxist and socialist feminist approaches share what she refers to as a 'categorical' approach to gender analysis

(Connell 1987). Here the focus is on men and women as two different units with opposed interests, and the emphasis is on specifying the relationship between these categories rather than looking at the processes and practices by which the categories are constituted. This categorical approach really captures only one limited dimension of what it is to be a social agent and also excludes from its analysis any treatment of the range, complexity and vitality of relationships between the genders. This is particularly unfortunate in the case of feminist theory because it really needs to be able to develop a nuanced analysis of gendered social and political practices precisely because it is committed to promoting progressive social change.

## Anti-essentialism

Many of the critics of the variants of structural-conflict theory and of liberal feminism take them to task for assuming that all women experience the world in the same way just because they are women. Attempting to ground feminist politics in a common or 'essential' experience of oppression effectively excludes women who are not white, Western and middle class from the theoretical picture and from political attempts to re-draw it. The rigidity of this 'identity politics' was seen as responsible for the fragmentation and disarray of feminist politics which became apparent in the 1980s in Britain and North America in particular. We can see this tendency towards essentialism as an inherent danger of structural-conflict theory in so far as it tends to make an unambiguous distinction between social groups based on their material or other interests. Whether we are discussing social class or gender, an individual is consigned to one category or the other and this allows no room for the complexity of real experience in which one is not just a woman, or a member of a particular social class or a member of a particular ethnic group.

However, the inherent determinism of structural-conflict theory is not the only factor at play in the deterioration of women's liberation into identity politics. In the more individualistic view of liberal feminist theory, the experience of white, middle-class women is taken to speak for all women. Yet, in reality, experience and **agency** develop from the complex ways in which these social structures enable and constrain us in and across different social settings. One of the most powerful criticisms of the essentialism of feminist theories comes from the writings of Black feminists. As Bhavnani and Coulson point out (in Evans 1994), the experience of racism means that black and white women

cannot be assumed to experience the same kinds of patriarchal structures and practices: 'Racism operates in a way which places different
women in different relationships to structures of power and authority in society' (Evans 1994: 337). These differences are lost when the
primary focus is on men and women as two homogeneous categories.
We need to ask how racism divides gender identity and experience
and how gender is experienced through racism, as well as how class is
shaped by gender and racism. Chandra Mohanty (1955–) develops this
critique of essentialism in her identification of a tendency to treat 'the
West' as the key referent and political actor in many feminist writings.
The corollary of this is to 'codify other feminists as non-western and
lump them together as a composite, singular "Third World Woman"'
(Mohanty 1988: 62). As she points out, this practice distorts Western
feminist practices and limits the possibility of (usually white) Western
feminists and working-class feminists and feminists of colour working
together to develop locally appropriate and detailed theoretical analyses and political strategies (see also Mohanty 2003).

We will now discuss some more of the most influential responses
to the theoretical and political limitations of structural-conflict and
liberal feminist theory. These responses draw on and contribute to
the more recent attempts by social theorists to re-think the relationship between social structures and action which we discussed in earlier
chapters. The issue of essentialism – of assuming that all women have
the same experience of oppression – is taken up in different ways
by Sylvia Walby, Connell and Butler. Walby (1990) adopts a realist
position in order to specify more clearly the interconnections and the
differences between the patriarchal structures that shape the experience of specific groups of women. Connell (1987) cites both Giddens
and Bourdieu as coming closest to meeting the needs of a theory of
gender that can recognize both the inventiveness of people's practical
attempts to transform their historical situation and the constraints
they face. She develops this more fluid approach to the relationship
between structure and agency in her subsequent work, which broadens
the focus away from the analysis of women to relations of domination
and subordination between men as well as between men and women.
Finally, we will discuss the ways in which Butler's work (1993) employs
a Foucauldian genealogy of the categories of identity. Her argument
suggests that feminist attempts to use categories relating to the unified
subject of **Enlightenment** philosophy to construct a feminist identity
and political solidarity are the source of the problems of exclusion and
fragmentation which beset the women's liberation movement in the
1980s. These theorists may thus provide a more tangible context – that

of gender practices and politics – within which to consider the theoretical and practical implications of realism, **structuration theory** and
post-structuralism.

## Re-theorizing patriarchy

Walby offers a theory of women's subordination under patriarchy
which both builds on earlier feminist conflict theory and attempts to
identify and repair its faults and weaknesses. Walby states that her
theoretical project is a realist one in that she wants to identify the
underlying structures of social life (Walby 1990: 19). This project
involves adapting some of the earlier feminist usages of the concept
of patriarchy so that it can both capture the range of experiences of
women of different cultures, class and ethnicities and also capture
'the depth, pervasiveness and interconnectedness of different aspects
of women's subordination' (Walby 1990: 2). Patriarchy is defined
by Walby in brief but stark terms as 'a system of social structures
and practices in which men dominate, oppress and exploit women'
(Walby 1990: 20). Her use of realism is evident in the claim that the
deep structures of patriarchy, although not immediately knowable,
can be discovered through systematic enquiry. She goes on to distinguish these more or less deeply rooted levels of patriarchy. At the most
abstract level, patriarchy exists as a system of social relations which
connects with capitalism and with racism. The patriarchal system of
social relations is composed of six structures which are the **emergent
properties** of specific sets of patriarchal practices: 'Any specific empirical instance will embody the effects, not only of patriarchal structures,
but also of capitalism and racism' (Walby 1990: 20).

Walby's outline of these six structures incorporates key features
of radical and Marxist feminism. The first structure, the patriarchal
mode of production, refers to the household; here housewives 'are the
producing class, while husbands are the expropriating class' (Walby
1990: 21). The second structure is that of patriarchal relations within
paid work. This structure emerges from practices that exclude women
from certain forms of work and segregate them into less well rewarded
and lower status ones. Walby argues that the state's 'systematic bias'
towards patriarchal interests in its policies and action means it should
be identified as the third patriarchal structure. Such policies include
not only those that regulate employment rates and conditions to the
benefit of men, as Marxist feminists claim, but also those condone
male violence towards women. Such violence, including rape, domestic

violence and sexual harassment is treated as the fourth structure of patriarchy. Here Walby incorporates the radical feminist emphasis on how violent acts have the effect of controlling the behaviour of all women through fear. Building further on radical feminist arguments, Walby designates patriarchal relations in sexuality as the fifth structure, including, for example, compulsory heterosexuality. The sixth structure she distinguishes is that of patriarchal relations in cultural institutions such as religion, education and the media, all of 'which create the representation of women within a patriarchal gaze' (Walby 1990: 21).

Walby uses this more elaborate theorization of patriarchy to address the essentialism found in earlier feminist theories. She argues that these six structures combine in different ways in relation to specific groups of women to comprise their different experiences of oppression, exploitation and domination. If we compare a young working-class woman, who is a lone parent and reliant on state benefits and part-time work, to a professional woman, a lawyer for example, who is without children, we can see that in each case state policies and employment conditions will combine to produce different kinds of regulation and control. The professional women will not be policed in terms of how much paid work she does and her financial relationship with ex-partners, but the lone parent will. But both women are likely to have to deal with unequal pay and promotion prospects compared to their male peers. Not only do such structures combine differently but one structure can act relatively independently. Thus women belonging to specific ethnic groups may well experience the effects of racism as a major determinant of their life-chances, but this racism will lock in differently for different groups, according to how it combines with economic exploitation or patriarchal oppression.

As we can see then, the deep structural triad of class, ethnicity and gender are presented as being ever-present for all women but not identically so. The different elaborations of this model, Walby claims, avoid the danger of reducing the effects of patriarchy to one cause and allow for historical change and cultural variation. This theoretical framework allows us to measure whether there have been changes in the degree and the form of patriarchal oppression in, for example, Britain over the course of the twentieth century. Walby offers an historical and empirical analysis which is intended to capture differences in the impact of these structures on specific groups of women. She argues that we can distinguish broadly between two forms of patriarchy – the one more private, the other more public. The former regime has the household as the main site of oppression while the latter is primarily located in sites such as employment and the state.

> In private patriarchy the expropriation of women's labour takes place primarily by individual patriarchs within the household, while in the public form it is more a collective appropriation. In private patriarchy the principal patriarchal strategy is exclusionary; in the public it is segregationist and subordinating. (Walby 1990: 240)

She argues that over the course of the twentieth century there has been a move from private to public patriarchy. First-wave feminists were instrumental in challenging the dominance of private patriarchy by succeeding in gaining citizenship and other rights for women to take part in the public sphere. This success also had an impact on the role of the state in the early to middle part of the twentieth century, so that welfare and social security policies offered more structural support for women in the public sphere. In the latter part of the twentieth century, the impact of equal rights legislation and other anti-discrimination law in relation to racism as well as educational polices both further increased the numbers of women in the public sphere and also served to reduce levels of inequality. For those women who have gained most from these changes, and who are able to work independently, there have been real advances towards equality. While they are still likely to experience segregation in relation to paid work, if they are married they are likely to experience a more egalitarian division of labour, and some can buy in services to minimize the impact of household labour. But for women who, for various reasons, have not been able to take advantage of these changes, a more private regime will be in play. Women who are older and therefore excluded from increased educational opportunities, working-class women, some ethnic minority women who live in patriarchal households, and women with young children who work part-time, are all likely to experience in differing degrees a combination of public and private patriarchal regimes. Women who head families and receive state support are subject to the more public regime of patriarchal regulation. In each case different structures work in different combinations and with differential impact, but despite all the gains no group of women is seen to be free of patriarchal power.

Walby's work can certainly be regarded as an important contribution to sustaining the project of feminist theory and research. Her removal of some of the inherent weaknesses of conflict theory means that more attention is given to historical changes to patriarchal structures. No longer do they appear as universal and constraining to all women.

However, her analytical framework has been criticized for its insistence that patriarchy is always integral to the structures of Western societies. We can note that Walby's later (1997) work still specifies the systemic features of society in terms of patriarchal rather than gender relations. As Connell suggests, such a claim fails to allow for the possibility of gender structures which are not inherently unequal or patriarchal but may instead be fundamentally democratic (Connell 2009: 76). This suggests a level of structural determinism which perhaps makes it harder to identify openings towards more egalitarian tendencies within gender structures and practices. While we might want to argue that some aspects of cultural institutions clearly only articulate patriarchal values, do we therefore want to say that cultural institutions which are the target of successive challenges to their values are still inherently patriarchal? To address this question do we need a more detailed discussion of the detail of specific political tactics, claims and strategies relating to all sides of the politics of a specific cultural form, or, as Walby seems to be claiming, do we need only to be familiar with the intentions of those deploying patriarchal practices?

While Walby evidently wants to be able to connect the deeper systemic properties of patriarchal societies to actual patriarchal practices, her account of change is expressed largely in terms of relations within and between structures. Arguably, Walby's development of the concept of patriarchy as an underlying structure of society leads her into adopting an analytical dualism between structure and agency which resembles Archer's morphogenetic theory, discussed in Chapter 7. This is not an analytical tool likely to capture the agency – the knowledgeability and action – of gender actors or the vitality and transformational potential of their practices.

Connell, like Walby, reminds us of the centrality of gender to the overall organization of society. Like earlier feminists Connell is also concerned to convey the extent to which current gender relations systematically benefit men and subordinate women. However, Connell's work offers a significantly different approach to feminist conflict theory than does Walby's, and one which moves towards a structuration-based approach to the question of analysing gendered structures and processes. Connell is clear that gender analysis requires a concept of structure to capture how powerfully determined patterns in social relationships define possibilities and consequences for action. But she also emphasizes that such structures should not be seen as mechanically deciding how people or groups act – 'Social structures are brought into being by human behaviour.' If 'we don't bring it into being, gender does not exist' (Connell 2009: 73, 74). Thus, agency, structure and change are brought into a much closer and fluid relationship in Connell's work than we have seen in other social theories – rather than standing opposed to each other, they become part of the same dynamic.

Whereas men and masculinity certainly loom large in Walby's account of the systematic nature of patriarchy they do tend to appear as a largely undifferentiated mass. Connell's work has been particularly influential in opening up the analysis of masculinity and of relationships between men to scrutiny. While many feminists were aware of the need to understand masculinity, once women's liberation movements became established the priority was to make visible women's experience after it had been hidden for so long and/or distorted by the patriarchal 'gaze'. Men, the argument often went, have been the sole focus of most of Western culture – the subject of its attention – whereas women had only ever been the object. Now it was women's turn to explore and understand their own experience.

However, Connell is one of several theorists who argue that, in fact, we cannot understand women's experience in isolation from their relations with men, and we cannot understand how the genders relate to each other without knowing a lot more about how men relate to other men. It is, Connell suggests, the multiple relationships between *masculinities* that also powerfully shape men's relationships to women. Thus, in order properly to analyse gender relations we need to include the situations and practices that occur *within* as well as between the genders. While Connell examines the processes at play within and between femininities and masculinities, the following account will focus on what she has to say about masculinity since it is here that her work has arguably made the most important contribution to gender analysis.

## Hierarchical masculinities

Connell's (1987, 1995, 2000, 2002, 2005) analyses of relationships of power and competition between men characteristically emphasize how such power is always provisional and the focus of contestation. Men compete over the resources they as a group gain from the overall subordination of women. These resources – summarized in the term 'the patriarchal dividend' – include money, 'authority, respect, service, safety, housing, access to institutional power, and control over one's own life' (Connell 2002: 142). They accrue to specific individuals and groups of men according to their position in the overall social order. Thus the inequalities arising from, most notably, social class and ethnicity feed into and are themselves re-enforced by the hier-archical ordering of gender within patriarchal societies. That form of masculinity which is culturally dominant at any one time Connell terms 'hegemonic masculinity'. This form of masculinity 'embodies the currently accepted answer to the problem of the legitimacy of patriarchy, which guarantees (or is taken to guarantee) the dominant position of men and the subordination of women' (Connell 1995: 76). As this definition implies, the superior position of any one hegemonic form is never secure; it is always subject to resistance and contestation both by other forms of masculinity and by oppositional femininities. However, also implicit in this definition is the degree to which many men who cannot themselves claim hegemonic status will still seek to attach themselves to it in order to reap the patriarchal dividend. This concept is now over twenty years old and it has inspired a large body of research-based and theoretical analysis of men and masculinities (see Connell and Messerschmidt [2005] for a useful overview and critique of the concept and the scholarship it has produced). It has been seen as offering a way to understand patriarchal power as a resource which is sustained and/or challenged within the detail of routine daily life as well as within the more regularized structures of society.

Earlier treatments of male power tended to see it as something bestowed on all men equally and as beyond challenge by women. However, if we consider that the category 'men' includes those who are gay, black and working class, then such 'essentialized' accounts of masculinity and male power have to be rejected. These other subordi-nated or marginalized forms of masculinity are ordered hierarchically in relation to the hegemonic form, with gay masculinity at the bottom and only one step up from femininity. Belonging to these subordi-nated forms of masculinity means being more at risk of various form of physical violence, stigma, humiliation and sometimes death at the hands of other men. But Connell also points out that any one form of hegemonic masculinity is always subject to challenge by those lower in the hierarchy. Thus, power, conflict and competition characterize most relationships between different masculinities. This is not all that these relationships consist of – friendship, solidarity and various other kinds of loving relationships are also possibilities.

This deliberately sparse framework for understanding masculinities offers the opportunity to treat gendered power as a resource which is always open to contestation and challenge, by other men and by women. Feminism and Gay Liberation movements are good examples of such challenges, but so are conservative men's movements which urge a return to nature and the religious right. Connell looks at how power operates within relationships between women too. She argues that although women do not tend to have the same kind of access as men to the resources of force and violence, this does not mean that women are not also caught up in competitive relationships with each other over social and material goods. As Connell argues, when a particular form of masculinity has a hegemonic status, those men who can make a claim to possess hegemonic qualities put themselves in a position in which they can also claim the privileges associated with masculinity. Women, with less power as a group, may find that the easiest and certainly the most advertised access to the same prized social resources will be to adopt the strategies of 'emphasized femininity' in order to make themselves attractive to the kinds of men that achieve them. Yet other groups of women will use more oppositional tactics to secure their own interests. Connell's rather tongue-in-cheek rendition of some of the characteristics of the strategies of emphasized femininity should alert us to the inadequacy of those social theories which portray social actors as unthinkingly obeying the dictates of gender socialization: this pattern of femininity includes, then, 'the display of sociability rather than technical competence, fragility in mating scenes, compliance with men's desire for titillation and ego-stroking in office relationships, acceptance of marriage and childcare as a response to labour-market discrimination against women' (Connell 1987: 187).

What women (and men) buy into – the values and behaviours they adopt in particular social settings – are not necessarily accurate reflections of what they are. In this light particular displays of masculinity and femininity are best seen as performances of social competence that are carried out to get by or to advance one's interests in particular social settings rather than as indications of internalized values – perhaps this perspective offers more of a sense of the contradictions *and* the reflexivity of gender that we alluded to at the beginning of this chapter. In an important sense then, gender, Connell suggests, is not something we can usefully understand as located within individuals, it does not originate in any practical sense in sexually different bodies. Gender is not a 'thing', a noun, but instead should be regarded as a verb, a series of practices and processes we engage in in relationships with others. Such processes are an organizational feature of the personal and collective social arrangements of institutional life.

## Gender regimes and the gender order

Connell distinguishes two levels of analysis of the ways in which gender organizes or structures social life. A 'gender regime' refers to the ways in which specific institutions such as schools or workplaces are organized by gender – who does what kinds of work, how emotional lives are conducted, etc. The 'gender order' is the overall pattern of power relations between men and women which gender regimes both shape and change (see Mac an Ghaill [1994] for an excellent example of research into the structuring of specific gender regime within a British school).

Connell's analysis of how relations between and within the genders feeds into wider social structures offers one way of thinking about how prized social resources such as political power, wealth, social status and access to elite goods can be successfully legitimized. The framework of hierarchical masculinities and femininities does not, as it stands, sufficiently identify the complexity and ambivalence of gender practices. However, it does go some way towards suggesting the routes by which we link reproductive practices to the rest of our lives in ways that reproduce the social conditions within which men both retain the balance of power vis-à-vis women and compete between themselves for the lion's share of the patriarchal dividend.

Analyses of gender regimes allows us to see the state of play in gender relations, and helps us identify those dimensions which seem more enduring and resistant to change as well as those that are more flexible. Connell distinguishes four structural dimensions of gender relations that can be found in contemporary society: power relations, production relations, emotional relations and symbolic relations (see Connell 2009 for a discussion of the more global dimensions to this model). Changes can occur within and between these structures. Connell suggests, then, that it is this approach to the analysis of gender – one that is ever-mindful of the open-endedness of the 'laws', conventions and values with which it is invested – that allows us to identify opportunities for moving towards more democratic gender relations.

## Post-structuralism and the politics of gender

Arguably, Connell's work allows us to recognize the play of agency and reflexivity in the politics and practices of gender relations. In order to understand how reproductive distinctions are brought into social processes we need to be able to recognize this play. Her work also suggests that this reflexivity can be lost, remaining invisible to those theories which treat social structures as only constraining of agency. Nevertheless, Connell's criticisms of the essentialism and structural determinism of some earlier feminist theories clearly move in the direction of a constructive critique rather than calling for the abandonment of the feminist project altogether.

Post-structuralist and Foucauldian critics of feminism such as Jane Flax, however, argue that the very idea of trying to use modernist theories to get at the causes of gender oppression is yet another example of the Enlightenment illusion that there is one neutral position from which we can grasp 'the truth'. According to Flax, then, feminists are fundamentally mistaken in believing that such abstract notions of truth can be of use in their own liberation, because such notions are contaminated by a history of being used to justify and also to conceal the domination and oppression of others. For these reasons, Flax argues that feminist theory must see itself as belonging to 'the terrain of postmodern philosophy', because it shares with **postmodernism** a recognition that Enlightenment concepts such as 'reason, knowledge, or the self' are 'neutralising and universalising facades' that serve to suppress the voices of those who are not 'white Western males' (Flax in Nicholson 1990: 42–3). Perhaps, Flax rhetorically suggests, reality can have '"a" structure only from the falsely universalising perspective of the dominant group . . . only to the extent that one person or group can dominate the whole will reality appear to be governed by one set of rules or be constituted by one privileged set of social relations' (Flax in Nicholson 1990: 49). On this argument, attempts to improve on theoretical accounts of the relationship between agency and structure are futile, because any attempt to impose a structural analysis of 'reality' will be but another example of the kinds of thinking that justified and sustained the domination feminists are attempting to challenge.

Judith Butler is similarly concerned to expose the ways in which modern structures of organizing the world under general concepts and categories rely on excluding and degrading those who fall outside of these concepts. For Butler, the fact that post-structuralism can reveal the ways in which theoretical concepts are implicated in the exercise of power offers a significant opportunity for renewing feminist politics. Butler argues that we can see the conflict and fragmentation which led to the breakdown of women's liberation movements in the late 1980s to be a direct consequence of the exclusionary impact of feminists' attempts to uphold a universal identity and solidarity among women:

> the premature insistence on a stable subject of feminism, understood as a seamless category of women, inevitably generates multiple refusals to

accept the category. These domains of exclusion reveal the coercive and regulatory consequences of that construction, even when the construction has been elaborated for emancipatory purposes. Indeed, the fragmentation within feminism and the paradoxical opposition to feminism from 'women' whom feminism claims to represent suggest the necessary limits of identity politics. (Butler 1990: 4)

However, she suggests, a new political project can emerge from the fall-out of these earlier divisions and exclusions within feminist theory and politics. This new politics can take shape from the radical critique of the categories of identity (Butler 1990: ix). In an argument which will be familiar from our earlier discussions of Foucault's analysis of discursive power, Butler claims that a feminist genealogy of identity politics will allow us to see the consequences of 'designating as an origin and cause those identity categories that are in fact the effects of institutions, practices, discourses with multiple and diffuse points of origin' (Butler 1990: viii–ix). In this context, the identity of 'women' is revealed as *an effect* of the legal, medical and political discourses which combined to produce modernist discourses of femininity. As we suggested above, those who fought for women's equal treatment before the law appeared to take political sustenance from the belief that they were 'more' than patriarchal society recognized them to be. Their political practice relied on placing themselves outside of and in opposition to patriarchy. Butler suggests that women's political agency must now be seen to arise from the fact that it is 'constituted' by power rather than created in external opposition to power (Butler 1990: 13).

She suggests that once we see agency to be constituted in and by power then new forms of resistance become possible which re-work and re-shape power. 'For what', she asks, 'is it that enables a purposive and significant reconfiguration of cultural and political relations, if not a relation that can be turned against itself, reworked, resisted?' (Butler 1990: 12–13).

Butler's 1993 work, *Bodies That Matter*, further explains the constitution of agency by power through the notion of performativity: the process by which discourse produces the phenomena that it names, regulates and constrains. As we may recall, in earlier feminist thinking, the distinction between sex and gender treats sex as the *prior*, natural foundation for the cultural elaboration of gendered norms. In Foucauldian vein, Butler reverses this account. She argues that the category of sex, and associated ideas of natural sexual difference, are brought into play or made visible as 'natural' only through the constant reiteration of these norms and values. This is not to claim that the body is created by culture, as some kind of artefact, but rather that the body can be regarded as 'fully material' because it is 'effect' of power. For example, in the early stages of life an infant is gendered by being shifted 'from an it to a she' (Butler 1993: 7). This 'girling of the girl' (Butler 1993: 8) is then reiterated 'by various authorities and throughout various intervals of time' to re-enforce this naturalized effect. Naming inculcates or leads to the internalization of the norm. Butler's reference here to the internalization of social norms may remind us of Parsons' structurally deterministic argument that individuals are conditioned to secure their society's 'needs' because they are socialized into its collective values. However, Butler's argument is somewhat different to that of Parsons.

For Butler it appears that the point of her feminist genealogy is to show how the dominant cultural script doesn't add up. Her approach is intended to uncover the erasures, the exclusions, the violent foreclosure and abjection, intrinsic to the process by which the subject is constructed. At this point we can more clearly see the basis for Butler's political investment in deconstruction: through revealing how concepts are implicated in the use of power, it thereby also opens up the category of women as a site of possible resignifications. These resignifications do not offer 'the truth' about what women really 'are' but they do offer the opportunity to develop strategies that 'expand the possibilities of what it means to be a woman' and to 'condition and enable an enhanced sense of agency'. It is through this release of the term 'woman' from fixed significations that 'something like "agency" becomes possible' (Butler 1992: 16).

For these reasons, then, Butler defines post-structuralism as the 'precondition' of a politically engaged critique (Butler 1992: 6). Feminism needs this theory not simply to refine its understanding of gender politics but, it would seem, also to sanction such politics. As we might recall, such a bold political investment in Foucauldian analysis stands in marked contrast to the much more distant stance from political engagement we saw Miller and Rose suggest in Chapter 6.

Arguably, what has helped to generate the controversy surrounding Butler's work since the mid 1990s is her explicit claim that post-structuralism has a directly and perhaps indispensably political significance. Indeed, both positive and critical reactions to Butler's interventions into feminist theory have played an important part in the more general exchanges between modernists and postmodernists which we discussed in earlier chapters. Without going into the detail of the feminist context of such exchanges we can usefully distinguish two broad avenues of discussion. On one hand, the challenge issued by postmodern and Foucauldian ideas has been seen to threaten the viability of any kind of rational analysis of social practices. For example, Sylvia Walby is one of several feminist writers who worry that postmodernist social theory 'has fragmented the concepts of sex, "race" and class, denying the pertinence of overarching theories of patriarchy, racism and capitalism' (Walby in Barrett and Phillips 1992: 31). Walby argues that this fragmentation threatens to destroy the capacity of social theory to analyse the larger structures – of global capitalism for example – that successfully concentrate power in relatively few hands. Walby's point here appears to be addressed to Foucauldian theorists, for whom power works through dispersal rather than through concentration in stable and identifiable blocs.

On the other hand, post-structuralist and postmodernist theory has been seen to undermine the possibility of any kind of collective politics. Lynne Segal offers a powerful summary of the issues involved when she comments that Butler's claim that resignifying what it means to be a woman offers new political possibilities can appear to be arguing that 'semantic' issues are more important than political struggles over material resources. In this way, Segal claims, Butler 'delineates a project which is distinctly different from the close attention to social *structures, relations* and *practices* which an earlier feminist project prioritized in pursuit of political-economic restructuring, and the transformations of public life and welfare' (Segal 1999: 13, original emphasis). Segal appears to be concerned, perhaps in similar ways to Walby, that post-structuralist and postmodernist feminist theories will replace modernist ones and thereby signal the end of the latter's critical and emancipatory ambitions.

This brief account of some of the contemporary debates in gender theory returns us to the themes with which this book began – the remit of social theory to describe and explain the social world as well as to diagnose its problems and propose solutions. We have now discussed some of the most important contributions to this task and can perhaps risk making the following generalization about the history of such theorizing. Theorists such as Habermas and Giddens identify the increasing importance of reflexivity within late modernity, both at the level of individual social agents and within the institutional structures of modern societies. Following this theme, we can usefully distinguish those theorists who recognize the importance of theoretical self-reflexivity as a resource with which to connect social theory with the real practices of social agents from those who produce theoretical systems that presuppose actors but provide no space within which to register the significance of their acts. Some of the ways in which structural theories have been used seem far more focused on telling us how or what social reality must be – how social order is possible, for example, or why structures may both constrain and cause conflict – rather than helping us to see what social practices are in play, and how. In this context, the theorists we have discussed from Chapter 5 onwards each contribute something useful, either to the 'internal' critique of social theories or to ideas about how to refine and develop sensitizing devices that will allow us to see the complexities, contradictions and innovations produced within and between social structures.

To return to the opening discussion of this chapter, if we consider social theory as the kind of activity which helps us to think through and against the many temptations to reify social structures as 'laws' that determine our fate then it seems necessary to have a range of different tools available for such a thinking through. Some social theories may rely on de-familiarizing social reality – making the familiar strange so as to invite us to reconsider what we thought we knew; others will instead offer ways of drilling down into the apparently mundane to reveal how much we do that we are mostly unaware of. In this context it seems unnecessary to treat post-structuralist analyses of discursive power as potential replacements for other sociological analyses of structure and action and instead better to view them as a useful resource to heighten theoretical reflexivity. Equally, however, the work of internal critique, of tracing the partial or exclusionary logic of certain concepts or ideas, is not all social theory should be limited to. Asking good questions of and about social agents and their practices, questions which focus on the vitality of those agents' own knowledge of their acts, is also arguably one of the most distinctive and important contributions of social theory.

## Further reading

Bradley, Harriet (2007): *Gender*, Key Concepts series, Polity.
Connell, Raewyn (2009): *Gender: in world perspective*, 2nd edn, Short Introductions series, Polity.
Segal, Lynne (1999): *Why Feminism?*, Polity.
Tong, Rosemarie Putnam (1998): *Feminist Thought: a more comprehensive introduction*, Westview

# POSTSCRIPT

So, now we are at the end of this book, where does this litany of debate and dispute in theorizing in sociology leave us? At least we are now in a position to ask appropriate questions. For example, as human beings, are we creative agents, writing our own life stories? Or are we constituted subjects, whose destinies are dictated by biographical forces outside our control? If so, how should we make sense of such forces? Are they normative, material, cultural, discursive or what? Or is human life best understood from both structural and action viewpoints such that, though we can try to be who we want to be, we nevertheless have to do so in structural circumstances not of our choosing?

Furthermore, how should we acquire knowledge of social life? Should we embrace science, reject it, or see the construction of scientific knowledge as itself a process requiring sociological understanding? Can the knowledge we acquire be judged true or false, or is human understanding inevitably relative – a product of a time and place? If so, should we dispense with the search for 'truth' altogether? If we choose to do that, how can we confront and attempt to manage the tremendous changes that characterize our times? The answers to these kinds of questions may be elusive, but the obligation to look for them is not just a price we have to pay for being human. It is also a privilege no other living thing can enjoy.

# BIBLIOGRAPHY

Abbott, Pamela and Wallace, Claire (1990) *An Introduction to Sociology: feminist perspectives*, London, Routledge.

Anderson, Perry (1976) *Considerations on Western Marxism*, London, New Left Books.

Anderson, R. (1979) 'Listening to conversation' in Meighan R., Shelton I. and Marks T. (eds.), *Perspectives on Society*, Sunbury-on-Thames, Nelson.

Archer, Margaret (1982) 'Morphostasis versus structuration: on combining structure and action', *British Journal of Sociology*, vol. 33.

Archer, Margaret (1995) *Realist Social Theory: the morphogenetic approach*, Cambridge, Cambridge University Press.

Archer, Margaret (1996) *Culture and Agency: the place of culture in social theory*, revised edition, Cambridge, Cambridge University Press.

Archer, Margaret (2000) *Being Human: the problem of agency*, Cambridge, Cambridge University Press.

Ariès, P. (1973) *Centuries of Childhood*, Harmondsworth, Penguin.

Ashenden, Samantha and Owen, David (1999) *Foucault Contra Habermas*, London, Sage.

Atkinson, J. M. (1978) *Discovering Suicide*, Basingstoke, Macmillan.

Badham, R. (1986) *Theories of Industrial Society*, London, Croom Helm.

Baert, Patrick and Carreira da Silva, Filipe (2009) *Social Theory in the Twentieth Century and Beyond*, second edition, Cambridge, Polity.

Barrett, Michèle (1988) *Women's Oppression Today: problems in Marxist feminist analysis*, London, Verso.

Barrett, Michèle and Phillips, Anne (eds.) (1992) *Destabilizing Theory: contemporary feminist debates*, Cambridge, Polity.

Bartky, Sandra (1990) *Femininity and Domination: studies in the phenomenology of oppression*, London, Routledge.

Bauman, Zygmunt (1978) *Hermeneutics and Social Science*, London, Hutchinson.

Bauman, Zygmunt (1992) *Intimations of Postmodernity*, London, Routledge.
Bauman, Zygmunt (1993) *Postmodern Ethics*, Oxford: Blackwell.
Bauman, Zygmunt (1998) *Globalization: the human consequences*, Cambridge, Polity.
Bauman, Zygmunt (2000a) *Liquid Modernity*, Cambridge, Polity.
Bauman, Zygmunt (2000b) *Modernity and the Holocaust*, New York, Cornell University Press.
Bauman, Zygmunt and May, Tim (2001) *Thinking Sociologically*, second edition, Oxford, Blackwell.
Beck, Ulrich (1992) *Risk Society: towards a new modernity*, London, Sage.
Beck, Ulrich, Giddens, Anthony and Lash, Scott (1994) *Reflexive Modernization*, Cambridge, Polity.
Becker, Howard (1967) *Outsiders: studies in the sociology of deviance*, New York, Free Press.
Benson, D. and Hughes, J. A. (1983) *The Perspective of Ethnomethodology*, Harlow, Longman.
Benton, Ted (1981) 'Some comments on Roy Bhaskar's "The Possibility of Naturalism"', *Radical Philosophy*, vol. 27.
Berman, Marshall (1983) *All That Is Solid Melts Into Air: the experience of modernity*, London, Verso.
Bernstein, R. J. (1976) *The Restructuring of Social and Political Theory*, Oxford, Blackwell.
Beynon, H. (1973) *Working for Ford*, Harmondsworth, Penguin.
Bhaskar, Roy (1979) *The Possibility of Naturalism*, Brighton, Harvester.
Bhaskar, Roy (1998) *The Possibility of Naturalism*, third edition, London, Routledge.
Bilton, Tony et al. (1981/2002) *Introductory Sociology*, Basingstoke, Palgrave (currently published in fourth edition, 2002).
Bloor, D. (1984) 'A sociological theory of objectivity' in Brown, S. C. (ed.), *Objectivity and Cultural Divergence*, Cambridge, Cambridge University Press.
Bocock, Robert and Thompson, Kenneth (eds.) (1992) *Social and Cultural Forms of Modernity*, Cambridge, Polity.
Bottomore, T. (ed.) (1988) *Interpretations of Marx*, Oxford, Blackwell.
Bottomore, T. and Rubel, M. (1963) *Karl Marx: Selected Writings*, Harmondsworth, Penguin.
Bouchier, David (1983) *The Feminist Challenge*, Basingstoke, Macmillan.
Bourdieu, Pierre (1977) *Outline of a Theory of Practice*, Cambridge, Cambridge University Press.
Bourdieu, Pierre (1984) *Distinction: a social critique of the judgement of taste*, London, Routledge.
Bourdieu, Pierre (1988) *Homo Academicus*, Cambridge, Polity.
Bourdieu, Pierre (1998) *Practical Reason*, Cambridge, Polity.
Bourdieu, Pierre and Wacquant, Loïc (1992) *An Invitation to Reflexive Sociology*, Cambridge, Polity.

Bowles, S. and Gintis, H. (1976) *Schooling in Capitalist America*, London, Routledge and Kegan Paul.

Bradley, Harriet (2007) *Gender*, Key Concepts series, Cambridge, Polity.

Brownmiller, Susan (1976) *Against Our Will*, Harmondsworth, Penguin.

Bryant, Christopher and Jary, David (eds.) (1991) *Giddens' Theory of Structuration: a critical appreciation*, London, Routledge (re-published in Routledge Revivals 2010).

Bryant, Christopher and Jary, David (2001) *The Contemporary Giddens: social theory in a globalising age*, London, Palgrave.

Burns, Tom (1992) *Erving Goffman*, London, Routledge.

Butler, Judith (1990) *Gender Trouble*, London, Routledge.

Butler, Judith (1992) 'Contingent foundations: feminism and the question of "postmodernism"' in Butler, J. and Scott, J. (eds.) *Feminists Theorise the Political*, New York, Routledge.

Butler, Judith (1993) *Bodies That Matter: on the discursive limits of 'sex'*, London, Routledge.

Butler, Judith and Scott, Joan Wallace (eds.) (1992) *Feminists Theorise the Political*, London, Routledge.

Cahoone, L. (ed.) (2003) *From Modernism to Postmodernism: an anthology*, second edition, Oxford, Blackwell.

Calhoun, Craig et al. (2007a) *Classical Sociological Theory*, second edition, Blackwell's Readers in Sociology, Oxford, Blackwell.

Calhoun, Craig et al. (2007b) *Contemporary Sociological Theory*, second edition, Blackwell's Readers in Sociology, Oxford, Blackwell.

Callinicos, Alex (1982) *Is There a Future for Marxism?* Basingstoke, Macmillan.

Callinicos, Alex (1989) *Against Postmodernism: a Marxist critique*, Cambridge, Polity.

Callinicos, Alex (2010) *The Revolutionary Ideas of Karl Marx*, London, Bookmarks.

Carlstein, Thoren (1981) 'The sociology of structuration in time and space: a time-geographic assessment of Giddens's theory', *Swedish Geographical Yearbook*, Lund, Lund University Press.

Castells, Manuel (1996) *The Rise of the Network Society*, Oxford, Blackwell.

Cheal, D. (1991) *Family and the State of Theory*, Hemel Hempstead, Harvester Wheatsheaf.

Cohen, I. (1989) *Structuration Theory*, Basingstoke, Macmillan.

Collier, Andrew (1994) *Critical Realism*, London, Verso.

Collins, Patricia Hill (1990) *Black Feminist Thought: knowledge, consciousness, and the politics of empowerment*, London, Unwin Hyman.

Connell, R. (1987) *Gender and Power: society, the person and sexual politics*, Cambridge, Polity.

Connell, Raewyn (1995) *Masculinities*, Cambridge, Polity.

Connell, R. (2000) *The Men and the Boys*, Cambridge, Polity.

Connell, Raewyn (2002) *Gender*, Cambridge, Polity.

Connell, R. (2005) *Masculinities*, second edition, Cambridge, Polity.

Connell, R. (2009) *Gender: in world perspective*, second edition, Short Introductions series, Cambridge, Polity.

Connell, R. and Messerschmidt, James W. (2005) 'Hegemonic masculinity: rethinking the concept', *Gender and Society*, vol. 19: 829–59.

Craib, Ian (1992) *Modern Social Theory*, second edition, Hemel Hempstead, Harvester- Wheatsheaf.

Craib, Ian (1997) *Classical Social Theory*, Oxford, Oxford University Press.

Cuff, E. C., Francis, D. W. and Sharrock, W. W. (2006) *Perspectives in Sociology*, fifth edition, London, Routledge.

Danaher, Geoff, Schirato, Tony and Webb, Jen (2000) *Understanding Foucault*, London, Sage.

Davis, Angela, Y. (1981) *Women, Race, and Class*, New York, Random House.

Delanty, Gerard (2000) *Modernity and Postmodernity*, London, Sage.

Delphy, Christine (1984) *Close to Home: a materialist analysis of women's oppression*, London, Hutchinson.

Dews, Peter (1987) *Logics of Disintegration*, London, Verso.

Ditton, Jason (1980) *The View from Goffman*, London, Routledge.

Dodd, Nigel (1999) *Social Theory and Modernity*, Cambridge, Polity.

Douglas, Jack (1974) *Understanding Everyday Life*, London, Routledge and Kegan Paul.

Downes, D. and Rock, Paul (eds.) (1979) *Deviant Interpretations*, Oxford, Martin Robertson.

Doyal, L. and Harris, R. (1986) *Empiricism, Explanation and Rationality*, London, Routledge and Kegan Paul.

Durkheim, Emile (1957) *Professional Ethics and Morals*, trans. C. Brookfield, London, Routledge.

Durkheim, Emile (1970) *Suicide*, ed. George Simpson, London, Routledge and Kegan Paul.

Durkheim, Emile (1974) *Sociology and Philosophy*, New York, Free Press.

Durkheim, Emile (1976 [1912]) *The Elementary Forms of Religious Life*, London, Allen and Unwin.

Durkheim, Emile (1982 [1895]) *The Rules of Sociological Method*, ed. Steven Lukes, trans. W. D. Halls, Basingstoke, Macmillan.

Dworkin, Andrea (1981) *Pornography: men possessing women*, London, Women's Press.

Eisenstein, Zillah, R. (1979) 'Developing a theory of capitalist patriarchy and socialist feminism' in Eisenstein, Zillah, R. (ed.), *Capitalist Patriarchy*, New York, Monthly Review Press.

Elliott, A. (ed.) (2009) *The Blackwell Reader in Contemporary Social Theory*, Oxford, Blackwell.

Elster, Jon (1985) *Making Sense of Marx*, Cambridge, Cambridge University Press, 1985.

Elster, Jon (1986a) *An Introduction to Karl Marx*, Cambridge, Cambridge University Press.

Elster, Jon (1986b) *Karl Marx: a reader*, Cambridge, Cambridge University Press.

Evans, Mary (ed.) (1994) *The Woman Question*, London, Sage.

Farganis, James (ed.) (2007) *Readings in Social Theory: the classic tradition to post-modernism*, fifth edition, New York, McGraw-Hill.

Fenton, Steve (1984) *Durkheim and Modern Sociology*, Cambridge, Cambridge University Press.

Fevre, R. (2000) *The Demoralisation of Western Culture: social theory and the dilemmas of modern living*, London, Continuum.

Feyerabend, P. (1981) *Philosophical Papers, vol. II, Problems of Empiricism*, Cambridge, Cambridge University Press.

Fidelman, Ashe (1998) *Contemporary Social and Political Theory: an introduction*, Milton Keynes, Open University Press.

Filmer, Paul et al. (1972) *New Directions in Sociological Theory*, London, Collier-Macmillan.

Firestone, Shulamith (1971) *The Dialectic of Sex*, London, Cape.

Flax, Jane (1992) 'The end of innocence' in Butler, J. and Scott, J. (eds.), *Feminists Theorise the Political*, New York, Routledge.

Foucault, Michel (1965) *Madness and Civilisation*, New York, Vintage.

Foucault, Michel (1975) *The Birth of the Clinic: an archaeology of medical perception*, New York, Vintage.

Foucault, Michel (1980) *Power/Knowledge: selected interviews and other writings, 1972–1977*, ed. Colin Gordon, New York, Prentice-Hall.

Freedman, Jane (2001) *Feminism*, Milton Keynes, Open University Press.

Friedan, Betty (1965) *The Feminine Mystique*, New York, Norton.

Fuller, Steve (2000) *Thomas Kuhn: a philosophical history for our times*, Chicago, University of Chicago Press.

Garfinkel, Harold (1984) *Studies in Ethnomethodology*, Cambridge, Polity.

Gellner, Ernest (1979) *Spectacles and Predicaments: essays in social theory*, Cambridge, Cambridge University Press.

Gellner, Ernest (1986) *Relativism and the Social Sciences*, Cambridge, Cambridge University Press.

Gellner, Ernest (1992) *Postmodernism, Reason and Religion*, London, Routledge.

Giddens, Anthony (ed.) (1971a) *The Sociology of Suicide*, London, Frank Cass.

Giddens, Anthony (1971b) *Capitalism and Modern Social Theory: an analysis of the writings of Marx, Durkheim and Max Weber*, Cambridge, Cambridge University Press.

Giddens, Anthony (1972a) *Emile Durkheim: selected writings*, Cambridge, Cambridge University Press.

Giddens, Anthony (1972b) *Politics and Sociology in the Work of Max Weber*, London, Macmillan.

Giddens, Anthony (1976) *New Rules of Sociological Method*, London, Hutchinson.

Giddens, Anthony (1977) *Studies in Social and Political Theory*, New York, Basic Books.

Giddens, Anthony (1979) *Central Problems in Social Theory*, London, Macmillan.

Giddens, Anthony (1984) *The Constitution of Society: outline of the theory of structuration*, Cambridge, Polity.

Giddens, Anthony (1987) *Social Theory and Modern Sociology*, Cambridge, Polity.

Giddens, Anthony (1990) *The Consequences of Modernity*, Cambridge, Polity.

Giddens, Anthony (1991) *Modernity and Self-Identity: self and society in the late modern age*, Stanford, Stanford University Press.

Giddens, Anthony (1999) *Runaway World: how globalisation is reshaping our lives*, London, Profile Books.

Giddens, Anthony (2001) *The Transformation of Intimacy: sexuality, love and eroticism in modern societies*, Cambridge, Polity.

Giddens, Anthony and Pierson, Christopher (1998) *Conversations with Anthony Giddens: making sense of modernity*, Cambridge, Polity.

Goffman, Erving (1968) *Asylums*, Harmondsworth, Penguin.

Goffman, Erving (1969) *Strategic Interaction*, Oxford, Blackwell.

Goffman, Erving (1990a) *Stigma: notes on the management of spoiled identity*, Harmondsworth, Penguin.

Goffman, Erving (1990b) *The Presentation of Self in Everyday Life*, Harmondsworth, Penguin.

Goffman, Erving (1997) *The Goffman Reader*, eds. C. Lemert and A. Branaman, Oxford, Blackwell.

Habermas, Jürgen (1981) 'Modernity versus postmodernity', *New German Critique*, vol. 22: 3–14.

Habermas, Jürgen (1984) *The Theory of Communicative Action, Vol. 1*, London, Beacon Press.

Habermas, Jürgen (1986) *Knowledge and Human Interests*, Cambridge, Polity.

Habermas, Jürgen (1987) *The Philosophical Discourse of Modernity*, Cambridge, Polity.

Hall, Stuart et al. (1988) 'New Times', *Marxism Today*, October.

Hall, Stuart, Held, David and McGrew, Tony (eds.) (1992) *Modernity and its Futures*, Cambridge, Polity.

Harré, Rom (2002) 'Social structure and social change: social reality and the myth of social structure', *European Journal of Social Theory*, vol. 5: 111–23.

Hartmann, Heidi (1979) 'Capitalism, patriarchy and job segregation by sex' in Eisenstein, Zillah, R. (ed.), *Capitalist Patriarchy*, New York, Monthly Review Press.

Hartmann, Heidi (1981) 'The unhappy marriage of Marxism and feminism: towards a more progressive union' in Sargant, Lydia (ed.), *Women and Revolution*, London, Pluto Press.

Harvey, David (1989) *The Condition of Postmodernity*, Oxford, Blackwell.

Harvey, David (2009) *Introduction to Marx's Capital*, London, Verso.
Harvey, David (2010) *A Companion to Marx's Capital*, London, Verso.
Held, David (1989) *Introduction to Critical Theory*, Cambridge, Polity.
Held, David and Thompson, John (1989) *Social Theory of Modern Societies: Anthony Giddens and his critics*, Cambridge, Cambridge University Press.
Heritage, John (1994) *Garfinkel and Ethnomethodology*, Cambridge, Polity.
Hesse, Mary (1974) *The Structure of Scientific Inference*, London: Macmillan.
Hollis, Martin (1994) *The Philosophy of Social Science*, Cambridge, Cambridge University Press.
Hollis, Martin and Lukes, Steven (1985) *Rationality and Relativism*, Oxford, Blackwell.
hooks, bell (1981) *Ain't I a Woman? Black women and feminism*, New York, South End Press.
hooks, bell (1990) *Yearning: race, gender, and cultural politics*, New York, South End Press.
Jackson, Stevi (ed.) (1993) *Women's Studies: a reader*, Hemel Hempstead, Harvester.
Jaggar, Alison, M. (1983) *Feminist Politics and Human Nature*, Hemel Hempstead, Harvester.
Jagger, Elizabeth (2000) 'Consumer bodies' in Hancock, Philip, et al., *The Body, Culture and Society*, Milton Keynes, Open University Press.
James, Joy and Sharpley-Whiting, T. Denean (eds.) (2000) *The Black Feminist Reader*, Oxford, Blackwell.
Jones, Colin and Porter, Roy (1994) *Reassessing Foucault: power, medicine and the body*, London, Routledge.
Kelly, Liz (1988) *Surviving Sexual Violence*, Cambridge, Polity.
Kemp, Sandra and Squires, Judith (1997) *Feminisms*, Oxford: Oxford University Press.
Kimmel, Michael. S. (2004) *The Gendered Society*, Oxford, Oxford University Press.
King, A. (2005) 'Structure and agency' in Harrington, A. (ed.), *Modern Social Theory: an introduction*, Oxford, Oxford University Press.
Kolakowski, L. (1978) *Main Currents of Marxism*, vols. 1–3, Oxford, Oxford University Press.
Kuhn, Thomas (1970) *The Structure of Scientific Revolutions*, second edition, Chicago, University of Chicago Press.
Kumar, Krishan (1978) *Prophecy and Progress: the sociology of industrial and post-industrial life*, Harmondsworth, Penguin.
Lash, Scott (1990) *Sociology of Postmodernism*, London, Routledge.
Lee, David and Newby, Howard (1983) *The Problem of Sociology*, London, Hutchinson.
Lemert, Charles (ed.) (2004) *Social Theory: the multicultural and classic readings*, third edition, New York, Westview Press.
Lemert, Edwin (1967) *Human Deviance, Social Problems and Social Control*, Englewood Cliffs, Prentice Hall.

López, J. and Scott, J. (2000) *Social Structure*, Buckingham, Open University Press.

Lovell, Terry (ed.) (1990) *British Feminist Thought: a reader*, Oxford, Blackwell.

Lukes, Steven (1973) *Emile Durkheim: his life and work*, Harmondsworth, Penguin.

Lyon, David (2000) 'Post-modernity' in Browning, Gary, Halci, Abigail and Webster, Frank, *Understanding Contemporary Society*, London, Sage.

Lyotard, Jean-François (1984) *The Postmodern Condition*, Manchester, Manchester University Press.

Mac an Ghaill, Mairtin (1994) *The Making of Men: masculinities, sexualities and schooling*, Buckingham, Open University Press, 1994.

McCarthy, Thomas (1984) *The Critical Theory of Jürgen Habermus*, Cambridge, Polity.

McHoul, Alec and Grace, Wendy (2002) *A Foucault Primer: discourse, power and the subject*, London, Routledge.

Mackinnon, Catharine (1982) 'Feminism, Marxism, method, and the state: an agenda for theory', *Signs*, vol. 7 (3): 515–44.

Mackinnon, Catharine A. (1989) *Toward a Feminist Theory of the State*, Cambridge, MA, Harvard University Press.

McLellan, David (1977), *Selected Writings of Karl Marx*, Oxford, Oxford University Press (second edition 2000).

McLellan, David (1973) *Karl Marx: his life and thought*, Basingstoke, Macmillan.

McLellan, David (1980) *The Thought of Karl Marx*, second edition, Basingstoke, Macmillan.

McLellan, David (1983) *Karl Marx: the first 100 years*, London, Fontana.

McLellan, David (1988) *Marxism: essential writings*, Oxford, Oxford University Press.

McLellan, David (2007) *Marxism after Marx: an introduction*, fourth edition, Basingstoke, Macmillan.

McNay Loïs (1994) *Foucault: a critical introduction*, Cambridge, Polity.

Malinowski, B. (1922) *Argonauts of the Western Pacific*, London, Routledge and Kegan Paul.

Mann, M. (ed.) (1983) *The Macmillan Student Encyclopaedia of Sociology*, Basingstoke, Macmillan.

Mann, Michael (1993) *The Sources of Social Power*, vol. 2, Cambridge, Cambridge University Press.

Manning, Philip (1992) *Erving Goffman and Modern Sociology*, Cambridge, Polity.

Margolis, Joseph (1991) *The Truth about Relativism*, Oxford, Blackwell.

Marshall, Barbara, L. (1994) *Engendering Modernity*, Cambridge, Polity.

Martin, Emily (1997) *The Woman in the Body*, Buckingham, Open University Press.

Marx, Karl (1954) *The Eighteenth Brumaire of Louis Napoleon*, Moscow, Progress Publishers.

Marx, Karl (2008) *Capital: an abridged edition*, ed. D. McLellan, Oxford World Classics, Oxford, Oxford University Press.

Marx, Karl and Engels, Friedrich (1969) *Basic Writings on Politics and Philosophy*, ed. Lewis S. Feuer, London, Fontana.

Marx, Karl and Engels, Friedrich (1976) *Collected Works*, London, Lawrence and Wishart.

Marx, Karl and Engels, Friedrich (2008) *The Communist Manifesto*, ed. D. McLellan, Oxford World Classics, Oxford, Oxford University Press.

Matthews, Betty (ed.) (1983) *Marx: 100 years on*, London, Lawrence and Wishart.

May, Tim and Powell, Jason (2008) *Situating Social Theory*, second edition, Milton Keynes, Open University Press.

Maynard, M. (1989) *Sociological Theory*, Harlow, Longman.

Meltzer, B. N. et al. (1975) *Symbolic Interactionism*, London, Routledge and Kegan Paul.

Meštrović, S. (1997) *Postemotional Society*, London, Sage.

Miller, Peter and Rose, Nikolas (2008) *Governing the Present*, Cambridge, Polity.

Millett, Kate (1977) *Sexual Politics*, London, Virago.

Mitchell, Juliet (1975) *Psychoanalysis and Feminism*, Harmondsworth, Penguin.

Mitchell, Juliet and Oakley, Ann (1986) *What is Feminism?* Oxford, Blackwell.

Mohanty, Chandra (1988) 'Under western eyes: feminist scholarship and colonial discourse' in *Feminist Review*, vol. 30 (Autumn): 61–88.

Mohanty, Chandra (2003) *Feminism Without Borders: decolonizing theory, practising solidarity*, Durham, Duke University Press.

Morrison, Kenneth (1995) *Marx, Durkheim, Weber: Formations of Modern Social Thought*, London, Sage.

Mouzelis, Nicos (1995) *Sociological theory: what went wrong?*, London, Routledge.

Mouzelis, Nicos (2000) 'The subjectivist-objectivist divide: against transcendence', *Sociology*, vol. 34.

Mythen, Gabe (2004) *Ulrich Beck: a critical introduction to the risk society*, London, Pluto Press.

Nicholson, Linda, J. (ed.) (1990) *Feminism/Postmodernism*, London, Routledge.

Norris, Christopher (1997) *Against Relativism: philosophy of science, deconstruction and critical theory*, Oxford, Blackwell.

Oakley, Ann (1972) *Sex, Gender and Society*, London, Maurice Temple Smith.

Oakley, Ann (1980) *Women Confined*, Oxford, Martin Robertson.

Oakley, Ann (1984) *The Captured Womb: a history of the medical care of pregnant women*, Oxford, Blackwell.

Oakley, Ann (1993) *Essays on Women, Medicine and Health*, Edinburgh, Edinburgh University Press.

Oakley, Ann and Mitchell, Juliet (1997) *Who's Afraid of Feminism? Seeing through the backlash*, Harmondsworth, Penguin.

O'Brien, Martin, Penna, Sue and Hay, Colin (1998) *Theorising Modernity: reflexivity, environment and identity in Giddens' social theory*, Harlow, Longman.

Outhwaite, William (1996) *The Habermas Reader*, Cambridge, Polity.

Outhwaite, William (2009) *Habermas: a critical introduction*, second edition, Cambridge, Polity.

Parker, John (2000) *Structuration*, Buckingham, Open University Press.

Parkin, Frank (1982) *Max Weber*, London, Tavistock.

Parsons, T. (1966) *Societies: evolutionary and comparative perspective*, Englewood Cliffs, Prentice-Hall.

Parsons, T. (1971) *The System of Modern Societies*, Englewood Cliffs, Prentice-Hall.

Pearce, Frank (1989) *The Radical Durkheim*, London, Unwin Hyman.

Plummer, Ken (1992) *Modern Homosexualities: fragments of lesbian and gay experiences*, London, Routledge.

Poggi, Gianfranco (2006) *Weber: a short introduction*, Cambridge, Polity.

Polanyi, Karl (1973) *The Great Transformation*, New York, Octagon Books.

Poster, Mark (1984) *Foucault, Marxism and History*, Cambridge, Polity.

Rabinow, Paul (ed.) (1991) *The Foucault Reader*, Harmondsworth, Penguin.

Radkau, Joachim (2009) *Max Weber: a biography*, Cambridge, Polity.

Rich, Adrienne (1980) 'Compulsory heterosexuality and lesbian existence', *Signs*, vol. 5 (4): 631–60.

Richards, Janet Radcliffe (1980) *The Skeptical Feminist*, London, Routledge.

Ritzer, George (2000) *The McDonaldization of Society: an investigation into the changing character of contemporary social life*, London, Sage.

Ritzer, George (2007) *Sociological Theory*, seventh edition, New York, McGraw-Hill.

Ritzer, George (ed.) (2002) *The Blackwell Companion to Major Social Theorists*, Oxford, Blackwell.

Ritzer, George and Smart, Barry (eds.) (2001) *Handbook of Social Theory*, London, Sage.

Robbins, Derek (2000) *Bourdieu and Culture*, London, Sage.

Roche, Maurice (1973) *Phenomenology, Language and the Social Sciences*, London, Routledge and Kegan Paul.

Rock, Paul (1979) *The Making of Symbolic Interactionism*, Basingstoke, Macmillan.

Rogers, Mary, F. (ed.) (1998) *Contemporary Feminist Theory: a text/reader*, New York, McGraw-Hill.

Rose, A. (ed.) (1962) *Human Behaviour and Social Processes*, London, Routledge and Kegan Paul.

Rowbotham, Sheila (1992) *Women in Movement: feminism and social action*, London, Routledge.

Sanger, Margaret (1916) *What Every Girl Should Know*, New York, M. N. Naisel.

Sanger, Margaret (1926) *Happiness in Marriage*, New York, Brentano's.
Sanger, Margaret (1928) *Motherhood in Bondage*, New York, Brentano's.
Sarup, Madan (1993) *An Introductory Guide to Post-structuralism and Postmodernism*, second edition, Hemel Hempstead, Harvester-Wheatsheaf.
Scambler, Graham (2001) *Habermas, Critical Theory and Health*, London, Routledge.
Schutz, A. (1962) *Collected Papers, vol. 1, The Problem of Social Reality*, Dordrecht, The Netherlands, Kluwer Academic Publishers.
Scott, Sue and Morgan, David (eds.) (1993) *Body Matters: essays on the sociology of the body*, London, Falmer.
Scott, Susie (2009) *Making Sense of Everyday Life*, Cambridge, Polity.
Segal, Lynne (1999) *Why Feminism?*, Cambridge, Polity.
Seidman, Steven (2008) *Contested Knowledge: social theory today*, fourth edition, Oxford, Blackwell.
Sewell, William (1992) 'A theory of structure: duality, agency and transformations', *American Journal of Sociology*, vol. 98.
Sharrock, W. W. (1977) 'The problem of order' in Worsley, P. (ed.), *Introducing Sociology*, Harmondsworth, Penguin.
Sharrock, W. W. and Anderson, R. J. (2010) *The Ethnomethodologists*, second edition, London, Routledge.
Shilling, Chris (2003) *The Body and Social Theory*, second edition, London, Sage.
Silverman, David (1998) *Harvey Sacks: social science and conversation analysis*, Cambridge, Polity.
Skidmore, W. (1975) *Theoretical Thinking in Sociology*, Cambridge, Cambridge University Press.
Smart, Barry (1988) *Foucault*, Key Sociologists, London, Routledge.
Smart, Barry (1992) *Postmodernity*, London, Routledge.
Smith, Greg (2006) *Erving Goffman*, Key Sociologists, London, Routledge.
Stanko, Elizabeth (1985) *Intimate Intrusions: women's experience of male violence*, London, Routledge.
Stones, Rob (2005) *Structuration Theory*, London, Palgrave.
Stopes, Marie (1996 [1916]) *Married Love*, Sussex, Orion Fiction.
Stopes, Marie (2000) *Birth Control and Other Writings*, ed. Lesley A. Hall, Bristol, Thoemmes Press.
Taylor, Steve (1982) *Durkheim and the Sociology of Suicide*, Basingstoke, Macmillan.
Thomas, W. I. (1966) 'Situational analysis' in Janowitz, M. (ed.), *Organisation and Social Personality: selected papers*, Chicago, University of Chicago Press.
Thompson, Denise (2001) *Radical Feminism Today*, London, Sage.
Thompson, John B. (1989) 'The theory of structuration' in Thompson, John B. and Held, David (eds.) *Social Theory of Modern Societies: Anthony Giddens and his critics*, Cambridge, Cambridge University Press.

Thompson, John B. (1991) 'Editor's introduction' in Bourdieu, Pierre, *Language and Symbolic Power*, Cambridge, Polity.

Thompson, Kenneth (2002) *Emile Durkheim*, second edition, London, Routledge.

Tong, Rosemarie Putnam (1998) *Feminist Thought: a more comprehensive introduction*, New York, Westview Press.

Trigg, Roger (1985) *Understanding Social Science*, Oxford, Blackwell.

Turner, Bryan (1981) *For Weber: essays on the sociology of fate*, London, Routledge and Kegan Paul.

Turner, Bryan (1992) *Regulating Bodies: essays in medical sociology*, London, Routledge.

Turner, Bryan (1995) *Medical Power and Social Knowledge*, second edition, London, Sage.

Turner, Bryan (2008) *The Body and Society: explorations in social theory*, third edition, London, Sage.

Turner, Bryan (ed.) (2000) *The Blackwell Companion to Social Theory*, second edition, Oxford, Blackwell.

Uberoi, J. Singh (1962) *The Politics of the Kula Ring*, Manchester, Manchester University Press.

Veblen, Thorstein (1998) *The Theory of the Leisure Class*, New York, Prometheus Books.

Walby, Sylvia (1990) *Theorizing Patriarchy*, Oxford, Blackwell.

Walby, Syliva (1997) *Gender Transformations*, London, Routledge.

Weber, Max (1947) *The Theory of Social and Economic Organisation*, New York, Free Press.

Weber, Max (1949) *The Methodology of the Social Sciences*, New York, Free Press.

Weber, Max (1968) *Economy and Society*, eds. G. Roth and C. Wittich, New York, Bedminster Press.

Weber, Max (1991) *Essays in Sociology*, eds. H. H. Gerth and C. Wright Mills, Abingdon, Routledge.

Weber, Max (2001) *The Protestant Ethic and the Spirit of Capitalism*, London, Routledge.

Whimster, Sam (2007) *Understanding Weber*, London, Routledge.

Whimster, Sam and Lash, Scott (eds.) (1987) *Max Weber, Rationality and Modernity*, London, Allen and Unwin.

White, Stephen, K. (1995) *The Cambridge Companion to Habermas*, Cambridge, Cambridge University Press.

Winch, P. (1970) *The Idea of a Social Science*, London, Routledge and Kegan Paul.

Wittgenstein, L. (1973) *Philosophical Investigations*, Oxford, Basil Blackwell.

Wootton, Anthony and Drew, Paul (1988) *Erving Goffman: explaining the interaction order*, Cambridge, Polity.

World Health Organization (1997) *Female Genital Mutilation*, WHO.

Worsley, Peter (1982) *Marx and Marxism*, London, Tavistock.

# GLOSSARY

**action**
In interpretive sociology, the term that stresses the consciously intended nature of human social behaviour.

**action theory / interpretive theory**
Approaches to human social behaviour that explain it as the product of the choices and intentions of actors, such as Weber's social action theory, symbolic interactionism, phenomenology and ethnomethodology. Social life is seen as the creation or accomplishment of conscious human beings whose mental abilities to interpret or attach meaning to reality enable them to make sense of each other and thereby interact in ordered ways.

**agency**
A term used by Giddens, distinctively to refer to the capacity of social actors to intervene in the world.

**alienation**
A crucial concept in Marxist thinking. It summarizes the nature of existence for a member of an exploited class. Forced to work for someone else in order to live, such a worker not only has little or no control over how this work is carried out but does not own what it produces either. Such workers are alienated from the work itself, its product, and from all those they live and work with.

**anatomo-politics**
A Foucauldian term which refers to the exercise of power in order to encourage people to think about and manage their bodies in particular ways.

| | |
|---|---|
| **anomie** | Durkheim's term for egoistic, self-centred, anti-social behaviour, which, for him, is always the result of inappropriate or inadequate socialization. |
| **belief system** | A set of interrelated ideas which together form a coherent view of the world. |
| **bio-medicine** | The approach to health and illness which treats these as matters essentially to do with the body and its constituent organs. |
| **bio-politics** | A Foucauldian term which refers to the exercise of power in order to promote particular forms of physical behaviour in a population of bodies. |
| **bourgeoisie** | The Marxist term for the owners of productive wealth in capitalism: employers, shareholders and investors. |
| **capital** | Prefixed by the terms cultural, economic, social, or symbolic and coined by Pierre Bourdieu to refer to an individual's, group's, or institution's resources. Mostly, types of 'capital' are self-explanatory. Hence 'economic capital' refers to resources such as income; 'cultural capital' defines manners, taste, knowledge and skills; 'social capital' relates to social relations or who one knows; and, perhaps less obviously, 'symbolic capital' is derived from honour and reputation. Social agents (individuals, groups, organizations) utilize forms of capital in order to dominate arenas of struggles for power. |
| **capitalism** | The hiring of workers to produce goods and services for sale in a competitive market in order to make a profit for their employers. |
| **class consciousness** | According to Marx, the ability of an exploited, oppressed class to appreciate the reality of its circumstances and to realize that it needs to act to free itself from these. |
| **compulsory heterosexuality** | The term employed by Adrienne Rich to describe the cultural privileging of male–female sexual relations over all others, and the resulting conviction that the only normal and natural source of sexual fulfilment is derived from penile-vaginal penetrative sex. |
| **consumption** | The activity of purchasing goods for personal use, as in shopping. |

| | |
|---|---|
| **critical realism** | A philosophy of science holding that objects of the social and natural world are real in the sense of possessing causal powers that may or may not be activated so as to bring into being an effect upon other social or natural objects. In social theory these 'real' objects are social or cultural structures which are said to pre-exist the social actions and activities of individuals. For critical realists social or cultural structures represent the conditions under which all social activity is enacted. The most well known exponents of this view are Roy Bhaskar, Margaret Archer and Andrew Sayer. |
| **depersonalization / mortification of the self** | According to Goffman, these are the principal consequences of institutionalization. The terms refer to the way in which the enforcement of organizational rules reduces the capacity of humans to choose who to be and to decide for themselves how to behave. |
| **discourse (1)** | The particular words chosen in order to express meaning. |
| **discourse (2)** | A depiction of reality and a set of prescriptions for behaviour based on a particular form of knowledge, as in medical discourse, religious discourse. |
| **discursive knowledge** | Used by Giddens to describe forms of social activity that actors are able to give an account of. See, in contrast, 'practical knowledge'. |
| **disenchantment / dehumanization** | Weber's term for the huge drawback of the dominance of rationalization in modernity. For him, the obsession with efficiency and calculability which typifies modern existence results in the absence of any real interest in the finer things in life – spiritual, emotional and aesthetic considerations in particular. |
| **division of labour** | Durkheim's term for the extent to which members of a society play different roles and live different lives. The more traditional a society, the simpler the division of labour; the more modern it is, the more complex the division of labour. |
| **doxa** | Bourdieu's term (originally from Plato) used to describe an actor's taken-for-granted or everyday activities. |
| **dualism** | The view that there is an ultimate and irreducible distinction between social structures and actors or |

agents. It is a position that is essential to structuralist sociology and to Archer's version of critical realism.

**duality**

Refers to the inseparable nature of, or synthesis between, social structures and the activities of agents or actors. For Giddens, the duality of structure and action prevents the two from being analysed individually.

**economic determinism**

Usually used pejoratively (as a criticism), this term refers to an analysis that sees economic activity as the only area of human life that needs to be understood in order to make sense of human behaviour.

**emergent properties**

First coined by G. H. Lewes in the nineteenth century to describe the way in which a combination of things or phenomena may produce a new entity possessing its own irreducible causal powers or properties. Archer utilizes the concept as a way of defining the different natures of social structures and of agents or actors.

**empiricism**

The exclusive reliance on the human senses, particularly observation, to demonstrate the existence of things.

**the Enlightenment**

The name given to the moment in history around the middle of the eighteenth century when it was realized that because human beings, uniquely among living things, have the mental ability to reason for themselves and thereby act rationally, they need no longer rely on religion-inspired accounts of reality, which typically explain it as the creation of non-human, higher beings, such as gods or spirits. This emphasis on the potential of human reason encouraged the establishment of scientific reasoning and practice as the embodiment of rationality and marginalized religious thinking and practice, a process known as secularization.

**epistème**

Foucault's term for the worldview promoted by a particular discourse.

**functionalism**

A theoretical approach to human societies which emphasizes their integrated, interdependent, structured features. Functionalists often portray the workings of social systems as analogous to those of organic systems.

| | |
|---|---|
| **globalization** | The name used to describe the ways in which the boundaries between different societies have been eroded. Those who claim that globalization is a central feature of contemporary life point to the worldwide transformations wrought by such factors as the power of transnational corporations, electronic communications, and global trading in both finance and manufacturing. |
| **habitus** | Used in the work of Pierre Bourdieu to refer to an agent's common-sense practical knowledge: taken-for-granted beliefs, mannerisms, ways of doing things and understanding what is going on. One's habitus is dependent on one's social or class position and these factors will colour the way in which an individual sees or interprets the social world and his or her positions or roles within it. |
| **hermeneutic** | Now largely used to refer to the significance of human communication in creating a meaningful world. |
| **historical materialism** | The term used to describe Marx's theory of history, in which he sees all human societies passing through the same epochs or times (though not at the same speed), and in which each epoch is defined by a different economic or productive system. |
| **ideal type** | A Weberian concept, this refers to the deliberate portrayal of an aspect of human existence in as stark and one-sided a way as possible. The point is to omit the complexity you are perfectly well aware exists in favour of making your selected emphasis as clear as could be. |
| **ideology** | Sometimes used as a synonym for a belief system (a set of interrelated ideas) but more sensibly used to refer to a set of beliefs which deny the believer an understanding of the true nature of reality. For example, Marxists and some feminists point to the ways in which ideologies obscure, or at least justify and legitimate, class- and gender-based inequalities. |
| **indexicality** | The term used by ethnomethodologists to refer to the context-bound, or contingent, nature of human action. That is, the decision to act in a certain way can only make sense in the social context in which the action takes place. It therefore follows that any |

action can only be understood properly by appreciating this social context.

**individualism**
An approach that explains human behaviour as the product of an individual's unique characteristics, such as their psychological make-up and personality traits.

**induction**
A form or method of reasoning, commonly associated with positivism, that involves making generalizations or laws based on empirical observations about particular instances of things.

**infrastructure / economic base**
For Marxists, the foundation or base on which any social system is built. In Marxist thought, the basis of any society is its particular form of economic or productive activity.

**institutionalization**
Goffman's term for the process whereby the establishments in which people live demand complete conformity from their inmates to rules of behaviour deemed necessary for organizational efficiency.

**instrumental rationality / instrumental reason**
For Weber the principal preoccupation in modernity, these terms refer to the application of the uniquely human ability to think and work out what to do solely in order to calculate the most efficient way of achieving something. That is, the pursuit of technical efficiency – for example, how to do things as cheaply as possible – prevails over all other considerations, such as working out whether something is good or bad, or whether it is the right thing to do.

**mechanical solidarity**
The type of solidarity found in pre-modern, traditional societies where social order is automatically, or mechanically, achieved because the inhabitants live similar lives and share similar beliefs.

**medicalization**
The exercise of medical power in order to regulate behaviour in realms of existence that have little or nothing to do with the body. This often means treating morality – concerns about right and wrong – as matters of health and illness, as in the medicalization of the family or the medicalization of sexuality.

**mode of production**
The Marxist term for a type of economy or way of producing goods and wealth. Apart from communistic economic activity, each mode – slavery, feudalism and capitalism – is based upon a dominant class

exploiting the labour of a subordinate class in order to produce wealth. This wealth then becomes the private property of the dominant class.

**modernism**
The belief that humans, by the use of reason, can discover certain, objective truth about the nature and meaning of things and events and can then use this knowledge to improve the conditions of human existence.

**modernity**
The name given to the Enlightenment-inspired changes which began to have a major impact in the nineteenth century and which matured during the twentieth; its central features included industrial capitalism, scientific activity, huge population growth, urbanization and the secularization of knowledge.

**moral relativism**
The view that all values and value-judgements are inevitably cultural constructions and therefore can never be held to be objectively correct and of universal validity.

**naturalism (1)**
An approach that explains human behaviour as a product of natural forces such as genetic make-up, evolution and the satisfaction of animal-like needs.

**naturalism (2)**
In social theory, the view that the methods of research and the mechanisms of cause and effect are the same for the social world as for the natural world.

**ontological security**
A term Giddens uses to refer to the sense of safety and security, or equanimity, that comes from the conviction that your world is morally and socially ordered and your place in it secure.

**organic solidarity**
The type of solidarity found in modern societies. Here people live very different lives from each other but because they are dependent on each other's different activities in order to survive, organic solidarity emerges. It is the solidarity that grows from the interdependence of different individuals.

**panopticism**
Foucault's term for the ways in which individuals regulate their own behaviour in case they are being observed. The panopticon was designed to be a prison in which the inmates knew they could never escape the surveillance of their guards.

| | |
|---|---|
| **patriarchy** | The exercise of power in all its forms by men over women. |
| **positivism** | The approach which argues that an account of reality can be accepted as true only if it can be proved to be so. |
| **postmodernism** | The view that contemporary existence is characterized by a loss of faith in the possibility, so central to Enlightenment ideals, that people can ever acquire objective truth or certain knowledge. Postmodernism holds that all human knowledge is inevitably a cultural creation. Since human beings can never stand outside the cultural influences that have made them who they are, human knowledge will always be a product of time and place. |
| **postmodernity** | The view that it is no longer accurate to say that we continue to live in modernity. According to postmodernists, the world has been so transformed in recent years that we have gone beyond modernity and now live in post-modern times. As a consequence, we need to develop new ways of making sense of this transformed existence. |
| **practical knowledge** | Defined by Giddens as an actor's knowledge that is understood only tacitly or in a taken-for-granted manner. See, in contrast, 'discursive knowledge'. |
| **project of modernity** | Activities based on the belief that the acquisition of certain knowledge by the use of reason will enable humans to achieve continuing progress for themselves and their societies. |
| **proletariat** | The Marxist term for the class in capitalism that sells its labour power to employers in return for the wages its members need in order to survive. |
| **rationalization** | For Weber, the hallmark of modernity – the process whereby modern humans become preoccupied with calculating how to do things efficiently. |
| **reflexive sociology** | Used by Pierre Bourdieu to refer to the need for the sociologist to recognize how his or her own social background might be a source of bias. This is not simply a methodological imperative but is derived from the view that an actor's understanding of the social world is not just a form of knowledge but a part of the material that creates and sustains that world. |

| | |
|---|---|
| **reflexivity** | The routine monitoring of yourself and your behaviour in order to decide who to be and how to live. |
| **reification** | The mistake of treating a concept as though it is a real thing. For example, to talk of the ideas or beliefs of a society, when in fact only human beings can have ideas and beliefs, is to reify the concept. |
| **relations of production** | The Marxist term for the ways in which individuals interact with each other in economic activity. Different economic systems or modes of production are characterized by different relations of production: for example, between the master and the serf in feudalism; between the employer and the wage-earner in capitalism. |
| **secularization** | The process whereby religious beliefs and practices lose social significance and influence. |
| **social solidarity** | Durkheim's term for the presence of social order in a society whose structure is solid and well organized. |
| **social structure** | The characterization of human societies as a set of interrelated and interlocking features that make up an organized whole. |
| **social system** | A description of the ways in which the different elements in a social structure work and change together over time, such as in the analogy between the workings of a living organism and the workings of a society often drawn by functionalism. |
| **stereotyping** | Associated with labelling theory, this term summarizes the decision to attribute a complete identity to someone on the basis of their possession of one characteristic alone, as in 'All black men are . . .' or 'All women are . . .'. |
| **structuration theory** | Developed by Anthony Giddens in the late 1970s and early 1980s, structuration theory argues that social structure and action are intimately tied together in synthesis. As such, social structures exist in a virtual realm as the memory traces of social actors who produce or reproduce them as outcomes ('instantiations') of action. Although they are virtual in character, social structural activities recursively mediated by individuals represent patterned systemic properties of society which may |

give rise to deeply entrenched inequalities that favour some individuals or groups over others.

**superstructure**    According to Marxists, all the elements in a social system that are not to do with its economy – the superstructure of non-economic activities, institutions, ideas and beliefs – are built upon and emerge from the economic base.

**value rationality**    A Weberian term, this involves the application of reason in order to decide what is right, or good, and what is bad, or wrong; that is, deciding what should be done.

**voluntarism**    The view that while social activity may be shaped by social structures it is based on free will or choice.

# INDEX

*Note*: Page references in italics indicate illustrations.